P9-ASL-482

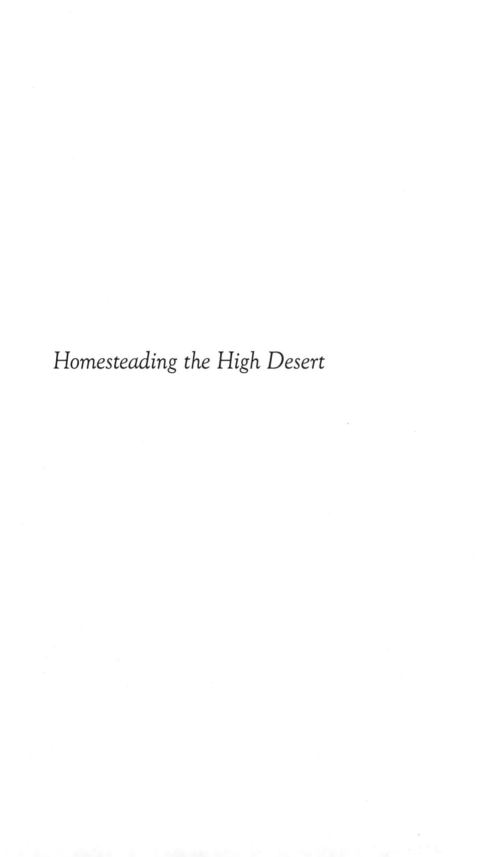

Homesteading the High Desert

HOMESTEAD CABIN IN THE FORT ROCK–CHRISTMAS LAKE VALLEY. *(B. Allen)*

University of Utah Publications in the American West

BARBARA ALLEN

Homesteading the High Desert

ILLUSTRATIONS BY MARY PAT ETTINGER

University of Utah Press   Salt Lake City   1987

VOLUME TWENTY OF THE
UNIVERSITY OF UTAH PUBLICATIONS IN THE AMERICAN WEST
UNDER THE EDITORIAL DIRECTION OF THE AMERICAN WEST CENTER.
FLOYD A. O'NEIL, DIRECTOR

Library of Congress Cataloging-in-Publication Data

Allen, Barbara, 1946–
  Homesteading the high desert.

  (University of Utah publications in the American
West ; v. 20)
  Bibliography: p.
  Includes index.
    1. Farm life—Oregon—Fort Rock Valley—History—
20th century. 2. Farm life—Oregon—Christmas Valley
Region—History—20th century. 3. Fort Rock Valley
(Or.)—History. 4. Christmas Valley Region (Or.)—
History. I. Title. II. Series.
F882.L15A44 1987   979.5'93   86-28125
ISBN 0-87480-268-7

for Lynwood

who lights the way

Contents

ILLUSTRATIONS

MAPS

Acknowledgments

The author of any study grounded, as this one is, in orally communicated history is most heavily indebted to the people who served as sources of information. My first thanks go, then, to the residents of the Fort Rock–Christmas Lake–Silver Lake area of northern Lake County, Oregon. They generously opened their doors and their minds to me during my initial visit in 1978 and graciously granted me permission in 1984 to use their words in this work. All are listed by name in the bibliography, but I would like to thank in particular M. K. (Mac) Buick, Russell and Mary Emery, Helmer (Shorty) Gustafson, Anna Linebaugh, and Roberta Miles for welcoming me back in 1985 and allowing me to copy some of their historical photographs. I am grateful also to Jack Pendleton of Lakeview, Oregon, who provided me with background information, both historical and contemporary, on land use in Lake County.

I was able to gather oral history in the community through the introduction provided by my sister, Mary Pat, and her husband Harry Dunn, who were living in the Fort Rock Valley in 1978 and who invited me to spend the summer with them while I conducted my fieldwork. Without that invitation, and their loving encouragement and support during that summer, this study literally would not have been possible. It is appropriate, then, that Mary Pat's evocative illustrations of the study area grace this book.

In the process of gathering the necessary documentary materials to supplement the oral information, I had the assistance of a number of enthusiastic and energetic librarians, including Hilary Cummings at the University of Oregon Library, Alden Moberg and Clair LaBarr at the Oregon State Library, and Joe Lauck, Linda Gregory, and Steve Hamp at the University of Notre Dame Library, as well as the efficient staffs at the Oregon Historical Society, the Oregon State Archives, the Oregon State University Archives, and the National Archives. Pat Pickens of the Bureau of Land Management Office in Portland was most helpful in locating the historical materials there that I needed. Cultural geographer Marshall Bowen of Mary Washington College in Fredericksburg, Virginia, provided me with useful advice at a critical juncture in my research. Laura Anderson Rice of Eugene, Oregon, sent me a copy of her grandmother's diary from the homestead era. To Laura and her father, R. E. Anderson, I am deeply grateful; they will see how extensively I have drawn upon that invaluable document in Chapters 2 and 3.

Several students also helped in the research stage of the study, including Paula Jean Wagener who scoured the Minnesota Historical Society on my behalf, and Patrick Ettinger and Tom and Lynn Hulsey who transcribed land record information from microfilm. When it came time to prepare the manuscript, I was blessed with the superb clerical assistance of Margaret Jasciewicz, Cheryl Reed, and Nancy Kegler who processed several drafts with consistent grace, intelligence, and cheerfulness. Hugh Ackert, with great good humor, reduced a jumble of information to cartographic order in the maps that appear here.

Completion of the research and preparation of the manuscript was supported by grants from the Institute for Scholarship in the Liberal Arts of the College of Arts and Letters and from the Jesse H. Jones Faculty Research Travel Fund of the University of Notre Dame. In addition, Dr. Carol Paul Brown of the Department of Modern Languages and Intercultural Studies at Western Kentucky University kindly provided me with a "home away from home" during summer and sabbatical leaves from Notre Dame while I was working on the manuscript.

I have saved the greatest debt until the last. For the past two years, Lynwood Montell has "lived" on the Oregon high desert with me, criticizing and counseling, editing and encouraging every step of the way. He has not only listened to and read every word in this manuscript—more than once—with the ear and eye of a professional colleague, but also, as a loving husband, has shared the day-to-day duties of our life together—all this while involved in writing a book himself. The dedication of this work to him is my public acknowledgment of a gratitude too great to be fully expressed.

Prologue

Travelers who cross the Cascade Mountains from western Oregon to the eastern part of the state witness a dramatic, even shocking, change in the landscape. Gone are the rolling terrain and lush greenery of the Willamette Valley. In their place are the flat plains, sparse vegetation, and muted colors of the desert, a barren and uninviting place in contrast to what has been left behind. In the mid-nineteenth century, emigrants on the Oregon Trail, traveling through what is now the northeastern quarter of the state, dismissed the land there as worthless for agriculture (just as they had the Great Plains) in their search for a landscape resembling the forested and well-watered regions of the Mississippi and Ohio river valleys with which they were familiar. The Overlanders found their wooded Eden in the valley of the Willamette River. A stream of settlers flowed steadily into Oregon from the 1840s onward, all apparently bent on taking up rich bottomlands in the interior valleys of which they heard such glowing reports.[1] Settlement proceeded so rapidly, in fact, that by the 1870s, as the first Oregon-born generation began to reach maturity, they found that the choice lands had already been appropriated. So they turned eastward across the Cascades to find land that did not need to be cleared of timber—land their parents had regarded as useless. To approach eastern Oregon from the west, then, is not only visually arresting but historically appropriate.

The first white land-seekers in eastern Oregon settled in the northeastern part of the state along the Columbia River. Together with southeastern Washington, this area comprised the Palouse, developed in the 1870s as wheat- and fruit-producing country. In the southeastern section of Oregon, stock raisers moved into areas where rainfall was insufficient for agriculture, but where cattle and sheep could find adequate water and ample pasturage on native vegetation.[2] The central portion of the state, however, east of the Cascades and south of the Blue Mountains, remained virtually empty of permanent agricultural settlement through the end of the nineteenth century. And understandably so, for with its high elevation and low rainfall, much of central Oregon is desert land. When settlement came to this region after the turn of the century, however, it arrived like a flood tide and receded almost as abruptly, leaving the inevitable debris in its ebb. If the settlement east of the Cascades was the backwash of the westward movement, then it was in the desert of central Oregon that the movement finally died, nearly one hundred years after John Jacob Astor established his fur-trading outpost at the mouth of the Columbia River and more than fifty years after the first Overlanders had arrived in the "Oregon country."

The central Oregon desert was my destination when I left the Willamette Valley in June 1978 and headed east in search of history. U.S. Highway 20 across the mountains followed nearly the same route used a century before by the first land-seekers; it brought me to the town of Bend on the eastern slope, a major trading and service center for the central region of the state. There I turned south on U.S. Highway 97. Some thirty miles later, I took State Highway 31 as it angled off to the southeast toward Lake County. After fifty miles of travel through timberland, the landscape shifted abruptly from pine forest to sagebrush plain. Suddenly the road tilted downward, the horizon opened up, and the desert lay before me.

At the foot of the slope I swung left onto a gravel road leading eastward through a low range of hills and into a broad flat valley. Rising three hundred feet from the center of the valley floor and dominating its emptiness as far as the eye could see was a spectacular rock

THE FORT ROCK VALLEY, LOOKING EAST. FORT ROCK IS IN THE
DISTANCE, JUST TO THE LEFT OF THE ROAD. *L. Montell.*

formation, looking for all the world like the ruins of a prehistoric for-
tification. From the descriptions of the area I had read, I recognized it
as Fort Rock, the eroded remnant of an ancient volcano.

From the top of Fort Rock, you have an unobstructed view of the
surrounding landscape. Scattered on every side are ranches, some near
at hand, others barely visible in the distance, all lying within a patch-
work of gray and green. The gray is the natural vegetation cover of
sagebrush, rabbitbrush, and greasewood; the green is irrigated fields
of alfalfa. Some of the fields are rectilinear, watered by "wheel lines"
stretching from one side of a field to the other and manually moved or
motor driven down its length. Other fields are round, irrigated with
"pivot line" radiating from central pumps and rotating in circles around
them. At the foot of the Rock, a mile to the south and east, is a cluster
of a dozen buildings making up the hamlet of Fort Rock. Twenty miles
across the level plain to the east is the Christmas Lake Valley, in which
the village of Christmas Valley lies; twenty miles to the south, beyond
the Connley Hills, is the Silver Lake Valley, with the small town of
Silver Lake at its heart.

With very little effort you can envision what the area looked like
in 1955 just before the advent of large-scale irrigation—a few patches
of green, a few ranch houses lying in a sea of sand and sagebrush.
Project yourself back another forty years and imagine the land dotted
with hundreds of small wooden structures—houses and barns, schools

and stores built by homesteaders who poured into the Fort Rock–Christmas Lake Valley in the 1910s—that have now vanished without a trace. Make one final mental leap into the past, beyond the turn of the twentieth century, and the land lies empty again—flat, monochromatic, desolate.

Seen from the heights of Fort Rock, the Fort Rock–Christmas Lake Valley impresses you with its immensity; contemplating its past, especially the homesteading era, leaves you wondering at the futility of human desires in the face of the forbidding appearance of the land-scape. What drew people here—more than 1,200 in all—between 1905 and 1915? Why was their tenure so brief and what made them leave? The formidability of the land itself suggests answers to the last two questions, but it makes the first even more difficult to resolve. Although I did not know it that first afternoon, these were the questions that my excursion into the central Oregon desert would raise, and that this book addresses.

At present, about 500 people live within the 2,000-square-mile Fort Rock–Christmas Lake–Silver Lake area, linked to each other by a system of county roads, some paved, some gravel, some simply dirt. Dating from the 1870s, Silver Lake is the oldest settlement in the area and now the largest, with a population between 150 and 200. It occu-pies a mile-long stretch of State Highway 31 which serves as the town's main street. Three "lanes" run parallel to the highway on the south and five or six lanes meet it at right angles. Along the lanes, Victorian-era cottages sit cheek-by-jowl with prefabricated houses, house trail-ers, and mobile homes, while abandoned buildings stare at each other across weed-choked vacant lots. Some of the houses are neatly painted and have meticulously kept yards; others, unpainted and ramshackle, are used only on weekends or during the hunting season. The public and commercial buildings of Silver Lake are clustered along the high-way: the unpretentious store and motel and two service stations lined up on the south side, facing the post office, the volunteer fire and ambulance service, and the tiny branch of the county public library tucked behind them. A block down the highway to the east is the old Baptist church, beyond it the school that houses grades one through eight. (The last high-school class graduated in 1942. Students are now bussed daily to the high school in Paisley, forty-five miles to the south.) Beyond the school, at the far end of town, sits a restaurant, the local gathering place for news and gossip, with the rodeo grounds behind it. The eastern outskirts of Silver Lake are marked by the small cemetery, a one-acre plot fenced off from an alfalfa field. Many of the people in town work "in the woods," either for the U.S. Forest Service, which operates the Fremont National Forest adjoining the Silver Lake Valley on the west and south, or for private lumber companies cutting timber on national forest lands.

A gravel road leads north out of Silver Lake through the Paulina Marsh and across the Connley Hills to the community of Fort Rock, seventeen miles away. Fort Rock is the only settlement left of the dozen or so that sprang up during the homestead period. All that remains there today is a handful of structures at the intersection of the Silver Lake road with the paved county road running east from Highway 31 toward Christmas Valley—a combined store–post office, a tavern, a county road maintenance station, the Grange Hall, a community church, an elementary school, and a few houses. A mile to the north is the bleak, windswept cemetery, holding the remains of people whose dreams died with them on the desert.

The road heading east from Fort Rock skirts the Connley Hills on the northeast. Fourteen miles from Fort Rock, another road branches off toward Christmas Valley, which lies eleven miles due east from that point. The original road continues through Arrow Gap, past Table Rock, and ends at Highway 31 seven miles east of Silver Lake.

The road to Christmas Valley runs through sagebrush-covered sand occasionally punctuated with faded notices advertising acreage for sale. Christmas Valley is the youngest community in the area, created in the early 1960s by a California developer who sold lots—sight unseen—to hundreds of people for vacation and retirement homesites. The expected boom never happened, although Christmas Valley today sports a golf course, restaurant, and two motels (all part of the original development), as well as a store, tavern, service station, realty office, community church, and a substation of the Silver Lake post office. As elsewhere on the desert, prefabricated houses and mobile homes are scattered throughout the community.

The Fort Rock, Christmas Lake, and Silver Lake valleys are bound together by more than roads, however, for people of each locality perceive themselves as linked to residents of the others by neighborly ties, fostered at least in part by isolation from the rest of the world and by some consciousness of a shared past. I had come to this postage stamp of a place, as I have said, in search of that past. More specifically, I had come to listen to people talking about local history. Over the course of the summer, I interviewed nearly three dozen people, literally from one end of the area to the other—from Russell and Mary Emery at their place on Buck Creek southwest of Silver Lake to Josephine and Alice Godon on their family's homestead at the foot of Cougar Mountain in the northern part of the Fort Rock Valley.[3] The choice of narrators was less my own than it was their selection from within the community, for one person often led me to another who was reputed to "know something about the history of this country." Sometimes the reputations were deserved, sometimes not. The majority of the people I talked with were natives of the area—"old-timers" in the local vernacular. But I also interviewed a few "newcomers," that is, people who had not been born in the area. These terms are strictly construed by the people who use them. For instance, one "newcomer" I talked with had moved into the Fort Rock Valley as a teenager in 1920; another had arrived in Silver Lake in 1909 as an eight-year-old child. The fact that such distinctions are so carefully drawn by residents gives some sense of the powerful influence of the local past.

The project I had undertaken could be called oral history of a sort, but with a twist. Rather than considering oral testimony as either a primary or a collateral source of information to be used in reconstructing local history, I was interested in it for its own sake. Trained as a folklorist, I was curious about how people would express themselves if asked to talk about their knowledge, experience, and perceptions of the past. The interviews I conducted were therefore largely unstructured in nature. Instead of asking people a battery of prepared questions designed to elicit specific kinds of information, I opened the interviews with very broad questions and allowed narrators every latitude in selecting and discussing topics as they saw fit. My rationale for allowing them to talk about local history largely in their own terms rather than mine was that, given the freedom to do so, people would concentrate their talk on those aspects of the community's history they considered to be the most significant. What would emerge from the range of subjects discussed and the intensity with which each was treated, I hoped, was a clear view of local history from the insiders' point of view.

As the summer wore on, I became convinced that my strategy was working. Even though individual interviews often covered a wide range of subjects, certain topics cropped up over and over again. This core of consistency from one interview to the next seemed an indication of the kind of unified community perspective on the past that I was after. An even more striking reflection of that perspective in the material I recorded was the divergence between the view of local history expressed by the people I interviewed and its depiction in written historical accounts.

My own understanding of the area's history, before I began the interviews, was based on such secondary sources, including four books about central Oregon (only one of which, published in 1905, was historical in nature) and a handful of periodical and newspaper articles.[4] No full-length scholarly treatment of the area was available anywhere. The materials I found, though scanty, were at least consistent, for they almost all mentioned or described what seemed to have been two key events in the area's past. One was a disastrous fire in Silver Lake on Christmas Eve, 1894, in which forty-three people died. The second was a "range war" between cattle ranchers and sheep owners just after the turn of the century, during which thousands of sheep were slaughtered and a man murdered. Since these subjects were emphasized in writings about the area, I expected to hear a good deal about them from the people I interviewed. Indeed, people did talk about the fire and the range war—among other things—but they did not dwell on them at any length. They preferred instead to focus on the homesteading that had taken place in the Fort Rock–Christmas Lake Valley in the first two decades of the twentieth century. This was a topic that had somehow remained beneath my conscious notice as I was reading, perhaps because it did not possess the obvious drama that characterized the fire or the range war.

By the end of the summer, however, it had become abundantly clear to me that, as far as area residents were concerned, homesteading was the pivot around which all local history revolved. Everyone I interviewed had something to say about it. When I tabulated the number of times various subjects were mentioned, homesteading topped the list. When I plotted those subjects on a time line, the homesteading period and the years surrounding it (1900–1925) dominated the chart. In contrast to what outsiders think is significant or noteworthy about the area's history, the people who live there regard homesteading as the key to their past.

If I had been surprised at the short shrift narrators had given the topics that I had expected them to talk about, I was certainly puzzled at the one they chose to emphasize. Why should they pass lightly over such patently dramatic topics as the range war or the Christmas Eve fire? Why should they prefer instead to talk about homesteading, which seemed in contrast so lacking in pyrotechnics? There was a whole range of considerations, in fact, working against homesteading as the key feature of the area's history. First of all, it did not affect all parts of the region equally: it was concentrated in the Fort Rock and Christmas Lake valleys, leaving the Silver Lake Valley largely untouched. Second, it did not represent the origins of white settlement in the area, for stockmen had settled the Silver Lake Valley in the early 1870s, nearly forty years before the homesteading rush began in the Fort Rock–Christmas Lake Valley. Nor, obviously, did the history of the area end with homesteading: although many small communities were abandoned toward the end of the 1910s, both Silver Lake and Fort Rock retained some viability as commercial centers, and people continued to live on farms and ranches scattered throughout the area. Finally, homesteading represented no triumphant peak of the area's history. It was, in fact, a dismal failure, for only about half of the homesteaders stayed long enough to gain title to the lands they had claimed, and fewer still managed to make a living from them afterwards. Of the estimated 1,200 people who had entered the area by 1915, only 300 remained in 1920.

Here was a paradox indeed: The key element in the area's history was a failed effort. Why should people celebrate, or at least dwell on, such an aspect of the past? What meaning did homesteading have for local residents that outweighed its manifest shortcomings as a source of historical pride? Did something inherent in the homesteading itself—perhaps its poignancy as a noble but failed effort—magnetize local feeling about it?

To find some answers and ultimately come to an understanding of the position of homesteading in the local view of the past, I found I had to turn from a consideration of its relevance in the present to an examination of its occurrence in the past. This meant moving beyond the emotionally charged but fragmentary information contained in orally communicated history to the dispassionate, and also often maddeningly incomplete, documentary traces that the homesteaders had left behind. I temporarily set my interview transcripts aside and delved into General Land Office tract books, census schedules, tax rolls, weather records, governmental agency reports, travelers' accounts,

newspapers, locally written historical accounts, and diaries. Reconstructing what had happened on the central Oregon desert between
1900 and 1920 from both oral and written sources, however, produced
only a sketchy picture of what actually happened. Although the documentary sources were often contemporary with the homesteading
effort—some even created by the homesteaders themselves—I found
them clumsy mediators between the past and the present. They told
me more or less clearly what the homesteaders had done, but they
shed little light on what the homesteaders had thought or felt or
believed. The oral information, on the other hand, conveyed some
sense of the human effort and emotion expended in the homesteading
period, but by its very nature—derived from the minds and memories
of people who were not involved in the homesteading themselves or
who recollected it only as a childhood experience—it too created a
sense of distance between the past and the present. Even when written and oral sources were judiciously and imaginatively combined,
the *immediacy* of the homesteaders' experience is still missing, irrevocably lost to us.

After synthesizing all the information I had gathered, then, I was
still left with a series of nagging questions: What drew people in such
large numbers to the desert? What motivated them to settle in such
an inhospitable and isolated place, where both environmental and
economic conditions worked against sustained agricultural success?
What did they hope to find or accomplish? Because the homesteaders
themselves had provided no answers to these questions, I had to transcend the local setting. The Fort Rock–Christmas Lake Valley homesteading was part of a larger movement that brought settlement to the
"last West" in various localities throughout the western United States
and Canada in the first years of the twentieth century, so I turned to
descriptions of the national scene at the turn of the century in order
to understand the economic, social, cultural, and intellectual climate
within which the homesteaders decided to settle on the Oregon desert.

In the following pages, I try to answer some of the questions I have
raised here. I begin in Chapter 1 with a description of the high desert
setting and of the human history that preceded the homesteading
period. The next two chapters reconstruct the homesteading itself,
from the first influx of settlers in 1905 to the peak of activity in 1915.
The exodus of homesteaders that began in 1916 is described in Chapter 4, culminating with the reversion of most of the land in the Fort

Rock–Christmas Lake Valley to government control by 1940. In Chapter 5, the context shifts from the local scene to an examination of the influences at work on the homesteaders, on both a regional and a national level, just before and concurrently with their attempts to settle the desert.

In a way, this final chapter is the crux of the study, for in it I try to establish a bridge between local events and the national scene. My purpose in doing so is not simply to point out the simultaneity of historical occurrences on two different levels of abstraction, but to demonstrate that the national mood had a critical role to play in local action and that what happened on the local level was a logical outgrowth of occurrences on a national scale. A third motive is involved here as well. If, as some have argued, all history is local somewhere, then the obverse may also be true: that all local history is somehow universal. The homesteaders on the Oregon desert were real people who lived and worked in a specific time and place, but their lives and actions can transcend time and space. They certainly have meaning to contemporary residents of the area; perhaps through them, we too can enrich our own understanding of the past.

Homesteading the High Desert

"As has often been said about hell, the Oregon Desert
might not be too bad a place to live if only it possessed
more water and a more attractive climate."[1]

1

The High Desert Setting

Human history does not take place in a vacuum. There is
always a physical environment in which people act and with which
they interact. The relationship between human activity and the natural environment is especially critical in the American West where
the sheer space the region encompasses, the range of geographical features it displays, its aridity and lack of timber, and the vagaries of its
weather are all factors influencing the pattern of human settlement
there. Certainly, in the settlement of the high desert of Oregon, as
much as anywhere else in the West, the physical environment played
a decisive role, for the land was eminently unsuited for the agricultural purposes to which the homesteaders in the Fort Rock–Christmas
Lake Valley attempted to put it.

THE NATURAL ENVIRONMENT

The Oregon desert is a term whose applicability varies. Most
broadly defined, it comprises the area east of the Cascades and south
of the Blue Mountains. More narrowly, the term refers to a roughly
triangular upland area, with an average elevation of 4,500 feet, bounded

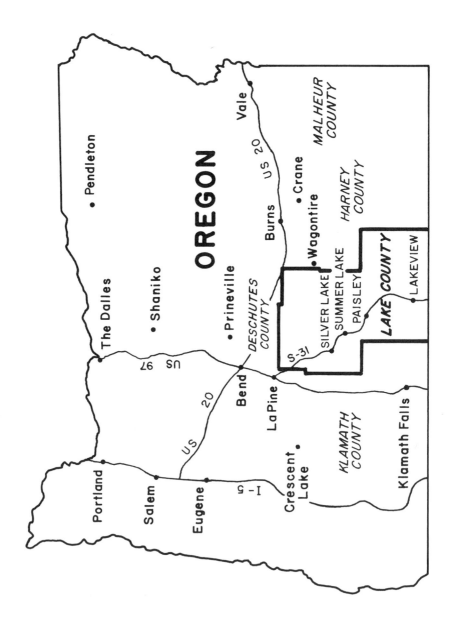

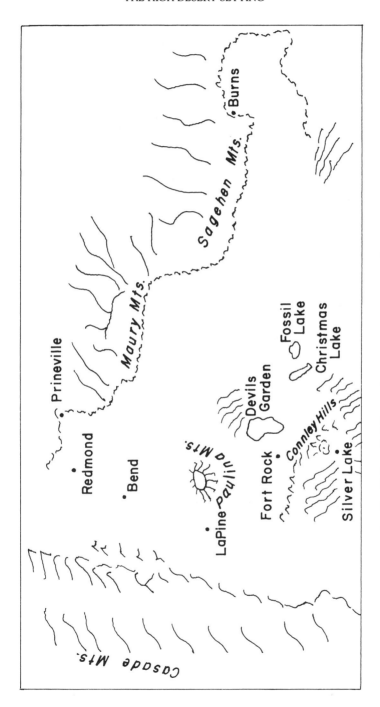

THE HIGH DESERT OF CENTRAL OREGON

on the west by the Cascade Mountains, on the east by the Maury Mountains and Sagehen Hills, and on the south by a series of scarps and valleys.[2] At the top of the triangle is the town of Redmond; its easternmost point is near Burns; and the Fort Rock–Christmas Lake Valley forms its lower edge. On old maps of Oregon, this area is variously referred to as Rolling Sage Plains, Great Sandy Desert, High Lava Plains, Sage Desert, Artemisia Desert, and High Desert.[3] The desert environment is created by the Cascades which block rain-bearing storms rolling in from the Pacific. The mountain barrier is the reason that the Willamette River Valley averages forty inches of precipitation per year, while the eastern part of the state receives less than half that amount, and the high desert only a quarter.[4]

The Fort Rock–Christmas Lake Valley, lying on the southern edge of the Oregon desert, forms the northwestern boundary of the Great Basin, and shares its characteristic aridity, extremes of temperature, loose porous soil, and internal drainage.[5] It is not a valley in the geographical sense of having been formed by the alluvial action of a stream. Instead it was created when the Columbia River lava flow moving from the north stopped short of the edge of the Basin and Range province on the south, resulting in the formation of a shallow depression with an average elevation of 4,300 feet, just slightly below that of the surrounding area. For that reason the valley is sometimes referred to as the "low desert."[6] The volcanic activity that created the valley in ancient geologic times also left its mark on the land, creating a moonscape of cinder cones, obsidian formations, eroded craters, rough outcroppings of lava, and caves formed by fast-flowing underground lava streams that left hollow tubes in their wakes. The most spectacular evidence of the volcanic activity that shaped the region is Fort Rock itself, the collapsed caldera of an ancient volcano.

Except for an anomalous rise or two elsewhere, the valley is as flat as a plate, stretching forty-five miles from sand dunes on the east to low hills on the west and ranging from ten to twenty-five miles in width. Topographically it looks like a somewhat misshapen butterfly veering on a slightly northwesterly course, its two "wings" separated by lava beds dipping down from the north and by the escarpment known as Seven Mile Ridge thrusting up from the south.[7] The eastern half of the valley, slightly lower in elevation, is usually referred to, both on maps and in local usage, as Christmas Lake Valley, while the term Fort Rock Valley commonly designates the western half.[8]

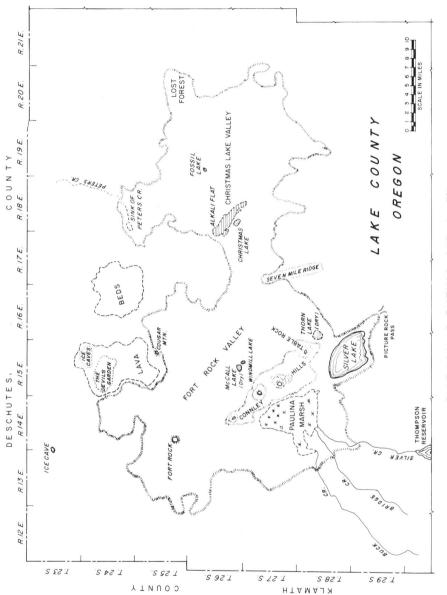

FORT ROCK–CHRISTMAS LAKE VALLEY

The soils best suited to agriculture lie in the northwestern part of the Fort Rock Valley and the north-central section of the Christmas Lake Valley. Elsewhere, the ground is extremely porous and heavily impregnated with alkalis, especially sulphate and lime. Because it contains very little humus material, the soil is extremely susceptible to wind erosion.[9]

The native vegetation cover—where it has not been disturbed by agricultural activities—consists of a dozen species of grasses, various wildflowers, sagebrush, rabbitbrush, saltbush, woolly sage, and greasewood. Before the advent of grazing and farming in the area, bunchgrass and wild rye were also reportedly abundant. On the hills surrounding the valley are juniper, pine, tamarack, buckthorn, manzanita, maple, cottonwood, and mountain mahogany.[10] Area wildlife runs heavily to small rodents, including rabbits, squirrels, mice, gophers, and skunks. Larger animals include foxes, badgers, bobcats, coyotes, antelope, and mule deer.[11]

Aridity is the critical element in the valley's environment. This is not to say there is no water there at all, but its presence is both limited and subject to fluctuation. There is no naturally occurring surface water in either valley at present, although the Christmas Lake Valley contains several shallow lake beds, or playas, including Fossil Lake and Christmas Lake, that periodically fill with runoff from the surrounding hills. As dry years follow wet ones, the playas dry up. Christmas Lake has been dry for much of the twentieth century, but in 1879 land surveyors reported that it covered about one hundred acres with alkaline water.[12] At Fossil Lake in 1889, naturalist E. D. Cope found the lake bed dry, but "clear water, somewhat alkaline to the taste at a depth of about eighteen inches."[13]

There were several springs in the Fort Rock and Christmas Lake valleys within human memory. In 1877, surveyors working six or seven miles northeast of Christmas Lake discovered "a remarkable spring called Ramsey's Spring" and another close by that they described as "excellent." There were springs as well at both Christmas Lake and Fossil Lake, at the latter of which, "it is claimed, range riders have drunk when the lake was dry."[14] Anna Long Linebaugh, whose family settled on Christmas Lake in 1900, recalled, "That country was full of springs. I've heard my mother tell that when they went there, they didn't have any water for a year except what they could get out of this spring."[15] The springs no longer run, as they are responsive to the general water level in the valleys.[16] The only other watercourse in either valley is Peter's Creek, an intermittent stream rising a dozen miles to the north of Christmas Lake and ending in a sink.

The lack of surface water is mitigated somewhat by the presence of deep water in both valleys, trapped by a bedrock layer of lava that creates three water-catching basins, one under Fossil Lake, one beneath Christmas Lake, and the third in the eastern end of the Fort Rock Valley. The depth of the water table within these basins varies from twenty-five to one hundred feet, depending on location and on current weather patterns.[17]

There is no water on the surface because so little falls. Precipitation in the valleys averages about nine inches per year. Most of that amount falls as snow in the winter; some rain falls in the late spring.[18] Exacerbating the scantiness of rainfall is its spottiness. Within the Fort Rock–Christmas Lake Valley, precipitation levels vary greatly between weather stations just a few miles apart, causing a corresponding variation in crop yields within the same general vicinity.[19] The critical fact of precipitation patterns in the valleys, however, is not the annual average amount, but rather the cycles of wet and dry years that may bring two inches of rain in one year and fifteen the next.[20]

The valleys' high elevation keeps the temperatures relatively moderate. The summers are mild, with daytime temperatures in the eighties; in the winter, temperatures during the day average in the thirties and forties.[21] The combination of high elevation and low humidity, however, means differences of twenty degrees or more between day and night temperatures, with occasional sharp rises and drops in air temperature over short periods. In September 1955, for instance, one private weather-recording station in the Fort Rock Valley, "had a temperature of 100 degrees and 30 degrees in the same twenty-four-hour period and a [daily] variation of 66 degrees or more in the next three or four days."[22]

The high elevation also creates erratic frost patterns, particularly in the open flats on the valley floors, where severe frosts can occur any time of the year. A "killing" frost in late spring or early summer can be as devastating to a crop as drought; although hardier crops, such as alfalfa, may not be killed, their growth may be severely retarded.[23] The possibility of frost year-round makes the length of the growing season—that is, the period between the last spring frost and the first fall frost—variable. While the average frost-free season is seventy-four days,[24] this figure is as deceptive as the annual precipitation figures, for it masks the difference between years with long, mild growing seasons of 150 days, and years in which spring and autumn frosts succeed each other within a few days in late July and early August.

The climatic conditions prevailing in the Fort Rock–Christmas Lake Valley were unknown to the homesteaders who began arriving after the turn of the century because systematic weather records were not kept there until 1909.[25] What made the area seem feasible for agriculture was its proximity to the Silver Lake Valley, where cattle and sheep ranching had been successfully pursued since the 1870s. The ranchers in the Silver Lake area, who wintered their stock on wild hay cut from the valley's marshes, had long been accustomed to using the Fort Rock–Christmas Lake Valley as a summer grazing range. According to one account, in fact, Fort Rock was named by a stockman, William Stephens, who was rounding up some of his cattle near there in 1873. (Stockmen reportedly used the Rock as a corral as its shape would allow a single cowboy stationed at the gap on its southeast side to pen an entire herd within its confines.[26])

THE SILVER LAKE VALLEY

While the Fort Rock–Christmas Lake Valley lies on the southern edge of the High Lava Plains, the Silver Lake Valley is the northernmost extension of the Basin and Range province that runs southward through California into central Mexico in a series of ridges or scarps alternating with flats or basins. In the Silver Lake Valley, the scarps rise abruptly 400 to 600 feet above the surface of the lake,[27] with gently rising slopes on the north and east, and steeply cut, clifflike faces on the south and west. The southern and western boundaries of the valley are formed by a series of scarps running generally from northwest to southeast; on the northeast the Connley Hills separate it from the Fort Rock–Christmas Lake Valley.

Geological evidence indicates that the Fort Rock–Christmas Lake Valley and the Silver Lake Valley formed a single geographical entity in prehistoric times.[28] But the environment of the Silver Lake Valley now is slightly wetter. The annual precipitation averages nearly eleven inches; most falls between October and March, with some rain in May and June.[29] In addition, several small streams rise from the mountains overlooking the valley from the south and west. These water-

courses—Buck, Bridge, and Silver creeks—empty into Paulina Marsh at the northern end of the valley; the marsh then drains into the slightly lower Silver Lake by underground seepage or, during wet periods, aboveground overflow.[30] The flow of Silver Creek into the valley is now controlled by the Thompson Valley Reservoir constructed in 1922 as part of the Silver Lake Irrigation Project of the U.S. Bureau of Reclamation.

Silver Lake itself is a large, freshwater playa with a well-documented history of cyclical filling and drying. In 1861, a gold prospecting party from Fort Klamath, headed for the John Day country in central Oregon, passed through the Silver Lake Valley. They found "Paulina Marsh to be practically a lake . . . and the west end of Fort Rock Valley . . . also submerged."[31] By the late 1880s, however, Silver Lake was completely dry. Local ranchers took advantage of the situation by cutting the natural grass for hay and even building stock fences on the lake bed.[32] This cycle of filling and drying continued beyond the turn of the century. In 1904, Anna Linebaugh recalled, "there was so much water in Silver Lake, the water would go clear on out to the desert [the Christmas Lake Valley]. You couldn't go through; you had to go around the south end of the lake to get to the town of Silver Lake." But by 1915, the lake was only three and a half feet deep.[33]

Since 1922, the Thompson Valley Reservoir has helped moderate the lake's fluctuations. Even the reservoir, however, was unable to keep the lake from flooding Highway 31 in 1964. In 1978, when I first visited the area, the lake bed was being used as a pasture, but it had filled again by 1984; along its edges could be seen the remnants of fences and small outbuildings used during the previous dry spell.

The moisture available in the Silver Lake Valley from both surface sources and precipitation supports a somewhat broader spectrum of vegetation than that found in the Fort Rock–Christmas Lake Valley. In addition to the species of sage and the variety of trees found in the Fort Rock–Christmas Lake Valley, the native vegetation of the Silver Lake Valley also includes several varieties of wild marsh grasses, as well as wild rye and bunchgrass. The presence of these natural grasses seems, in fact, to have been the most striking feature of the valley to the first white settlers. "My ancestors told me that this used to be all grass country," said Roberta Miles, the great-granddaughter of early settlers in the Silver Lake Valley. "When my grandmother came here, she said that there was grass all over the country. She was in a side saddle, just a little kid, but she said that she could remember that the grass was so tall that if anybody dropped out of the horse train, they'd stand up in their saddles and look ahead to see where the grass was waving to catch up with the others."[34] Even as late as 1898, after cattle ranching was well established in the Silver Lake Valley, "you could sit in the saddle and the tops of the bunch grass clumps would brush your feet in the stirrups as you rode over the range."[35] Government geologist Gerald Waring praised the Silver Lake Valley in similarly lush imagery. "Over nearly all of this area," he wrote in 1908, "bunchgrass and rye grass grow in sufficient quantity to furnish range for thousands of head of stock, while from the marshes many tons of wild hay are cut every year for winter feed."[36]

The environmental differences between the Fort Rock–Christmas Lake Valley and the Silver Lake Valley are significant enough to residents that they perceive the two areas as separate locales. No one name, in fact, is used to refer to the area as a whole, except perhaps "this part of the county." Instead, people speak of the "Silver Lake country" on the one hand and the "Fort Rock country" (which includes the Christmas Lake Valley) or "the desert" on the other. These designations reflect not just a perception of environmental differences, but a recognition of the different ways in which each area was settled, ways that were themselves largely influenced by environmental factors. The relatively wetter Silver Lake Valley had been settled as part of the general movement eastward across the Cascade Mountains from the western interior valleys in the 1870s. The impetus for moving into the Fort Rock–Christmas Lake Valley, on the other hand, came largely from the passage of the Enlarged Homestead Act in 1909. The first white settlers in the Silver Lake Valley were stockmen looking for good grazing lands, while in the Fort Rock–Christmas Lake Valley, the land was taken up by people intending to farm. Nevertheless, the Fort Rock–Christmas Lake–Silver Lake area presently constitutes a single social, cultural, and economic entity, and the history of one component cannot be understood in isolation from the other.

EARLY DEVELOPMENT

The settlers who arrived in the area in the nineteenth century were, of course, not the first human inhabitants of the region. Although archaeological evidence is scanty, various groups of hunters and gatherers apparently occupied the area beginning as far back as 13,000 years ago, alternately inhabiting caves in the Fort Rock Valley when the climatic conditions were cool and moist, and abandoning them when the weather cycled into hot and arid periods.[37]

Little evidence remains of the types or duration of occupancy from the time that the current climatic conditions were established two thousand years ago up until white contact in the early part of the nineteenth century. Within the past two centuries, however, the Fort Rock–Christmas Lake–Silver Lake Basin was part of the territory ranged by Northern Paiutes, whose homelands included the western part of the Great Basin—southeastern Oregon, northeastern California, southern Idaho, and northern Nevada. Although there is little agreement among anthropologists on which tribes occupied what territories in eastern Oregon, the Fort Rock–Christmas Lake–Silver Lake area probably served as hunting and temporary camping grounds rather than as a permanent habitation site. The Deer-Eater band of the Northern Paiutes, in particular, may have used the Silver Lake Valley as a hunting and gathering site.[38]

These early inhabitants left several kinds of physical evidence behind, among them a series of petroglyphs found near the southeast end of the Silver Lake Valley at the summit of the rim separating the Silver Lake and Summer Lake valleys.[39] More widespread and abundant are the numerous flaked obsidian artifacts in the Fort Rock–Christmas Lake Valley. The concentration of these artifacts near Fossil Lake in particular, where hundreds of prehistoric skeletal remains of birds and mammals have been recovered, reveals that site to have been a prime hunting ground.[40] Ironically, it is now the artifacts themselves that are hunted. Reportedly, some early arrowhead hunters collected up to ten thousand specimens; nearly every resident today owns at least a few stone points.

The most spectacular archaeological remains of local Native American occupancy were discovered in 1938, when anthropologist Luther Cressman of the University of Oregon excavated a remarkable cache of seventy nine-thousand-year-old sandals, woven from sagebrush, buried in a thick layer of volcanic ash at the rear of a cave near Fort Rock.[41] When Cressman published news of the discovery in 1940, his report attracted a good deal of attention from scholars and the general public alike, and the discovery itself remains a strong point of local pride.

The Fort Rock–Christmas Lake–Silver Lake area experienced only peripherally the violent encounters between Native Americans and whites that occurred throughout the Great Basin from the mid- to late-nineteenth century as mining activities and agricultural settlements encroached on Indian territories. According to one account, in the fall of 1872, Paiutes attacked the ranch of Willard Duncan on the shore of Silver Lake, frightening two brothers grazing a band of sheep there. While the white men were putting up wild hay, "a band of fierce Indians looked on. I'd look at Tom and Tom looked at me and we just pitched all the harder," one of the men later recalled.[42] Five years later, when the Bannocks left the Malheur Reservation in southeastern Oregon, the stock ranchers in the Silver Lake Valley decided that "the women should return to the Willamette Valley until the trouble was over. During the war, renegade Klamath, Modocs, and other Cascade [tribes] passed through Silver Lake Valley on their way to join the Bannock war, killing sheep and cattle, and helping themselves to whatever they wanted."[43]

White settlers were quick to move into south-central Oregon once the perceived threat of trouble with the local tribes was extinguished by the end of the 1870s.[44] After that, relations between the two groups in the Fort Rock–Christmas Lake–Silver Lake Basin were limited to occasional and peaceful encounters. When the Longs moved to Christmas Lake, for instance, "Mother stayed all alone at first with my brother and me while my dad worked away," said Anna Long Linebaugh. "Mother said there was an Indian that used to come there every year. I don't know what he did but he came through the country. And I've heard her tell the first time he came and asked for Mother, he stood way out from the house and asked if he could stay. And I guess he slept in the barn. He opened his arms and he meant no harm; he was friendly."

As late as the 1920s, people in the Silver Lake Valley were accustomed to seeing Indians from the Klamath Reservation in and around the town during their annual fall trek to gather wild plums in the

Summer Lake Valley. Longtime area resident Russell Emery recalled that "a lot of them [would] go plumming just about this time of year [August]. They'd have a team and an old buckboard of some kind, and four or five kids a-horseback and some dogs."[45] Anna Linebaugh also remembered the Klamath clearly: "The Indians came through here frequently when we had our store [in Silver Lake] in the '20s," she recalled. "They'd come through the forest and come to Summer Lake every fall to get wild plums. There'd be quite a few come. They'd come to the store, and they'd have their baskets and things to trade for groceries." M. K. (Mac) Buick, the brother of Roberta Miles, recalled that the Indians also made gloves to sell to the white residents: "On the Klamath reservation, a lot of them over there made buckskin gloves. In the spring of the year, they'd bring a bunch of them into the stores and sell them to the stores. And sometimes they'd peddle them around the country. But they were pretty good gloves they made. They'd smoke-tan them; you could smell them for a mile. It wasn't a bad smell, but they smelled smoky. They were real comfortable, nice and soft."[46]

The early settlers who began moving into the Silver Lake Valley in the 1870s had also been preceded by explorers such as Peter Skene Ogden, Ewing Young, and John C. Fremont who had reportedly traveled through or near the area. Emigrant trains and gold prospectors also left ghostly trails through the Oregon desert.[47] But in the view of contemporary residents, the curtain rises on local history in 1873 when a group of ten stock raisers arrived in the Silver Lake Valley looking for open rangeland for cattle, horses, and sheep.[48] Like most of the people who moved into the valley in the 1870s and 1880s, these men came from the Willamette Valley, traveling over a military wagon road completed in the fall of 1872 through McKenzie Pass.[49] Other early settlers came from the Rogue River Valley via a route known as "the southern trail" that crossed the mountains somewhere near Upper Klamath Lake. A third contingent came from northern California, traveling the old mining road from Yreka, California, along the eastern edge of the Summer Lake Valley into the Christmas Lake Valley.

Most of the first entrymen in the valley established stock ranches, taking up land with grass and water on it.[50] Many had already had success as ranchers or farmers in other places and brought their experience to bear on the conditions they found in the Silver Lake Valley. The area was ideally suited for cattle ranching, for the native grasses that abounded around Silver and Thorn lakes and in Paulina Marsh to the northwest provided excellent forage. The land along the north edge of Silver Lake in particular "is good natural meadow," wrote the surveyors in 1874, "affording locations where settlers can cut large quantities of hay for stock." In the northeastern part of the same township, they noted, was an "extensive bunchgrass range for stock of all kinds."[51]

The early ranchers acquired title to their lands under every conceivable provision of the land laws. They filed preemption, homestead, timber culture, desert land, and swampland claims, or bought the land outright from the government.[52] Swampland claims were especially popular, as the law allowed a stockman to extend his holdings considerably beyond the 160 acres permitted under the Homestead Act and therefore to increase the number of animals he could support on his home range. Although much of the northwestern end of the Silver Lake Valley was marshy, far more swamp acreage was claimed there than actually existed. The law stipulated that settlers wishing to take up swamplands had to offer proof of the wet nature of the plots they were claiming by swearing that they had traveled over them in a boat. Lawrence (Bussie) Iverson of Silver Lake explained that fraud was often perpetrated by some "old-timers [who] put a boat in a wagon and went around [the land] that way."[53]

From the beginning, the population in the Silver Lake Valley grew steadily. A post office was established in the winter of 1874–75 at Lone Pine, the George C. Duncan ranch nine miles east of the present town of Silver Lake.[54] (Teased about the $1 annual salary that he received as postmaster, Duncan reportedly quipped, "But think of the honor!"[55]) Weekly mail service between The Dalles and Lakeview, via Prineville and Silver Lake, was established in 1876, assuring newcomers that they had not totally severed ties with the outside.[56] By 1875 there were fifty-four people residing in the valley, and by 1880, despite a hard winter that year, "with blizzards and deep snow,"[57] the population had nearly doubled to ninety-two. Most of the adults shown on the census for that year had been born in Oregon, as had nearly all of the children. Native Californians comprised the next largest component of the population, although they were only half as numerous as native Oregonians. People born in Missouri made up the third largest element of the population; it is likely that these were the children of overland emigrants from the 1840s and 1850s.[58]

During the early years of settlement, each household in the valley had to obtain its own supplies, which meant making the long trip back across the mountains to the Willamette Valley. One long-time resident of Silver Lake romanticized what must have been an arduous journey as a jolly family outing: "Each rancher took his whole family in the fall and went to the Willamette Valley to bring home a year's supplies of everything needful[,] not only groceries but hardware, shoes, and whole bolts of calico. Pa's shirt was apt as not to match the baby's dress, or all the girls' dresses [to look] alike. These trips were gala occasions for the young people. It took about three weeks to make the round trip over the old military road, which was the one most used. Usually two or three families traveled together to give each other neighborly help."[59] People traveled across the mountains to the Willamette Valley rather than making the relatively easier trip to The Dalles because they were eager to combine the trip for supplies with visits to family and friends "back home."

Although settlers were scattered throughout the Silver Lake Valley, a concentration quickly developed in Township 28 South, Range 14 East. As early as 1875, two-thirds of the population either lived or owned land there. The township lay on the southwestern side of the valley, where land was less marshy than to the north and east, and where fresh surface water for irrigation was available from Silver Creek. In 1885, H. F. West took up 160 acres in Section 22 of that township where, in 1888, he platted the town of Silver Lake, allotting fifteen blocks for its future development.[60] By that time, there were already two stores, two hotels, a saloon, and a sawmill in town. A physician, William B. Owsley, had arrived in 1881, and a blacksmith, Sam Allison, set up shop in 1888.[61] Several school sessions had been held in private homes beginning in 1879, but the first public schoolhouse was built in 1886 with $700 raised by subscription. Reportedly, the heaviest contributors were local cowboys who wanted to use the schoolhouse for dances. The new school opened its first term with fifteen students.[62]

The post office, which had been discontinued at the Duncan ranch near the lake in 1880, was reactivated at the C. P. Marshall ranch just west of town in 1881 and eventually relocated in the Clayton store in 1886.[63] According to one colorful (if unverifiable) account, the post office was moved from the Marshall place because "the folks got smallpox and everybody was afraid of them. There was a couple of

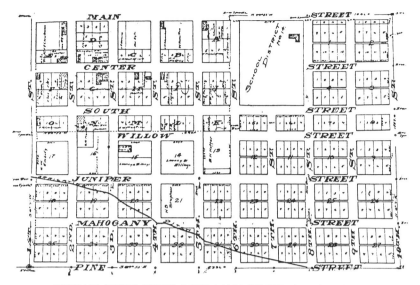

TOWN PLAT FOR SILVER LAKE. MAIN STREET, AT THE TOP, IS NOW STATE HIGHWAY 31.

Mexicans that were shearing sheep that came into the country along about the time the folks were the sickest and they already had it. They went in and took care of them to the best of their ability and when they died, they took them out south of town and buried them. And then they fumigated the land and after a month they burned the house. Then the post office moved into the town of Silver Lake."[64]

Once stores were established in Silver Lake, their supplies were freighted from The Dalles, a major shipping point on the Columbia River for northeastern Oregon, indeed for the whole Columbia River Basin.[65] Although two hundred miles north of Silver Lake, The Dalles was the closest railhead to the valley until 1900, when the Columbia Southern Railway was constructed from The Dalles to Shaniko, shortening the distance some sixty miles.[66]

Some of the merchants in Silver Lake, such as Francis Chrisman, hauled their own freight. Chrisman "used twenty-four mules and two wagons," recalled Lawrence Deadmond. "It was one hundred and fifty miles across the desert. They crossed the creek at Prineville from Shaniko. Then the old wagon road cut back in not too far from [the village of] Brothers and came through the Connley Gap across the desert."

A number of independent freighters also hauled goods for both businesses and individual ranchers in the Silver Lake area. "One freight team that used to come here," recalled Russell Emery, "had twelve mules, belonged to a fellow named Creed Conn. He run a store down here, one of the stores. And he couldn't find a driver." Eventually Ed Henderson, a fabled driver, approached Conn and made him an offer. "Well, I'll take your team and if I can't drive them, the trip won't cost you anything." So they let him take this team and drive them. He was an old mule-skinner.

"They had quite a lot of curves in the road. And going around the turns, by the time these twelve mules got around and the three wagons, why, the back wagon would cut in here. So he trained those mules so they'd jump the chain [that connected them] and pull up the hill and keep the wagons so they wouldn't cut across. . . . So they figured he was a pretty good mule-skinner, by the time he got back. They kept him on for years."[67]

Even after the entry of professional freighters into the area, some families continued to haul their own supplies as they had done in the 1870s. "After Klamath Falls kind of got built up," recounted Lawrence Deadmond, "George Emery and Dad and Jeff Howard and Miles and some others would take a couple of wagons and six horses and go to Klamath Falls and get beans and coffee and stuff like that."

The federal census for 1890 showed a population of 264 in the Silver Lake precinct. By that year, virtually all of the usable land in the Silver Lake Valley had been taken up for the stock ranching operations that were the economic mainstay of the area and for the production of hay crops such as rye and alfalfa.[68] The village of Silver Lake seems to have prospered during the first part of the 1890s. By 1894, more than fifty people were living there; nearly 200 more were scattered throughout the valley. In December of that year, the townspeople planned a special Christmas event for the children. The ill-fated "Christmas Tree" program was to include dramatic and musical performances, followed by a distribution of gifts. The program was held on the second floor of the Francis Chrisman building, above the J. H. Clayton store. Between 160 and 200 people gathered for the event, some coming from as far as Summer Lake.[69] A man who had attended the program later recalled its tragic ending: "Christmas eve came. The tree was loaded with presents. The program had been very enjoyable. I remember that I was in one of the plays. The choir was singing the last song, when a man got up, for some reason or other, and started back toward the door and bumped his head against one of the Rochester hanging lamps. The lamp was hanging between me and

FREIGHTING OUTFIT IN THE SILVER LAKE VALLEY AROUND THE
TURN OF THE CENTURY. *Courtesy of Russell and Mary Emery.*

the door and I started toward the lamp, but Uncle Charley got there ahead of me and pulled the wick down, but there was considerable oil in the wick and the flame burned high. This would have soon died down, if they had kept their composure, but some of the women screamed. One man removed his coat and put the sleeve of the coat down in the top of the lamp globe, trying to smother the flame, but this was no effect. There were too many people, each trying to do something. Then some of the men started to take the lamp down. Creed Conn, Francis Chrisman . . . , Florey Edwards, Haze McCall and the postmaster were all helping. The oil ran down on Francis Chrisman's hand and burned him and he dropped the lamp on the floor. Jep [Jeff] Howard picked up the lamp and carried it outside, but by that time most of the oil had spilled on the floor and was burning. Different ones were trying to whip out the flames with their coats. I tried two or three times to go and help put out the fire, but somebody would always get in front of me, and this is what probably saved my life, because every time I started, it put me a little closer to the door. The burning flames reached the wall, and it went up with a roar before anyone could say 'Jack Robinson.' There was no stopping the people now. George Payne tried to keep them quiet and line them up. I thought then this could not be done. Nothing could be done with these people now. They were all trying to get out the door."[70]

The only way out of the room was down a narrow outside stair-way. The door opened inward and the panicked crowd pushing to escape the flames made it nearly impossible to keep the door open. The weight on the stairway soon caused it to collapse, leaving the remainder of the crowd inside. A few people managed to climb through a window onto a small porch in the front of the building, but that too was unable to sustain much weight and fell to the ground. Within minutes, the entire building was consumed. Forty people were burned to death that night; many more were injured, three of them fatally.

At some point shortly after the fire started, a young man named Ed O'Farrell took off on horseback for a doctor. Reportedly, the only physician in Silver Lake at that time, a Dr. Thompson, had gone to Paisley to treat a patient. The nearest available doctor was Bernard Daly in Lakeview, one hundred miles away. Maurice Ward recounted O'Farrell's heroic ride for help: "He was just a common, ordinary cowboy around there, and he had a bit better clothes than some of the rest of them. They rustled him up an extra good horse. He'd go into a ranch down at Summer Lake or someplace like that, tell them there's been a big fire up at Silver Lake and he needed a good horse to go on. Everybody'd give him a horse and away he'd go."[71]

At each stop, O'Farrell arranged for a buggy team to be ready for Dr. Daly's return trip. In spite of severe cold and deep snow, he reached Lakeview in nineteen hours, arriving there at 4 P.M. on Christmas Day.[72] Dr. Daly and Willard Duncan (whose family lived in Silver Lake) left immediately, reaching the scene of the disaster sometime the following day, December 26.[73]

The forty-three deaths suffered in the fire amounted to nearly one-fifth of the total population of the Silver Lake Valley at the time. Virtually every family in the community lost at least one member; others lost many more. Especially hard hit was the Buick-Owsley family, eleven of whom were killed. Three other members of the family—all brothers-in-law—were away from home on a cattle-selling trip. While waiting for a cattle buyer in Yreka, California, "an acquaintance rushed up to them thrusting a newspaper into their hands, and exclaiming that their families had perished." In an agony of fear and grief, the men immediately headed for home, two hundred miles away, on horseback.[74]

The speed with which the news of the tragedy spread brought anguished inquiries about its victims from all over Oregon. One young man, responding to a letter from an anxious aunt, explained how he had managed to escape the disaster:

SILVER LAKE CEMETERY MONUMENT TO THE VICTIMS OF THE
CHRISTMAS EVE FIRE, 1894.

Dear A[u]nt:
I received your letter of Jan. 20 and was glad to hear from you[.] we
was not at the Xmas tree and I am glad we was not[.] a lot of us had just
got home on Sunday before with our cattle from Klamath Marsh and
had to seperate all day monday and was tired and worn out so we staid
at home[.] we would have been there if I had got home 2 or 3 days before[.]
we was in bed a sleep at the time it hapened and did not know it till
morning.[75]

The victims of the fire were interred together in a mass grave in the
Silver Lake cemetery. In 1898, an impressive stone monument was
erected there, engraved with the names of all those who died in the
tragedy. For years after the event, survivors refused to talk about the
fire or would burst into tears at a reminder of it.[76] A small item in the
Silver Lake Leader on November 26, 1903, however, mentions plans
for a Christmas Tree program that year, indicating that after ten years
had elapsed the townspeople had begun to put the horror behind
them.[77]

The fire not only dealt the community a severe emotional blow,
but produced an economic setback as well. The federal census for
1900 listed only 229 persons in the Silver Lake precinct, compared
with 264 in 1890. This figure not only reveals the loss of population
due to the fire and to bereaved residents moving away afterwards, but
also reflects a significantly retarded rate of growth in the Silver Lake

Valley during the last decade of the nineteenth century, compared with the preceding twenty years. The area's difficulties during this period were undoubtedly compounded by the national economic depression of 1893 and the slow recovery that took most of the rest of the decade to accomplish. With agricultural prices generally low during those years, people had little incentive to start up new stock and hay ranches. Nevertheless, sheep and wool production grew dramatically during this period. Although cattle had been the dominant kind of livestock raised in the area during the first decade of settlement, sheep gained in importance during the 1880s, increasing over tenfold between 1880 and 1900.[78]

The expansion of sheep raising in the Silver Lake Valley paralleled its growth in Lake County as a whole and in other sections of central and southeastern Oregon in those years.[79] Shortly after the turn of the century, however, tensions mounted between the cattle ranchers and sheep owners in central Oregon, including northern Lake County, over grazing rights. The fundamental issue in the conflict was the cattle ranchers' accusation that sheep cropped the grass too short and fouled water sources. They complained that nonlandowning sheepmen grazed their flocks on public lands without having any stake in the land itself, while cattle ranchers owned and maintained ranch buildings and fences, constructed ponds, and made other improvements. Sheep owners countered by pointing out that sheep ate plants cattle would not touch, thus making efficient use of the range. They also charged that cattlemen often owned only single acres of land scattered over a wide area, the improvements on each consisting simply of a well and a watering trough for their animals drifted out on the open, public range.

Friction between the two sides came to head in northern Lake County in July 1903, when the self-styled Crook County Sheepshooters Association attacked a band of sheep near Benjamin Lake in the northeastern corner of the county. Eleven masked horsemen bound and tied the two herders and shot twenty-four hundred sheep.[80] Seven months later, three thousand sheep owned by a Silver Lake man were killed. After the herder had corralled the sheep for the night,

five masked men rode up to him, emerging from a hiding place nearby, where they had evidently awaited this opportunity, compelled him to stand with his arms up and his back to the crowd while they placed a

sack over his face and tied his hands. He was then compelled to stand by
a juniper tree, while, with rifles, pistols, knives and clubs . . . , the masked
men proceeded to slaughter sheep.[81]

After killing 75 percent of the herd, the men warned the herder
to keep sheep off the range and to keep quiet about what he had witnessed. "Some of the people who were involved, who went out and
killed sheep, I guess, lived here in Silver Lake, but no one was supposed to know who did it," said Mary Emery. "Yeah, there were several of them," agreed Russell. "This Creed Conn, that run this one
store, he sold them the ammunition." The sheep slaughterers were
apparently afraid that Conn might reveal their identities, for a threatening note was pinned to the door of his store, and a string of his
wagons was burned as a warning to him against leaking information.[82] In early March, "he come up missing, and they didn't know
where he was," said Russell Emery. "They couldn't find him." Toward
the end of April, Conn's body was recovered from Bridge Creek near
Silver Lake, with two bullet wounds in the chest. The coroner's inquest
brought in a prudent verdict of suicide, although "the general belief
was that he was murdered."[83] According to a woman in Fort Rock, "if
one of the old-timers was sick, you know, and liable to pass away . . .
then some of this old bunch [involved in Conn's murder] would sit
with him to be sure that he didn't tell the straight of it in all these
killings."[84] The day after Conn's body was found, a flock of eighteen
hundred sheep in Christmas Lake Valley was driven off a cliff by masked
riders. Those animals that did not perish from the fall were finished
off with guns. (The cliff is still known locally as Sheep Rock).[85]

It seems not coincidental that the range war occurred about the
same time that the federal government was closing considerable amounts
of acreage in the area to homestead entry for the proposed Warner
Mountain Forest Reserve and the Silver Lake Irrigation Project. The
process began in 1903. By 1906, however, with the formation of the
Fremont National Forest and the temporary abandonment of irrigation plans, a good deal of the forest land reserves and virtually all of
the reclamation project land had been restored to entry. In that same
year, the federal government moved to end the violence over range
rights by granting stockmen of both persuasions grazing permits
in the newly created forest reserves bordering the Silver Lake and
Fort Rock valleys on the southwest and northwest. After the "war,"

however, the sheep industry in Lake County never returned to the peak it had reached in 1900; in ten years the number of animals dropped by 100,000.

With the conflict between the two major agricultural interests in the area resolved, Silver Lake experienced slow but steady growth. Its position as a trading center for the northern part of Lake County was assured because of the area's isolation from rail service. " 'Th' town [of Silver Lake] couldn't help but grow,' an old-timer confided to me," wrote George Palmer Putnam, touring central Oregon in 1909. " 'Yer see, it was such a durn fierce trip, after a feller tried it once he never wanted ter repeat—so he stayed with us!' "[86] The trip referred to would have been by passenger stage which, along with regular freight and mail service between Silver Lake and Prineville three times a week, offset the lack of a railroad to some extent.[87] Talk of a railroad coming into the area was standard copy in booster literature, but Silver Lakers also liked to boast that, at a distance of 140 miles from Shaniko, their post office was reputedly farther from a rail line than any other in the United States.[88] They repeated with relish the story of a local youngster who, upon hearing adults talking about "railroad tracks," asked his father, "Pa, are railroad tracks anything like bear tracks?"[89]

Silver Lake's social and cultural life had actually begun to take an upward swing around the turn of the century. In 1899, the first of several fraternal lodges—the Woodmen of the World—was organized. Two years later, the townspeople constructed a telephone line to link them with Lakeview. By 1906, with a population close to a hundred[90] the town consisted of "2 General Merchandise stores, 2 hotels, 2 newspapers, 2 sawmills, 1 blacksmith shop, 1 shoemakers shop, [and] 1 saloon run by Silvertooth," as well as livery stables, a barber shop, a Methodist church, and a school. Several buildings in town were "furnished with electric light from the plant of Mr. F. M. Chrisman, which uses power generated by a distillate engine."[91] Three newspapers were published there during the first years of the century and the town was even on the minstrel show circuit.[92] By 1909 there were two physicians in town—Dr. J. W. Thom, who arrived in 1904, and Dr. Adeline Kenney, whose father was the town druggist. A Baptist church was organized by 1908, and Reverend George Washington Reynolds of Surprise Valley, California, became the church's pastor in 1909.[93]

While this bustle of activity was going in the Silver Lake Valley, the "desert" to the north still lay vacant, except for cowboys and shepherds in the summer and for a handful of permanent settlers. But things were destined to change drastically—and rapidly—during the next ten years.

Indian
Paintbrush

"That was hectic out there on the desert. . . . They didn't have nothing, just a-looking for a home."¹

2

Homesteading the High Desert: 1905–1912

While the development of the Silver Lake Valley as a stock- and hay-raising area took place over a period of nearly forty years, the Fort Rock–Christmas Lake Valley was settled and then nearly abandoned within the span of a decade by people attempting to farm. The settlement on the desert occurred between 1905 and 1915, at the same time that tens of thousands of people were moving into other areas of the arid West, including much of the Great Basin and the northern Plains. Under the twin stimuli of cheap land and high wheat prices, these twentieth-century homesteaders attempted to extend the agricultural frontier to its full limits.² The scope of this effort was monumental; nationally, more land was taken up under the various laws governing the disposition of the public domain in the twenty years after 1900 than in the forty years before.³ Within the Fort Rock–Christmas Lake Valley, the statistics are equally dramatic: in 1904, 95 percent of the land there was still in the public domain; by 1915, over 90 percent of it had been claimed under one or another of the homestead laws. Almost overnight, the desert was transformed—sagebrush was cleared, buildings were erected, roads criss-crossed the valley. People planted seed and hoped to harvest crops in an effort to create a new American garden according to the old American dream. On the Oregon desert, they had their work cut out for them.

The transformation occurred in two stages. The first, lasting from 1905 to 1908, involved primarily desert land entries and attempts at irrigation; the second phase, from 1909 to 1914, was prompted by the passage of the Enlarged Homestead Act in 1909.

PHASE I—1905–1908

A few white settlers were already living in the valley before the homestead rush began. John Jackson and A. L. Chase seem to have been the earliest. They were living at Christmas Lake—one at the eastern end, the other at the western—when government land surveyors came through in 1882.[4] In addition, a few people had taken up scattered timber claims on the northern fringes of the Fort Rock Valley in the 1890s. In 1900, Alonzo Long, who had been a stockman in Lake County for a number of years,[5] purchased the Jackson homestead on the southwestern edge of Christmas Lake from a Thomas Farrell, and moved his wife, Mary, and their three children, Everett, Reuben, and Anna, from Lakeview to the desert. "We came from Lakeview via the east side of Summer Lake," wrote Anna Long Linebaugh. "My father drove a six horse team with two wagons. Reuben and I rode with mother, who drove a team with a buckboard. Brother Everett and a hired man were [on] horseback, bringing the cattle and loose horses."[6]

"The homestead included a log cabin and a good-sized barn," Anna remembered. The barn was built of "hand-hewn timbers, with pegs to hold it together."[7] To supplement the family's first 160 acres, Mary Long proved up on a desert land claim of 320 acres, and Alonzo filed on one 160-acre homestead claim in 1903 and on another in 1909.[8]

The Longs frequently provided accommodations for travelers through the desert during their first years at Christmas Lake because, according to Anna, "four major travel routes intersected in our neighborhood. Mother ran an informal inn, where travelers stopped for rest and rejuvenation on journeys through the desert. Meals were served family style for 50 cents. Mother's sister and family stopped over, when they moved from Jackson County to Idaho in 1904. The ZX [a local ranch] cowboys were seasonal guests."[9] The family had no permanent neighbors in the Christmas Lake Valley until 1904. "That's when they started settling [the desert]," Anna told me. "I remember that because of a little chair that a locator gave to me. He used to come from Prineville and stay at our place. He brought me that chair when I was four years old. That's when they first started settling the desert."[10]

This first wave of settlement was concentrated in the Christmas Lake Valley, beginning "in February, 1905, [when] a party of a dozen or more men, neighbors and residents in Willamette Valley, were brought in by a 'locator' and took up claims in the region north of Fossil Lake, now locally known as 'Sucker Flat.' In the fall of the same year and in the spring of 1906, others came in and settled, chiefly around Christmas and Fossil Lakes."[11]

At least one motivation for taking up land in the desert at this time was the possibility that the Oregon Eastern Railroad would soon be built through the Fort Rock–Christmas Lake Valley. Incorporated in 1905 as a subsidiary of the Union Pacific, the Oregon Eastern pro- jected a line from Vale, the terminus of the Oregon Short Line, to the Natron cutoff on the eastern slope of the Cascades. The route to be taken through the valley passed just south of Christmas Lake. By January 1906, the Oregon Eastern was reportedly ready "to start work east from the Natron area." Surveys within the Fort Rock– Christmas Lake Valley were made and rights-of-way acquired begin- ning in 1907.[12]

In addition to the people who filed claims near the proposed rail line in the Christmas Lake Valley, a few people took up land in town- ships in the Fort Rock Valley through which the projected route was to pass. (Other townships to the east and south either had been with- drawn from entry as forest reserve land in 1903 or were as yet unsurveyed and therefore ineligible for entry.) Although the railroad was never built and the rights-of-way were finally relinquished in the late 1920s, people who filed on claims along its proposed route, as well as those who acquired and developed commercial property in both valleys, must have done so on the strength of the promise of growth offered by railroad construction and operation. Randall Howard, a journalist who visited central Oregon in 1910, hinted as much when he wrote that "settlers, in their haste to reach Central Oregon ahead of the railway and to get a better choice from the open Government lands, took a chance, freighted their goods a hundred or two miles to the interior, built their homesteaders' cabins and waited."[13]

A second impetus for settlement in 1905 may have been the Reclamation Service's proposed Silver Lake Irrigation Project. In

December 1904, 140,000 acres in the Christmas Lake and Silver Lake valleys were withdrawn from entry, pending a study of the feasibility of an irrigation project in the area. The lands taken up by homesteaders in 1905 and 1906 bordered the reclamation project area. The withdrawn lands were restored to entry in June 1906, and by November of that year, "about 120 claims had been filed on in the valley."[14]

These claims were clustered in three locales—at Christmas Lake, at Fossil Lake, and near the sink of Peter's Creek—where water was more accessible, albeit in some places only intermittently.[15]

While the early settlers found water in both lakes and springs rather readily, these sources were not always reliable, as fluctuations in precipitation levels caused them to dry up periodically. Anna Linebaugh recalled that when her family first settled at Christmas Lake, "the lake had a spring on either end of it, there was a meadow on the north side of it and a pasture on the south side. The lake was one mile long and a half mile wide. It was alkaline water except the south end where there was a spring and fresh water. . . . I heard the folks say that in 1902 Christmas Lake went dry, filled up again and went dry again in 1904. Then it filled again and it didn't go clear dry again 'til 1913–14."

Ironically, it was often the consequences of settlement near water sources that caused them to fail. A spring on the western edge of Christmas Lake, for instance, was "soon buried by sand . . . when the willows and nearby sage were cleared off."[16]

Settlement had proceeded to such an extent by the end of 1906 that post offices had been established at Lake and Cliff (named after the locator who brought the settlers in) and a school district formed. The Lake post office was located at the Long place on Christmas Lake, and the Cliff post office near Fossil Lake, with weekly service between them and Silver Lake. A third post office was established in Fort Rock the following year. By 1908, the U.S. Weather Bureau was using temperature and precipitation data from a volunteer observer in Christmas Lake.[17]

The boom began in earnest in 1908. William Powers, who had arrived in the Christmas Lake Valley in 1907, reported that "a year after we located there was a big rush to the valley."[18] Homestead filings in the Fort Rock–Christmas Lake Valley tripled from thirty-five in 1907 to eighty-seven the following year.[19] Most of the homesteading activity in the Fort Rock Valley took place near Fort Rock itself and to the west where the town of Fremont was developing. In the Christmas

Lake Valley, the greatest activity continued to center around the lake itself.

Most of the people arriving in that vicinity between 1906 and 1909 filed on desert land claims in addition to their regular homesteads. In the township in which the fledgling community of Lake was located, for instance, forty-three of the eighty-six land claims filed were on desert land. These claims were made possible by the Desert Land Act of 1891 which permitted an individual to acquire up to 320 acres of the public domain, with the stipulation that the land be irrigated and producing a crop within a period of three years.[20] There was no residence requirement, as the government allowed an individual to file a desert claim in addition to a regular homestead claim upon which an entryman was required to live. The flurry of desert land claims around Lake, especially in 1907 and 1908, seems to have been the result of the visit of government water resources geologist Gerald Waring to the area in the fall of 1906. In his report, published in 1908, Waring pinpointed two potential reservoir sites in the Christmas Lake Valley, one near Peter's Creek and the other south of Christmas Lake, both of which might store runoff water from the surrounding slopes.[21] Waring's conclusions must have become common knowledge before his report was published—most likely from conversations he had had with local residents while he was conducting his survey. The desert land claims thus represent people's attempts to acquire land that could most easily be irrigated.

Elsewhere in the west, fraud regularly attended desert land claims, but in the Christmas Lake Valley most such claims were taken up in conjunction with regular homestead entries, indicating that the entrymen were not interested in land speculation.[22] William Powers, who had filed on a desert land claim himself, stated emphatically in a letter to the General Land Office in 1912 that "the people who have settled on this desert land are not speculators but people who are trying to make homes for their families."[23] In spite of honest intentions, however, two-thirds of the desert land claims were relinquished, that is, voluntarily given up, between 1907 and 1912; only one ever came to patent. While people tried in good faith to fulfill the conditions of the law by putting their land under irrigation, they found themselves unable to do so, primarily because there simply was not enough water.

Compounding the water problem was the poor quality of the soils. In many parts of the valley, the soil was very porous, making flood irrigation virtually useless. And everywhere, irrigation brought salts in the soil to the surface, creating a hardpan over the top of the ground. Waring described the alkaline nature of the soils in the Fort Rock–Christmas Lake Valley in some detail, although he concluded, with an optimism that characterizes his entire report, that care in irrigation and cultivation would keep their harmful effects to a minimum. He predicted, with prophetic irony, that "troubles from excessive irrigation and rise of the ground-water level [are not] apt to be serious in the valleys of Lake County, because of the fairly low present water level and the improbability of development of water to such an extent that it will be used lavishly."[24]

Excessive salts in the soils eventually proved of less concern to the people trying to irrigate than the alkalinity of the groundwater they were pumping. On his claim in the western Christmas Lake Valley, for instance, William Powers pumped "very little water [at all] and lots of that so bad from minerals that it isn't fit for house use and some of it not fit for stock water."[25] Farther west, another homesteader found that "the water he got was so badly charged with alkali that nothing would grow after he put the water on the land."[26] Thus, in spite of the determined efforts of those who took up desert land claims, the land simply could not be bent to their purposes.

People were eager to take up desert land along with their regular homestead claims because the 160 acres allowed under the Homestead Act was simply insufficient to produce a living for a family on the high desert. Filing on both a regular homestead and desert claim gave an entryman 480 acres; if two adult members of a family filed both homestead and desert land entries, the total could be boosted to 960. It became, in fact, common practice for family members—husbands and wives, brothers and sisters, cousins—to take up blocks of land in adjoining claims. This is what Henry Morgenstern proposed in a letter to his father-in-law in 1908:

Bend, Sept. 29
Dear Father—
I have been up to the land of which I sent you the papers.
I think that is the best proposition I ever saw. I will sent you $100 and I want you and Frank to come as soon as you can. I could buy a team and meet you at Shaniko, but it would take so much longer to get there that the expenses would be about as much for the round trip.

I know of no place where all of us can get together in as good a place as that appears to be. The water is from 6 to 22 ft. and as good as you ever drank. I won't say any more for I want both of you to come. You can take 160 Desert yet Mother can take 320. Frank can take Homestead Desert all 320. Roe can do the same when he gets of age. I can take 320. If we all could get together it would be a bunch of 1440 acres. We ought to be able to do well with that. As far as you and I are concerned we could do well here but for the boys there is nothing left here that I know of [i.e., in terms of employment]. A person must be here to file and the land won't last long.

It is about 87 miles from here East and South and warmer.

If you think enough of this to investigate do so as soon as you can for the way people are coming in it won't last very long. At least it won't be so as we can get it all together as we can now and have our pick. The land is all level and sage brush from 8 to 6 ft. high and very easily cleared. No rock. There are about 50 who have located there already, and some are building, etc. There are disadvantages but I want you to look this up and bring any friends with you you want to.

Should you come let me know so I can get things ready.

I can go anytime after the 14th.

I am going to drive stage until I hear from you.

Hoping that I will be of some advantage to you some way. I will let you have all the money you need for filing. Also Frank if he can come. Desert land costs 1.25 in money .25 cash per acre balance in four years or sooner if desired.[27]

When the Enlarged Homestead Act was passed in 1909, the entries on desert land dropped dramatically, for the new law allowed people to claim up to 320 acres of land without having to irrigate it.

PHASE II—1909–1915

The Enlarged Homestead Act allowed an entryman to take up 320 acres of public land designated by the Secretary of the Interior as "nonmineral, nonirrigable, unreserved, and unappropriated surveyed public lands which do not contain merchantable timber."[28] The law thus excluded entry on lands that could be obtained under any of the other existing land disposition laws. There were both advantages and disadvantages to the new law from the point of view of the homesteaders. On the one hand, it doubled the amount of acreage permitted under the original Homestead Act of 1862 and removed the onus of irrigation. On the other hand, it required five years of residence on the land instead of the usual three, along with cultivation of at least one-eighth of the acreage within three years.

In Oregon, most of the lands opened to entry under the Enlarged Homestead Act, beginning in February 1909, were in the central desert.[29] Fifteen townships in the Fort Rock–Christmas Lake Valley were designated for enlarged homestead entry on April 27, 1909. Omitted were lands in the forest reserve on the northern edge of the valley and an area east of the Connley Hills included in the U.S. Reclamation Service's Silver Lake Irrigation Project as potentially irrigable.[30]

The opening of the public lands in Oregon under the new homestead law was well publicized. Newspapers carried announcements of the openings, and the General Land Office published maps showing exactly what lands were eligible for entry. Railroads with interests in central Oregon also boosted the area. In addition to these sources of information there was the informal and unofficial promotion of central Oregon by people who came to the area early on and who wrote enthusiastically to relatives and friends about the potential of the desert.[31]

The response to the opening of the land in central Oregon under the Enlarged Homestead Act was tremendous. By the end of 1909, 224 new homestead claims had been filed in the Fort Rock–Christmas Lake Valley, sixty-one of them in September alone.[32] Most of the entries were concentrated in three locales: near and west of Fort Rock, in the eastern end of the Fort Rock Valley at the foot of the Connley Hills, and northeast of Christmas Lake. Oddly enough, although people had apparently been attracted to the desert because of the publicity surrounding the Enlarged Homestead Act, most of them did not take up 320-acre claims, preferring instead to file on regular 160-acre homesteads. In 1909, for instance, only 38 of 224 entries were for 320 acres.

There were obvious advantages to the 160-acre claims. The residence requirement was shorter, and the claim could be commuted and title gained by paying $1.25 per acre after fourteen months. An enlarged homestead claim, in contrast, could be commuted only after three full years of residence. The smaller percent of enlarged homestead entries may also reflect the limited amount of acreage open to such entry. Only fifteen townships were opened to entry by April 1909, although eight more townships or parts of townships were opened by the end of 1913.[33]

By that time, the people coming into the Fort Rock–Christmas Lake Valley reversed a four-year-old pattern by filing more enlarged homestead claims than regular homestead entries. One stimulus for this was the relaxation in 1912 of the residence requirement for larger homesteads from five to three years. In addition, an entryman was allowed five months' absence each year from his claim and could commute the entry after fourteen months of continuous residence. Not only did the number of actual enlarged homestead entries soar after 1912, but people who had already claimed 160 acres took advantage of the favorable turn of events by filing second claims for 160 acres, in order to bring their total holdings up to the 320 acres to which they were entitled under the law.[34]

The people who began pouring onto the desert in 1909 arrived, literally, from all over the world. A good many of the homesteaders came from within the Pacific Northwest, some from the western interior valleys such as the Willamette, others from the wheat-growing regions of southeastern Washington and northeastern Oregon. More than half of them were originally from midwestern, plains, or southern border states; a few came from the East Coast. In addition to native-born Americans, there were Germans, Irish, and Norwegians, along with Britons, Scots, French, Swiss, Swedes, Danes, Finns, Russians, Bohemians, Poles, Lithuanians, and Canadians. These foreign-born individuals made up 10 percent of the area's population in 1910.

Judging from the birthplaces of their children, some of the homesteaders had made several moves before arriving in central Oregon. For instance, an Illinois couple's four children were born successively in Kansas, Illinois, Iowa, and Idaho. Another family's five children had been born in Oklahoma, Kansas, California and Oregon.

In addition to the "professional" pioneers who had taken up and relinquished homesteads elsewhere, the Oregon desert also attracted a fair number of "greenhorns" with no farming experience. By and large these were people from Portland, Seattle, and other urban centers, "city men and women who saw here a chance to make a beginning."[35] Many had worked for wages or salaries before taking up homestead claims.[36] Peter Godon, for instance, who brought his wife and five young daughters from Philadelphia to the Fort Rock Valley in 1909, was a French-born hotel chef. Most of the homesteaders "were professional people from the city who came out here," long-time resident Eleanor Long told me. "They didn't stay very long because they just didn't know how to cope with it." Edwin Eskelin explained that some people who had never farmed before were attracted to the area "because they seen the others was here. They'd see a little straw stack and thought they could farm here. That's what brought Henry Ostrum here. He never farmed in his life; he was a carpenter. . . . He come out here and he seen this straw stack. Somebody'd thrashed some grain, and so he thought, boy, that's what he's going to do."[37]

The homesteaders arrived on the desert singly, in pairs, and, often, in extended family groups. While half of the households in the 1910 census contained married couples, a third of the homesteaders were single men,[38] and a handful were single women—a situation that must have given rise to many scenes like that experienced by Anna Steinhoff, who homesteaded near Christmas Lake in 1910. "This afternoon one of the bachelor neighbors came. He brought me a rabbit and then told me of his hunt etc. We talked of very sensible subjects until dusk. Then his conversation drifted off on matrimony etc. I was honored with a proposal and he with a refusal before he left."[39]

Although Anna had taken up her claim as a single woman, she was not alone on the desert. She and her sister, Millie, had joined their cousin, Alvin Miller, who was already there, and had filed on adjoining claims, building their houses on the line between them. (This was apparently a common practice on the desert—one house was used for cooking and living space, the other for sleeping quarters.[40]) The Steinhoff sisters were not the only homesteaders who settled on the desert as an extended family group. William Powers came to the Christmas Lake Valley in 1907 with four of his sons.[41] Seventy-six-year-old Civil War veteran Manius Buchanan moved to the same vicinity with his son. Mother and daughter Emma and Augusta DeForest homesteaded on adjacent claims south of Fort Rock. Alonzo Long's brother settled at Sink. The General Land Office tract books, in which homestead entries were recorded, are strewn with family names shared by four, five, or six different individuals.

People who were considering homesteading were repeatedly advised in government publications and even in promotional literature to bring sufficient capital with them to make the initial outlay for stock, equipment, seed, and building materials, and enough cash to cover living expenses until the homestead could begin producing an income-earning crop. The *Oregon Voter* sounded a typical warning, advising that "the homesteader should have enough money to last him two or three years until his place is in producing condition"; the editor suggested between $1,000 and $2,000 as a minimum.[42] How much most of the entrymen in the Fort Rock–Christmas Lake Valley actually brought with them is unknown, but it is likely that most of them arrived with very little, for the land itself was free, or virtually so; people with a substantial amount of capital would likely find more suitable land for purchase elsewhere. The land offered by the government in the Oregon desert, after all, was among the least desirable of all the land remaining in the public domain at that time. Those willing to take it up must have had little alternative.

Because they had little or no reserves to sustain them through lean years, many of the homesteaders began leaving as soon as dry years and hard times set in between 1913 and 1916. Although Reub Long wrote that "those with the least stayed the longest,"[43] his axiom did not likely hold true in all cases. Roberta Miles met one of the former homesteaders in later years and asked him why he had left "after he'd built his house. 'Well,' he said, 'I had that much money and I spent it. And when I spent it then there was nothing else to do.' He couldn't live on nothing, so he left."

Even those who managed to hang on until they had gained title to their land were by no means well off.[44] The monetary value of their improvements, equipment, and other moveable property ranged from $300 to $2,500; few of the homesteaders were worth more than $1,000. Compared with the capital investments in ranches in the Silver Lake Valley, ranging from $17,000 to $127,000 during the same period, the homesteaders' assets were indeed modest.[45]

ARRIVING ON THE DESERT

Most of the homesteaders arrived in the Fort Rock–Christmas Lake Valley with little more than hope, determination, and whatever equipment and furnishings they could load on a wagon or pay to have shipped from their former homes. Those coming from the East or the Midwest rode the Great Northern or Northern Pacific as far as Spokane or The Dalles, then traveled to Shaniko via the Columbia Southern or—after 1911—to Bend on the Oregon Trunk Railroad. The rest of the journey was made by stage. When the Godons came west from Philadelphia, "the end of the railroad was Opal City [Oregon]," said Jo. "And that's where we came to. We waited there for the wagons to come and take us on in." Fred and Marie Eskelin arrived as home-steaders in the Fort Rock Valley in 1909. Fred had been born in Fin-land, Marie in Norway. They were living in Michigan when they decided to migrate to Oregon. "From Pendleton, Mother came by train as far as Shaniko, which was the end of the track at that time," their son Edwin wrote. "Then by horse drawn stage past the town of Bend which at that time had very few buildings, arriving at the homestead July 15, 1909. The area then was known as Arrow, because it was served by Arrow post office, located 3 miles South and 1/2 mile east of the homestead."[46]

Even the trip from western Oregon was an arduous one. Anna and Millie Steinhoff left Portland at 10 A.M. on November 1, 1910, traveling via Shaniko, Prineville, and Bend, and arriving in Silver Lake by stage forty-one hours later. From there, after a day's rest, they took another stage to the Christmas Lake Valley that dropped them off in the middle of emptiness a mile and a half from their claims. They walked the rest of the way, carrying what they had brought with them to set up housekeeping: "grips, a quilt, one length of stove pipe, and a broom." Anna noted in her diary that when they reached their land, they found that "the shacks were done but [had] nothing in them."

While the Steinhoff sisters had filed on their claims before they moved to the desert, other people arrived in the valley hoping to find suitable tracts. The greenness of most newcomers made them uncertain of their own abilities to gauge the suitability of land for agriculture. Even those who had some knowledge of farming may have been hesitant to rely on previous experience when confronted with the desert landscape. Thus "locating" settlers on government lands became a thriving business. Locators represented themselves as familiar with the area and offered their expertise to landseekers looking for a good piece of land on which to file a claim for fees ranging from $30 to $300.[47] "These locators and real estate people actually made quite a bit of money bringing people out here and selling them wheat land," said Hazel Ward. "Well, they couldn't sell it to them. It was government land. They did what they called locating. They were paid a fee for locating."

George Palmer Putnam, during his trip through central Oregon in 1909, encountered a locator at a stage stop between Shaniko and Bend and heard part of his promotional spiel:

> "Well, when it comes right down to getting something worth while—
> something for nothing, you might say—the claims down by Silver Lake
> can't be beat." He launched into a rosy description. . . . My informant
> was a professional "locator" whose business it is to combine the landless
> man and the manless land with some profit to himself, in the shape of a

fee for showing each "prospect" a suitable tract of untaken earth hitherto the property of Uncle Sam.[48]

Locators advertised in local newspapers, hoping to attract the attention of the homeseekers who had not yet filed on land. A typical ad in the *Silver Lake Leader* in 1909 read: "U. S. Dickey. We do a general locating business and can locate you on the choicest lands in the famous Fort Rock and Christmas Lake Valley's which is the comming wheat-producing section of Oregon."[49]

Fred Eskelin was one of the homesteaders who used the services of a locator because "difficulty in speaking the English language, lack of knowledge of farming in the new land, and lack of money made it difficult for Father to search for suitable farm land. . . . When Father and John [Uksila, a fellow land-seeker] arrived in Silver Lake, the weather was nice, and there was no snow. This was in early Feb. 1909. . . .

> M. S. Buchanan was engaged to locate a homestead for Father and Mr. Uksila. Mr. Buchanan escorted [them] to the most suitable places around Christmas Lake, but all the while, Father had his eye on the place next to Hayes hills [the northern end of the Connley Hills]. On the way back to Silver Lake Father had Mr. Buchanan stop so he could look at the land that seemed desirable to him. The section Father wanted had been surveyed (all the land north of that section in Fort Rock Valley had not been surveyed). Father got off the wagon and standing on the South-East corner of the section said "dhis my homsted." Locators under those circumstances quite often explained that the land they showed had better soil, but Father had no way of knowing what soil was good and what wasn't.[50]

SETTING UP ON THE CLAIM

Once his claim was filed, the first tasks facing the homesteader were to construct a dwelling and to secure an adequate supply of water. The law allowed a grace period of up to six months before an entryman had to take up residence on his claim. Some people used this time to build their houses before moving themselves and their families onto the homestead site. Others waited until the last minute to move onto their land and met their immediate needs for shelter by pitching large tents until permanent dwellings could be built. The Ray Nash family of Fort Rock lived in a tent when they first arrived. "I was the first baby to be born at Fort Rock—March 31, 1908," wrote oldest son, Dwight. "I was born in a tent, in a snow storm and a resulting

A HOMESTEADING COUPLE IN THE FORT ROCK VALLEY, IN FRONT OF
THEIR TENT. *Courtesy of Shorty Gustafson.*

wind that blew the tent down."[51] Such a flimsy housing arrangement
in unfamiliar surroundings makes the behavior of another homestead
family understandable. During their first few weeks in the Christmas
Lake Valley, Marie Jetter wrote, her parents "took turns at night sitting outside the tent with a gun, in case any wild animals came around.
This probably wasn't necessary, but they must have felt more secure
in doing it."[52] Reportedly, some families "lived in a tent all the time
they were there." Others simply made do with what shelter was available before their houses were built. The Godons, for instance, lived in
a shed on a neighboring homestead for a month before their cabin
was completed.[53]

When the homesteaders were ready to build, they discovered that
natural building materials were scarce on the desert. Juniper, although
plentiful enough, was generally too small, too hard, and too gnarled
to produce logs suitable for construction. Most of the pine growing on

HOMESTEAD CABIN IN THE NORTHERN FORT ROCK VALLEY. *Courtesy of Shorty Gustafson.*

the surrounding hills was either protected in forest reserve land or located too far from building sites to be transported feasibly. Only the earliest structures in the valley were built of native timber. The Jackson cabin near Christmas Lake, erected shortly after 1880 and purchased by Alonzo Long in 1900, was one such house. (The house stood on its original site until 1981.)[54] Reub Long, who grew up there, wrote that the logs for the house had been hauled from Pine Ridge (also called Lost Forest), an anomalous stand of pine surrounded by sand dunes about twenty miles northeast of Christmas Lake.[55] At least two log houses were constructed in the Fort Rock Valley. One was built by three brothers, Lee, Tom, and Bill Edwards, east of the Devil's Garden. The other, a 14 x 24, one-room log structure, was erected north of the town of Fremont by a Penrose family.[56]

Most of the homesteaders, however, used pine logs only for foundation sills; for the remainder of their building needs they relied on milled lumber hauled from sawmills in the Silver Lake Valley. Most accessible to the Fort Rock–Christmas Lake Valley was the Embody mill, thirteen miles northwest of Silver Lake town and about nine miles south and west of Fort Rock. Present-day maps show a tangle of unimproved roads leading to and from the once busy location, although nothing now remains at the site where the mill stood. When the Eskelin house was built, Ed wrote, "the lumber for the house was hauled July 21 [1909], the house was completed July 26, then Father left for work July 29. The lumber was purchased from Embody saw mill located 23 miles almost due West of the homestead. . . .

"Father rented Walter Buick's team of horses and wagon to haul the lumber. The rent was $2.00 per day for team and $2.00 per day for wagon. Total cost of the house was $51.00. Mother always recalled how happy she was to be able to go into her own house (a 10 by 16 rough board cabin)."[57] Homesteaders calculated that "if you got one load of lumber, that built you one room. If you got two loads of lumber, then you had two rooms," said a woman whose parents homesteaded in the Fort Rock Valley in 1913. I asked her how big her parents' house had been. "They had two loads of lumber," she laughed.[58]

The houses the homesteaders built were small and simple, of box-frame construction with board-and-batten or, occasionally, shiplap exteriors.[59] These "box houses," as the homesteaders called them, were erected over foundations of field stone or, more commonly, "of two logs, or more, laid on either side of a pit (used as a root cellar) with the floor planking nailed to the logs."[60] Nearly every house had a cellar, usually two feet smaller than the outer dimensions of the house itself and five to six feet deep. The cellars were used to store root crops, canned foods, and other items that needed protection from freezing temperatures. The roofing for the houses was "mostly of wood shingles, the source of which was the Ponderosa pine forest that is found to the north and west of Fort Rock, at a distance of about five to ten miles."[61] Tarpaper and "rubberoid" roofing were also used; one family simply stretched a tent over the house to serve as a roof. Though volcanic rock, plentiful in the area, was reportedly used for chimneys and was locally designated "chimney rock," stovepipes seem to have been more common than stone chimneys. One homestead house, still standing in 1981, even sported "two homemade chimneys constructed of five gallon cans."[62]

The houses varied in size, representing a balance between the amount of living space needed and the amount of money available for lumber. They ordinarily ranged from 10 x 16 feet to 16 x 20, and stood a story or a story-and-a-half high. The most common sizes were 12 x 14 and 12 x 16; a few were as large as 24 x 24.[63] Most houses consisted of either one or two rooms, though three- and four-room houses were apparently not uncommon. Single-room houses were sometimes partitioned with curtains into living and sleeping areas, and lofts, used for sleeping and storage, were often erected to create more space. A house could also be enlarged by adding a room, a lean-to shed, or an ell onto the original structure.[64] Some houses had exterior porches, and a few of them sported picket fences. They were only rarely painted; as the wood weathered, the houses took on the browns and grays of the surrounding landscape. Thus the buildings, though rising abruptly and rectilinearly from the ground, soon appeared to be natural outgrowths of it.

Inside, the dwellings were usually "double-boarded" or ceiled with dressed lumber; sometimes the floors were also of a double thickness of lumber. One house, still standing in 1981, had tongue-and-groove flooring.[65] But the construction methods and materials used in most structures afforded only minimal protection from the elements. Anna Steinhoff recorded in her diary for May 13, 1911, that she "spent some time poking paper into the cracks in the side of my house." Venita Branch, who grew up on a homestead southwest of Fort Rock, recalled, "Quite often it was 20 below zero and 40 below. Even if our house had wallpaper, the nailheads had frost on them from the inside. That's when there was family togetherness. We were all around the big stove!

"Our neighbor had a one-room house with gables," she continued. "I remember staying there as a little kid, sleeping overnight and waking up and seeing those open gables [i.e., open to the outside]." Another family in her neighborhood had "a house that had cracks in the floor and bugs would come up," she remembered. The youngest

member of the family "was just old enough to crawl and he had a big spoon. And he'd see one coming up and crawl over and bang it with the spoon. She didn't have any trouble keeping things out!"[66]

In order to insulate as well as decorate the insides of their houses, the homesteaders often finished the interior walls with a covering of some sort, including purchased wallpaper, "blue building felt," or paper readily at hand (such as newspaper). Reub Long claimed that many of the children on the desert learned to read from the newsprint on the walls of their homes.[67] One homesteader, according to Roberta Miles, "was kind of an artistic guy, so he'd do his own pictures, make his own calendars to decorate the wall."

Household furnishings were usually sparse and simple because homesteaders often sold most of their belongings before departing for the desert. "Mother told me that back east they had beautiful furniture and all kinds of cut glass," said Jo Godon. "And that was all left behind." Replacing them were homemade tables and chairs, cupboards and shelves. Alvin Miller built furniture for Anna and Millie Steinhoff. Ed Eskelin's father furnished his family's house with items fashioned from native juniper.[68] Beds were simply rough frames or flat shelves, covered with straw ticks for mattresses. In his homestead cabin, Manius Buchanan had "a bed and bedding, cook stove, cupboard, five shelves, dishes, and clothing." Spanish-American war veteran Gilbert Smith's cabin contained "4 chairs, table, bed, bedding, stove, cooking utensils, clock, lamp, trunk, wardrobe, clothes, food, 2 guns, fishing tackle, and small library." The walls were "decorated with lithographs and one large Phillipine [sic] flag captured from Aguinaldo." The Lewis Haines family was a little more prosperous. They owned "a range and a heating stove, 2 beds, a cot and bedding for the same, a reasonable amount of dishes and cooking utensils, 1 dresser, 1 library table, 1 sewing machine [a rare luxury], 1 dining table, 3 trunks, a reasonably good housekeeping outfit, clothing, provisions." Likewise the Ernest Fenn family was relatively well off with "2 stoves, a bedstead, springs and bedding, chairs, table, stand, cupboard, trunk, phonograph, clothing, cooking utensils, carpet, a few pictures, curtains and window shades, books."[69]

Aside from the houses themselves, the homesteads comprised varying numbers of outbuildings of log, pole, or lumber construction. At a minimum, the homesteader built a privy, as well as a barn for whatever livestock he owned. Eventually, he might add stables, chicken

ESKELIN HOMESTEAD.

houses, and hog pens as needed. According to long-time resident Shorty Gustafson, one Fort Rock Valley homesteader conserved on building materials by constructing his house on stilts and enclosing a space beneath it for his stock. On the Eskelin homestead, "the side walls of the barn were made of 8 ft long fence posts lapped in such a way as to make a snow tight wall; the ends were made of lumber, and roof of long, comparatively knot-free, foot-wide boards. The roof came to within 4 feet of the ground on the East side, the lower portion being an additional chicken house." The Eskelin children took advantage of the low-sloping roof. "When the roof was frosty, brother John and I would go to the top of the roof with a barrel stave, then sit on the stave and slide down on that portion of the roof that extended close to the ground."[70]

Concurrent with building shelter for themselves and their animals, the homesteaders had to establish adequate and dependable water supplies. Some obtained water on a temporary basis by hauling it in barrels from a nearby well until their own supply was secured. In the northern part of the Fort Rock Valley, "when this [area] was first settled, there were so few wells, water was a real problem," said Hazel Ward, daughter of a homesteader. "I guess ours was probably the first well up in this area because the people east of here hauled water from here in a wagon and barrels. The Derricks [neighbors to the north] came down here and got water. . . . Down in the flat [i.e., on the valley floor] that wasn't such a problem," she explained, "because they could hand dig thirty feet and get water." Jo Godon remembered that her mother "used to pack [carry] water—two buckets of water—from that house over there [one-quarter mile away]. She had to pack water by hand. Imagine, had to do all the washing for us by hand. The drinking water was portioned out, just a glass every so often." The Steinhoff sisters also had to haul water when they first arrived on the desert. Anna's diary entry for Saturday, November 19, 1910, reads, "We took the washtub and went to Beckett's [a neighbor's] for water.

We put it half full and carried it home—1 1/4 miles." She added lacon-ically, "Found it hard work." Christmas Lake Valley homesteader Arthur Donahue complained directly to the Secretary of the Interior about the difficulty he encountered in securing water on his claim:

> April 1st, 1908 I filed on a homestead in Christmas Lake Valley. . . . Within 6 mo. after filing I was there with my family, but when I dug my well I struck water that was so bitter it could not be used. As I could not at that time procure barrels for hauling water I was obliged to live off [away from] my land until the last of Jan. 1909. . . . For six months in 1910 the family was alone but remained on the claim and hauled water on a hand cart 3/4 mil., over a road mostly filled with drifted sand. Such a task, my wife says, must be performed to be fully appreciated.[71]

One homestead family in the western end of the Fort Rock Valley "never did have a well," Bill Mattis told me. "They had two kids. And they'd have to pack their water. There was a well way down there at Fremont and it must have been a good two miles up to their place. Well, she would carry two buckets and each kid would have a gallon bucket. And that's the way they'd take their water home. For years they lived that way."[72]

Although there were a few natural springs in the Christmas Lake Valley, surface water in the area was virtually nonexistent. Wells were therefore a necessity; as early as 1906, twenty-five wells had been dug there.[73] Many homesteaders in the Christmas Lake Valley found water at relatively shallow depths (from seven to thirty-five feet), but others, especially near the hills and in the Fort Rock Valley, had to sink their wells deeper. Josiah Fox had to dig eighty feet and Ross Noel ninety-one feet ("54 feet through rock") to obtain water north of Fort Rock.[74]

The water quality from the wells in both valleys "generally speak-ing . . . is good, especially . . . in the west end of Fort Rock Valley where the water is only slightly alkaline to the taste," wrote two Rec-lamation Service engineers in 1915. "In the eastern end of Fort Rock Valley near Seven Mile Ridge the water from wells is distinctly alka-line to the taste, while in Christmas Lake Valley some of the wells have been abandoned as unfit for use on account of their strong min-eral character."[75]

Not everyone who dug wells found water. A few people even failed to find it on their land before proving up on their claims. Manius Buchanan was one of them; he obtained his water from his son's homestead for three years, as none of the eight wells he had dug was successful. Harry Baker listed a "43-foot well (dry)" as part of the improvements on his homestead. Frank Polte told the Department of the Interior that "for 2 years I was unable to get any water on the land, for the reason that I could not dig a well of sufficient depth to obtain the same." Mary Ashworth of Fort Rock, petitioning the General Land Office to grant her title to the desert land claim she had been unable to irrigate, testified

> that the wells on adjoining lands have proved insufficient even for domestic uses. That a well about 60 rds from this place on an adjoining 80 [acres] has been dug 65 ft with no signs of any water; that on the SE1/4 SE1/4, S. 24, T. 26S, R. 14E., and just across the section line a well was dug about 100 ft deep, and there is not even sufficient water there for domestic use; that a well has been dug on the adjoin[in]g tract (Lot 3) 80 feet deep and was discontinued because there was no water at that depth and it was solid rock where work was discontinued; that her husband has a well on the adjoin[in]g tract to the east of this entry which is 84 ft deep and only sufficient water for house use; that when he thrashed his grain in the summer of 1915, they had to haul water for the thrashers as our well supply gave out.[76]

Reub Long joked that "in some parts of the desert the homesteaders claimed it was as far to water straight down as it was to haul it from a source ten miles away."[77]

Most homesteaders dug wells themselves or with the help of neighbors. "I don't remember just when they started digging our well," said Jo Godon. "My dad dug that and my mother and my oldest sister pulled all the dirt up. You passed down a bucket and they had to pull it up with a windlass." The dug wells measured from three to six feet square at the top and were "cribbed" by boards, posts, flat rocks, or cement. Frames were built over them that held rope pulleys; some wells had windlasses. One homesteader with forethought dug his well beside the house and built an enclosed porch over it, so the family could get water in cold or stormy weather without stepping outside.[78]

Well digging sometimes proved a dangerous enterprise. "The well used to go dry and it would have to be deepened," explained Jo Godon.

> One time our well went dry and it had to be deepened so Ivy Stingley [a neighbor] came and said he'd go down to deepen the well. So he was down there and he hit rock and he had to dig rocks out. I don't know how he did it, when I think about it.
> We had a barrel, a nail keg. So Ivy, he loaded this barrel down heavy with the rock, and he said, "Now take this one real easy 'cause I've got it

loaded with rock." So we said, "All right." So we was going real easy, then when we got the thing to the top . . . the bottom dropped out of it. Nobody said a thing, we were so scared. And finally, Ivy hollered up to us. All that saved him—he was a quick thinker. He had a shovel and he said it turned dark in there when that thing [the barrel] started to come down there. He first thought the well was caving in. But he took up that shovel and he got up against the wall and put it over his head and that stuff come right in front of him.

Jo recalled the death of Raymond Duchaplay, a Fort Rock home-steader who was killed while helping a neighbor dig a well. "There's gas that forms in those wells," she said. "That gas'll kill you."

> This fellow that homesteaded this place, [Raymond] Duchaplay, he went over to help the Briggs. They were digging a well, and he went over to help them. I guess at noon they stopped and ate dinner, and they waited a while. He was anxious to get the well finished up. He wanted to hurry up and I'll be jeetered if he didn't get gassed and killed. They used to keep talking, hollering down when they're putting them down to see that they're all right, to see that they land all right. Well, he didn't answer and didn't answer. I guess he fell off the bucket and they felt the bucket lighten and knew something had happened.
> This Briggs, he wanted to go down there right away and his wife wouldn't let him, or he wouldn't ever have come out. They hooked him out and he was buried over there in the Fort Rock cemetery. It was when we first come here.

Most early wells were dug rather than drilled because of the pro-hibitive cost of well-drilling equipment. Not until 1915 was there a well-drilling rig in the valley, a steam-powered machine that "would transport itself from one job to another but the road speed was slow—a little over a mile an hour."[79] The advantage of drilled wells was their greater depth; people who were able to sink shafts deep enough to reach the water table usually managed to procure an adequate amount of good water. Fred Stratton drilled a 197-foot well in the township south of Fremont; southeast of Cougar Mountain, Josiah Rhoton had a well 210 feet deep that provided "plenty of water for livestock." Law-rence Frizzell, on his homestead south of Fort Rock, had two 15-foot dug wells and a 200-foot drilled well.[80]

Although most wells were located on private property, there was reportedly at least one community well in the valley, located at Fremont. The well was dug in the middle of the road, providing water for stage and freight horses as well as the people living there. In stormy weather,

"it provided 'running water'—the people would run to the well and back to their homes with the water pail," wrote Ed Eskelin tongue-in-cheek.[81]

Ranchers had dug a few wells in the Fort Rock–Christmas Lake Valley before the turn of the century to supply water for their stock, but most of the water for livestock during the early years of homesteading was available mainly from ponds or springs. "There were water holes when they first started settling up," said Hazel Ward. "It must have been wetter because I've heard so many people tell about water holes which have not been around very much in my lifetime."

To insure a steady flow of well water for domestic use, livestock, and irrigation, many homesteaders installed windmills. But there is conflicting testimony about the amount of wind on the desert and therefore their efficacy. Reub Long, who lived in the area all his life, said that the wind blew almost constantly.[82] Anna Steinhoff made frequent mention of the wind in her diary. "The wind blew all night and was so bad all day that we could scarcely step outdoors," she

wrote on May 18, 1911. "The air was full of dust and sand, and it was
very cold." At times the wind would blow "just like a hurricane," Ed
Eskelin told me. "The rabbits would run sideways. The wind would
catch them and they'd roll over and over 'til they hit a sagebrush." In
contrast to the testimony of permanent residents, visitors to the area
claimed that windmills were only a qualified success, for during the
hot, dry periods in which water was most needed, there was little or
no breeze.[83] Government irrigation engineers noted in 1915 that one
of the chief complaints of valley farmers was a lack of wind.[84] Although
considerable at times, the wind could not be relied on as a steady
source of power. Therefore, people who could afford to, especially those
attempting to irrigate desert claims, bought gasoline-powered pumps.
William Powers, for instance, had a "centrifugal pump with a four
horse power engine." His chief difficulty was not the lack of wind,
however, but the fact that there was not "water sufficient to supply an
ordinary windmill pump."[85]

CULTIVATING THE DESERT

Once homesteaders had secured shelter and water for themselves and their families, they got down to the business at hand—raising a crop. The first step was to fence their land in anticipation of
clearing, plowing, and planting. Fortunately, juniper, while unsuitable for other building purposes, made excellent fence posts as it is
extremely hard and durable enough, as the local jest asserts, to "outlast
three sets of post holes." The gnarly posts were strung with either two
or three strands of barbed wire. Not only was fencing required by the
homestead law, it was also necessary to protect field crops from cattle
turned out on the desert range. One early homesteader ruefully reported
that his 1908 crop had been destroyed by range cattle.[86] Stockmen
accustomed to running stock in the valley apparently did not take
kindly to the miles of homestead fencing, as revealed in a tersely worded
advertisement that appeared in the *Silver Lake Leader* on August 20,
1909: "Warning! To the parties who have been cutting wire fences in
the Fort Rock neighborhood."

Once the land was fenced, it had to be cleared of the ubiquitous
sagebrush—a tedious undertaking. One method was to set fire to the
sagebrush and burn it off. "During the summer of 1906 it was found
that on a hot day, with a steady, moderate breeze, the denser patches
of sage, once fired, burned completely, the fire often following the roots

BARBED WIRE FENCE WITH JUNIPER POSTS, JUST SOUTH OF
CHRISTMAS LAKE. *L. Montell.*

below the surface." A second means was to dig or "grub" it out with a
hoe, which "owing to the loose nature of the soil . . . is comparatively
easy and gives a field nearly free from brush roots."[87] Most people
chose this latter method as a surer, if slower, way to clear their fields.
Peter Godon "grubbed the sage first by hand," explained Jo. "Then
my mother and us had to take it and pull it and burn it. Then he
plowed it. And we had to follow him and pick up the roots.

"It was real hot and we were barefooted," she went on. "And in
those days, you wore dresses. We followed him around and my legs got
sunburned. I can remember my mother carrying me in out of the field
and they were all blistered."

Marie Eskelin, whose husband was often away from the homestead working for wages, "had to learn to chop wood (she had never
used an axe before she came to the homestead). She also grubbed
sagebrush. It did not take long for her to learn that the dresses worn
by women during those days was a poor 'uniform' to grub brush in, so
she would don Father's trousers which were much, much too big for

SAGEBRUSH IN THE CHRISTMAS LAKE VALLEY, SOUTH OF LAKE
TOWNSITE. *L. Montell.*

her. Mother was self-conscious about wearing a man's clothes. She
would keep a wary eye all directions and if she saw any one come
along the road, she would dash into the house to change clothes."[88]

Occasionally, other methods of removing the sagebrush were tried,
such as dragging with a heavy beam where the brush was too thin to
burn readily, not a very successful technique as the sage was not brittle
enough to snap off easily.[89] One ingenious homesteader cleared his
land "with a homemade sage grubber, consisting of a heavy sled with
heavy knives extending out diagonally on either side of the runners.
The sled was drawn by a traction engine and the brush piled on the
sled to use [later] for fuel. . . . It was estimated that an acre could be
cleared by this method in one hour when working steadily."[90] Once
removed from the fields, sage was cut up and burned as firewood. Anna
Steinhoff spent many hours chopping up sage for this purpose. After
one long evening of playing cards and checkers with visitors until 3:30
A.M., she noted in her diary that by the time the guests had left, "we
had burned all our sage that was cut."

People had come to the Fort Rock–Christmas Lake Valley expecting to raise wheat by dry farming. Once their fields were cleared, they
faithfully followed the precepts of that agricultural method: plowing
deep, harrowing after each rain to create a dust mulch, and summer-
fallowing their fields to conserve winter moisture. Their knowledge of
these techniques came not only from the word-of-mouth advice of

earlier settlers, but from published sources as well, including Hardy Campbell's *Scientific Farmer*. The homesteaders paid particular attention to fallowing, regarding it as a "process necessary to produce paying crops."[91]

The homesteaders planted grain crops, including wheat, barley, oats, and rye, but the twin demons of the high desert—drought and frost—severely limited their success rate. After their hopes for raising wheat had been considerably dampened by several disastrous crop years, they turned almost exclusively to rye. "That's about all you could grow," said Jo Godon. "See, there was no water, no irrigation at all." Rye became the most common crop in the valley because of its resistance to frost and drought and because if the grain did not head out, it would still produce a crop of hay or, at worst, could be used for pasture. By 1915, between 20 percent and 30 percent of the land in the Fort Rock–Christmas Lake Valley had been broken for cultivation, and most of it planted in rye.[92]

Relying on one crop made the homesteaders especially anxious about its welfare. Fred Eskelin, for instance, raised rye for hay. "Father did not have a hay rack; he just piled the hay onto a wagon. Each shock made a wagon load of hay," Ed wrote. In the summer of 1913, after a second cutting of hay, "one of the neighbors was to haul the hay into the barn, but he did not do it. I had received a wagon for Christmas. The weather looked like it would rain, so Mother would pile all the hay on my little wagon she could, and holding the hay on the wagon the hay was hauled in. It was near midnight when the last load was hauled in. It did not rain."[93]

FOOD FOR THE TABLE

While the homesteaders were primarily engaged in cash rather than subsistence farming, they also spent a good deal of energy raising foodstuffs since their cash supply was meager, the few goods available in desert stores expensive, and the long trip to Bend to lay in supplies too costly in time to be undertaken more than twice a year. Almost all of the homesteaders attempted to raise vegetable gardens, and usually cleared just enough land in the first year for that purpose. Arthur Donahue planted a half acre in garden during his first season in the Christmas Lake Valley; Arthur B. Fields put one acre in garden in 1912; George King had half an acre planted in his first season,

followed by three acres the following year.[94] The size of the garden depended on the size and industriousness of the family. The plots were often enclosed with extra fencing to keep out pesky jackrabbits.

"Years ago, they did have some beautiful gardens," said Jo Godon. "There's a place over there by Loma Vista—I think it was the Metke place—and they raised a beautiful garden." East of Fort Rock, "my grandmother had a garden and Dad had a garden," said Hazel Ward. "We had the hardy things. You can't grow a lot; seems like you could grow more then than you can grow now." As she suggests, the home-steaders had their greatest success with weather-resistant crops such as cabbages, rutabagas, and turnips, although the Lewis Haines family planted peas, radishes, and onions as well. People also tried raising potatoes, but often lost them to unseasonable frost. On July 7, 1911, for instance, Anna Steinhoff ruefully noted the occurrence of "a hard frost which got all my potatoes." Certain localities were more favor-able than others for raising vegetables. Hillside locations in particular were sheltered from the winds that blew across the valley floor itself and thus were protected from the harshest frost conditions.

While there was confident talk early on in the homesteading years of the possibility of growing fruit commercially in extreme northern Lake County,[95] plans for orchards like those in southeastern Wash-ington never materialized, as the realities of the abbreviated growing season made themselves manifest. Nevertheless, a few homesteaders raised fruit on their claims. For instance, Vincent Kasperonez, a Rus-sian immigrant who homesteaded near Cliff, had "27 fruit trees, goose-berries and other bushes" when he filed for final proof in 1913.[96]

The homesteaders also provided for their fresh food needs by keeping hogs, cows, and chickens. The Eskelins, for instance, began raising chickens after "Mother subscribed for the *Farm Journal*. In it she read that a small flock of chickens did not need much feed because they would scratch and pick much of what they needed from the barn yard and around the house. So [in 1912] Mother bought 6 Rhode Island red hens and a rooster from Walter Buick.

"The Rhode Island red hens of that day were good setting hens. . . . Mother [would place] eggs into luke warm water—if the eggs floated, they were not fertile, and were not placed under the setting hen. The chicken industry was a success from the start and helped immeasurably with the food supply."[97]

"Everyone had chickens," said Hazel Ward. "When the neighbors came for dinner—very few people had fresh meat, so if somebody came, you killed a chicken or two." She chuckled as she recalled one particular occasion when her family had company: "One time—I don't remember who this fellow was, somebody that was staying up there with the Derricks [neighbors to the north]—but my grandmother had told him to go out and shoot a chicken. It was the only way you could get them.

"It was the time of the year when fryers were big enough to eat, so he took the .22 and went out there and kept shooting and shooting. Finally came in with a couple of chickens, which she dressed and we had for dinner. And later, us kids were running around out there playing, and we found a dead chicken and pretty soon we found another chicken. He'd hit them and they'd gone away and died. Oh, she was mad!"

Chickens were useful not only as food for the table but also as a means of supplementing the family income through egg sales. The milk, cream, and butter from dairy cattle were another important source of both food and cash. "Most of those people relied on cows for milk, and sold cream for their cash," said Hazel Ward. The creameries established in Fort Rock in 1913 and Fremont in 1914 bought cream from the homesteaders and then transported it to Bend. "Everybody had to load their cream and take it to Fort Rock," Hazel continued. "Of course, you'd keep it a week before you had enough to take. . . . It went to the creamery and made enough cash for homesteaders to get by on." A five-gallon can of cream brought $4.00.[98]

There was relatively little that the desert afforded the homesteaders in terms of natural foodstuffs. Though there were wild plums growing in the Summer Lake Valley to the south, the only native fruit in
the Fort Rock–Christmas Lake Valley reportedly was a wild cherry
that the settlers made into jelly and preserves.[99] Wild game, particularly deer, was fairly plentiful, however, as a source of fresh meat. Hazel
Ward recalled that "anybody that wanted to hunt went in the wintertime. A lot of us had our meat that way in the wintertime. In the fall,
they'd get several wagon loads of men and horses and they'd go up in
there [to the woods north of the Fort Rock Valley] and spend a lot of
time getting deer." Her husband, Maurice, added, "They'd camp out.
Get a bunch of deer so everyone could have some meat. Kill a whole
bunch, you see, and in cool weather they'd keep for a while."

Not all the hunting took place during the legal season. DeForest
Stratton, whose mother had homesteaded in the Fort Rock Valley as a
young woman, recounted a favorite anecdote about a local man who
"always had illegal venison around. And they got a real hard-boiled
[forest] ranger in the country here, Bill LeSater, that was also a game
warden; he started to crack down on the guys that had illegal venison.
So he went up there. And Tom Parker was back in the bushes and
saw Bill LeSater coming, heading about where he had a deer hanging
up. So he thought he oughta discourage him from getting closer. So
he fired outa the bushes over Bill's head. That didn't faze the old boy;
he kept right on coming. So finally, in desperation, Tom, who was a
crack shot with a rifle, pulled down and shot his saddlehorn off his
horse, off his saddle. And that was too much for LeSater and he turned
around."

Jack Parker, Tom's brother, also had a reputation for violating
game laws. "They would almost assign a state police just to follow him
around the woods," DeForest told me. "They tell a story up at LaPine
and I'm sure it's true because it's just typical of Jack. He shot some
deer during the hunting season and he was kinda looking at it, wondering how to get it out of the woods, out where the pickup was. And,
anyhow, a state policeman came up behind him and says, 'Well, Jack,
I hope you've got a tag to put on that deer.'

" 'Oh, yes, yes, I got a tag.' And he got his billfold out, went all
through that.

" 'Gosh, I know I had a tag here somewhere.' That, 'course, went
on and on and on. And finally the cop decided he was just bluffing

ANNA LONG AND HOMESTEADER LAURA ANDERSON WITH
JACKRABBITS THEY HAD KILLED IN THE CHRISTMAS LAKE AREA,
1912. *Courtesy of Anna Linebaugh.*

and didn't have a tag at all, which didn't surprise him.
   " 'Well, I'm going to have to give you a citation,' he says.
   " 'Yeah, I suppose you're going to confiscate my deer, too.'
   " 'Yeah.'
   " 'Well, you confiscate the deer, you're going to have to carry it
out of here.' And so the cop got the deer on his shoulders and went
staggering out through the jack pine, got out to the road where the
pickups were. And Jack says, 'Oh, now I remember where that tag is.'
[Reaching into his breast pocket] 'It's in here!' "
   If deer were scarce, jackrabbits were plentiful—so much so, in fact,
that they constituted plagues in some years. In the absence of other
sources of fresh meat, however, the homesteaders often relied on rabbit, although as Maurice Ward said, "We wouldn't eat one nowadays.
Feed them to the dogs and the cats now." Hazel said, "Well, it wasn't
supposed to be good to eat anyway. They had worms or rabies or

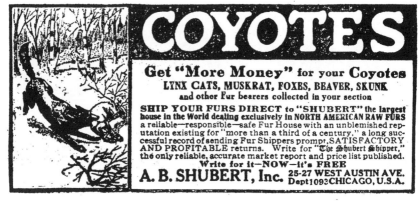

ADVERTISEMENT IN THE *FORT ROCK TIMES*, NOVEMBER 11, 1915.

disease of some kind. But I don't think it ever hurt anybody then. At least, everybody ate them."[100] Anna and Millie Steinhoff regularly hunted rabbits, carrying shotguns on virtually all occasions. Anna even dug a pit as a rabbit trap—perhaps inspired by a rabbit falling into her newly dug well. When the lakes had water in them, the homesteaders hunted wild fowl, including ducks, geese, and swan. They also hunted or trapped fur-bearing animals, such as coyotes, bears, and wildcats, and sold the pelts to supplement their slim incomes.[101]

Fred Eskelin was one such trapper. He was looking for work one fall "when a Frenchman by the name of DeMoss came and asked Father to go in partnership with him in trapping coyotes. Father agreed. Mr. DeMoss was a good trapper, and I recall seeing the north side of the house covered with furs—coyote, wild cat, badger, weasel, civet cat. The furs were shipped to Funsten Fur and Hide Company in Chicago. It is remarkable how soon after the fur shipment was made that the check for the shipment was received. One fur shipment was a large one and Mr. DeMoss disappeared with the check. Father trapped on his own till March but the price of furs dropped. However, the money Father received did help, but his dream of buying a horse that spring was not realized."[102]

Aside from wild game, the only other natural resources the homesteaders could use were salt and ice. Homesteaders mined salt from several playa lakes in the Christmas Lake Valley, including Alkali Flat, just northeast of Christmas Lake, McCall Lake, and Windmill Lake, all of which contained water during the homesteading era. The salt lay on the bottom of the lake in deposits from one to three inches

ALKALI FLAT, NORTHEAST OF CHRISTMAS LAKE, WHERE
HOMESTEADERS MINED SALT. *L. Montell.*

thick. It was broken up with potato forks, then loaded into a shallow
boat. The boat was pulled to land via a long rope attached to a horse
on shore.[103] The salt was occasionally used for stock, "sometimes with
injurious effects on the animals."[104] "It was kind of alkaline," explained
Ed Eskelin. "The first time the cattle would use it, it would give them
kind of a diarrhea effect, but when they got accustomed to it, it was all
right." The salt was also used for human consumption, though Ed
warned, "You had to be careful how you handled it. If you quickly
rinsed it with cold water and let it dry and then ground it and cooked
with it, you couldn't tell the difference from any other salt. But once
your food was cooked and then you sprinkled that on, you could taste
the alkaline."

The homesteaders also took advantage of the ice that formed in
hollow lava tubes or "ice caves" in the northwestern part of the Fort
Rock Valley. There was not enough ice to "harvest," so people con-
tented themselves with visiting the caves in the summer and making
ice cream on site.[105] The caves "contributed quite a bit to the social
life of the community," said DeForest Stratton, "because that was way
before the days of refrigeration. If we ate ice cream, why, we had to
assemble at one of the ice caves and make it right on the spot."

GETTING SUPPLIES

For the most part, then, the high desert homesteaders had to
rely for food on what they could raise themselves. Everything else—
along with equipment, clothing, and hardware—had to come from

the outside. Some people hauled their own supplies, as ranchers in the Silver Lake Valley had been doing for years. "It was always exciting in the spring and fall when the men went for supplies," recalled Marie Jetter. "Mother would spend days making up a list. A careful check had to be made so that nothing was left out, as we had no other source of supplies, with the exception of a small store in the valley that kept only the barest necessities."[106] "When I was a kid, it used to take all day to go to Bend in an old Model T Ford," remembered Mac Buick. "My mother would make a bunch of sandwiches and we'd get out in the pine timber some place about lunchtime, stop and build a fire, make coffee and eat sandwiches. By the time you'd get to Bend, it'd be three, four, five o'clock in the evening. You'd usually stay and do everything you had to do while you were there, because you couldn't afford to go again for a while.

"It used to be a lot of fun, but sometimes it'd get kinda bad too. The old car would break down or something. They didn't used to have as good tires as now. Used to be normal to have two or three flat tires on the way and back. If you made it without a flat tire, you'd make a mark on the wall!"

The homesteaders laid in large supplies of staple, nonperishable foods, such as beans, rice, cornmeal, and dried fruits. "Sugar was bought by the hundred-pound bag, flour by the barrel, dried fruits by the hundred-and-fifty-pound lot," wrote Marie Jetter. "There were cans and cans of baked beans and Pet milk, and dried codfish and mackerel."[107]

In addition to their annual or semiannual expeditions for supplies, the homesteaders sometimes made special trips in the summer to the fruit orchards around Summer Lake. "Folks would take their kids and their wagons and go down, spend all night, load up with vegetables and stuff out of the garden and fruit out of the orchards," recalled a woman who grew up in Summer Lake. "It'd take a couple of days. They'd leave early in the morning to go pick and they'd stay all night, because that twenty-five miles by horse and buggy or wagons was quite a jaunt."[108] Ed Eskelin recalled that "it didn't make no difference what you bought—fruit, vegetables or grain—it was all three cents a pound." When the homesteaders got home with the fruit, they preserved what could not be eaten immediately by canning or drying it.

Between their gardens and food animals, along with the staples purchased on supply trips, the homesteaders had an adequate, if some-

times monotonous, diet. A typical winter meal for Anna Steinhoff included "beans, rabbit, and some corn bread." Breakfast consisted of "a dish of mush and a pancake as usual."

The homesteaders also made heavy use of mail orders, especially for items such as seeds, dry goods, and hardware as "the only means of getting commodities that Mother couldn't make and Father was unable to buy in the little general store or . . . when he went for provisions."[109] Mail order catalogs were standard articles in the homesteaders' cabins. "Everything is brought to them [the homesteaders] by parcels post," remarked the county agricultural agent in 1916. "In the spring it is quite a sight to see 50 lb. sacks of seed piled on the stage."[110]

By that time the sight would have been impressive indeed, for the desert had filled rapidly in the preceding dozen years. According to the federal census of 1910, 996 persons were living in the Silver Lake precinct, which included the Fort Rock–Christmas Lake valleys, compared with 229 in 1900. Because most of the land in the Silver Lake Valley had already been taken up, the population increase between 1900 and 1910 can be largely attributed to the rush of homesteaders into the Fort Rock–Christmas Lake Valley before the actual census enumeration in April 1910. At that point, there were probably over 700 people on the desert. Between 1910 and 1912 (the peak year for number of homestead entries filed) 371 new homestead entries were made, representing approximately 630 new residents. Given a certain attrition rate among people who had either proved up or given up on their claims by then, the population in the Fort Rock–Christmas Lake Valley in 1912 had likely reached its maximum level of around 1,220 people,[111] all busy constructing houses, clearing land, plowing fields and planting crops, fighting jackrabbits, fearing frost, and praying for rain. They were involved as well in building a social fabric within which their individual efforts could be given meaning. As diverse as the homesteaders were in background, experience, and temperament, they found themselves bound together by shared dreams for a place of their own and a common adversary in the inhospitable desert environment. From those bonds, and the day-to-day interactions in which the homesteaders engaged, emerged a full range of community activities that served both economic and emotional needs, as we shall discover in the next chapter.

"Little towns began to spring up everywhere."[1]

3

Homesteading the High Desert: 1912–1916

The social and economic institutions that appeared on the desert in the wake of the homesteading rush were natural outgrowths of the settlement there. The earliest evidence of social organization was the establishment of post offices, followed in quick succession by stores and schools, eventually churches and community associations. A few communities developed into commercial centers, offering a variety of services to the people on the desert. Today, though little tangible evidence of their existence remains, the homestead-era hamlets remain ghostly presences on the land—as though the bustle of human activity can still be heard and felt seventy-five years later.

THE DEVELOPMENT OF COMMUNITIES

The first post offices in the Fort Rock–Christmas Lake Valley were opened at Lake and Cliff in 1906, followed in rapid succession by post offices at Fort Rock and Fremont (1908), Arrow and Viewpoint (1910), Sink (1911), and Connley (1912). Still others were established at Fleetwood and Loma Vista (1913), Woodrow and Burleson (1914), and Wastina (1915).[2] A weekly stage from Silver Lake served the desert post offices,[3] carrying both passengers and mail.

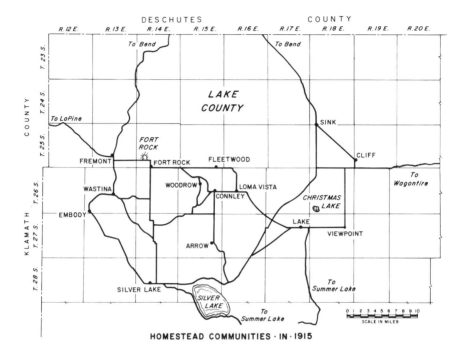

HOMESTEAD COMMUNITIES · IN · 1915

Some early post offices in the valley were little more than provisional postal stations maintained in homes. Other offices were housed in the small stores that were soon established in the valley, with the storekeeper or a family member serving as postmaster. The store–post office combination was mutually beneficial to patron and proprietor alike, making goods and services available in a single location and bringing people into the store on a regular basis. The stores prospered because they provided a common ground for social encounters and exchange of neighborhood news. Tuesday was mail day at the Lake post office, where the Steinhoff sisters received their mail. "After breakfast I took all our mail and went to Lake," Anna Steinhoff wrote on December 13, 1911. "Besides posting our letters I got the milk and bought some thread. Saw Mr. Sims there and talked a while."

Ray Nash established one of the first stores in the valley at Fort Rock in the spring of 1908. Nash had previously owned a store in Falida, Washington. When he moved to the Fort Rock Valley, he "contacted his wholesaler—Lang & Co. of Portland—for his first stock of store goods and opened in his woodshed before building was complete."[4] Storekeepers found it difficult at first to keep adequate

FREIGHTER JOHN DENEEN WHO HAULED GOODS FOR RAY NASH, IN
REDMOND, AUGUST 1911. *Courtesy of Lee Nash.*

stock on hand because demand was high and freighters were scarce.
Some merchants, at least in the early years, hauled their own goods. A
journalist traveling through central Oregon in 1910 encountered a
party of three men from northern Lake County near Klamath Marsh.
Two were homesteaders and the third "was now freighting in from
Klamath Falls a load of supplies for his little grocery store on his ranch—
a store more than a hundred miles from the present nearest railway."[5]
    Ray Nash himself had difficulty securing freighters in the first years
of operation, but eventually had as many as eight working for him at
one time, each driving two wagons in tandem and six to eight horses.
"At the age of three to five," wrote his son Dwight, "I can remember
plainly the arrival of freight—times when men on horse and by wagon
would wait a day or two for freight to arrive—sometimes all the freight
would be sold off the wagon."[6] Eventually, the stores were all supplied
by freight drivers, working either as independent operators or under
contract to the store owners. The building in Fort Rock that is now
the local tavern had been a delivery barn or warehouse for freight
from Portland and The Dalles. Among other things, "they were hauling barrels of whiskey to these different places, you know, fifty-gallon
barrels," Bill Mattis told me. One of the drivers explained to him that
"they'd take a hammer and a blunt instrument or something, and
they'd raise one of them iron hoops. And they'd take a brace and bit

and drill it in there. And then, with a rye straw, they'd siphon off maybe a couple gallon or so and then plug the hole.

"Shucks," Bill chuckled. "He said all the time he was freighting, he was drinking free whiskey!"

By 1915 at least a half dozen stores were scattered across the Fort Rock–Christmas Lake Valley, at Lake, Arrow, Connley, Woodrow, Fleetwood, and Fremont. Most of the stores were small, casually run operations. In one of the smaller stores in the Fort Rock Valley, for instance, the storekeeper's children were reportedly allowed to play with the dried beans and macaroni. When they were through playing, the storekeeper would simply scoop the materials up off the floor and put them back into the open barrel, ready to be sold to customers.[7]

The key reason for the heavy concentration of stores and post offices in the valley—some less than a half dozen miles apart—was the kinds and conditions of the roads. The editor of the *Silver Lake Leader*, traveling through the Christmas Lake Valley in August 1909, remarked in fine booster style that the roads were sixty feet wide throughout the valley and "where it was settled up the roads are grubbed clean of sage brush [their] entire width." He noted in addition that each section (square mile) of land was also bordered by a road, "making travelling convenient, as well as adding materially to the . . . convenience of every settler getting in and out of his holdings."[8] But Ed Eskelin painted not quite so rosy a picture. "The roads were where people started to travel," he wrote. "If one set of ruts became too deep, they would drive beside the deep ruts, or if in the timber the storms blocked a road, the people would drive around the blockade. They would cope with dust in the summer and snow and mud in the winter."[9]

In the spring of 1911, Anna Steinhoff recorded a five-mile, three-and-a-half-hour trip to a neighbor's home. "We had to walk through the sage and over sand ridges to keep out of the mud," she wrote. The condition of the roads affected freighters and the mail stages as well.

"A lot of times in the winter, trucks couldn't get through so then they'd use horses," Mac Buick pointed out. "Same with the mail stage. When the weather was good, they'd use automobiles, but when it got bad, then they'd have to fall back on horses. So it'd get a little slower getting the mail in."[10]

Weather and road conditions were natural concomitants. Though the average annual precipitation on the desert was low, snowfalls of two or three feet at one time were not uncommon. A horseback rider traveling from Silver Lake to Fort Rock one winter "went right over the top of the fences, the snow was so deep."[11] The wind blowing over the flat terrain drove the snow into drifts that filled the roadbeds.

Poor roads and adverse weather conditions meant that the home-steaders usually restricted activities to their home neighborhoods. "I knew most of the people in our area, but I didn't know the ones around Fort Rock," said Anna Linebaugh, "because we didn't get around. There was no way unless you were on horseback or in a wagon." "I didn't get to know many people except the ones in our neighborhood [Wastina]," remarked Venita Branch. "We didn't go that far to mix with people." For the Godons, "Going to Fort Rock was an all-day affair. And there was a lot of people [along the way] and they'd stop you to visit, you know, so that was a sort of a pleasure trip for us," Jo recalled. "We just never was any hand to [do much socializing other-wise]. We always was tied down. . . . If we went any place, we had to get back to milk."

The enforced isolation of localities within the valley meant that each neighborhood developed its own identity. The post offices and stores contributed to this process, as did the numerous schools that were quickly established on the desert as families with children moved in. Frank Anderson organized the first school in 1907 at his two-room house at Lake. "He lived in one room and taught school in the other," wrote Ed Eskelin.[12] Soon thereafter, schools opened at Fort Rock, Connley (1909), and Sink (1910). By 1912, there were twenty schools on the desert.[13] Although the schools were often named after the near-est post office, they were not always located in proximity to them because, "according to law, children living more than three miles from school did not need to attend school." For that reason, schools were so located that no child needed to travel more than three miles.[14]

The minimum number of children needed to open a school was six; often children as young as four years old were enrolled in order to reach the quota. For instance, "shortly after January 1915, there were only 5 children attending Clover Leaf School," wrote Ed Eskelin. "Six children were required to maintain a school, so Lily Jalo, Esther Jaskari and my brother John, all born in 1910, were placed in school so as to have their attendance counted."[15]

Newly organized schools were often held in empty buildings until schoolhouses could be constructed. The Godons, for instance, first attended school in a woodshed at Fleetwood until the Cougar Valley school was built. The Glendale school met during the 1912–13 term in a vacant house.[16] When schoolhouses were built, they "appeared to have been cast on one mold, then scattered or distributed into different parts of the valley," according to Ed Eskelin.

"They were usually 26 x 30 feet with a porch on one end of the building, flanked on either side by an ante-room. In one ante-room the children kept their togs and lunch pails, in the other, the teacher kept her supplies and administered spankings to unruly children."[17] Most schoolhouses were finished on the exterior with shiplap construction.[18] On the inside, the furnishings were spartan. In the Clover Leaf school, for instance, "when school first started, smaller boxes were used for seats and larger boxes with planks across the top was used as the desk, the children sitting side by side in a row."[19]

Children walked to school or rode horseback. Marie Jetter's father bought her a pony for her three-mile ride to school. During very cold weather, her mother would wrap her feet in burlap to protect them from freezing.[20] The pupils often had responsibilities for maintaining the school and performing certain chores, such as building the fire in the school stove in the winter and hauling water year round. The Lake School did not have its own well during the homestead era, so the children hauled water from a nearby source. "I recall I would carry or help carry water more than a quarter of a mile to school," wrote Ed Eskelin. "Generally, a 3 gallon water pail would be suspended from a stick about 3 feet long with one boy holding each end of the stick. We were careful to walk so we were out of step. If we walked in step, the water in the pail would spill over the edge of the pail. If we walked out of step, the water would ripple but not splash."[21]

Recreational equipment at the schools was, naturally, limited, but the Clover Leaf school had a makeshift merry-go-round "which consisted of a hollow juniper post on which a 2 x 12 plank was placed. A hole had been drilled into the center of the plank thru which a long

1/2 inch diameter bolt went through into the hollow of the post." The children soon tired of their new play equipment, however, because "automobiles were all the rage in those days and we went to driving our automobiles, which were sticks about 4 or 5 feet long with a can lid nailed to it with one nail through the center of the lid so it turned like a wheel barrow wheel. We would generally make the hole in the lid a little oblong so the wheel would rattle as we pushed it, because the more noise it made, the better car we had."[22]

The teachers were most often homesteaders themselves. Occasionally young single women from outside the region would come out to the desert to teach, many eventually marrying local men. Roberta Miles's and Mac Buick's mother, Louise Ware, "came to Silver Lake as a school teacher," Roberta told me. "She was originally from Colon, Michigan. She came west with friends . . . who homesteaded in Christmas Valley." Louise married Kinnear Buick in 1911.[23] At the Fort Rock school, "Miss DeForest [who had homesteaded south of Fort Rock] was teacher for 2 terms. She was married to Roy Stratton during the 2nd term. She was an excellent teacher."[24] Sometimes teachers took up homesteads and taught while proving up on them. Others boarded with local families; occasionally even those who had taken up claims lived as boarders. The Patison sisters, for instance, Nellie, Stella, and Belle, each had a homestead by the Lake area and boarded with the Taylor family.[25] Few teachers stayed in a school more than a year or two. The Clover Leaf school had an almost continuous turnover of teachers from its opening in 1913—six teachers between then and 1918 when "all schools were ordered closed because of the flu (LaGrippe) epidemic."[26]

Valley schools provided instruction only for elementary grades. Students wishing to attend high school had to travel to Silver Lake. They either boarded with friends or relatives in town while school was in session or commuted from the desert. Often when a family in the Fort Rock–Christmas Lake Valley had a child or two in high school, one parent would move into town with the children during the school term. After Anna Linebaugh had finished eighth grade at the Lake school, for example, "We rented a house in Silver Lake, and I finished high school there." The *Silver Lake Leader* for September 22, 1916, noted that "the population of Silver Lake has taken a sudden leap upward. That their children may enjoy the excellent school privileges of this little city, the following named families have moved to town

NOTICES IN *FORT ROCK TIMES*, NOVEMBER 11, 1915.

within the past week or two. . . . " Those mentioned included people from Fleetwood, Arrow, and Christmas Lake.

By mid-decade, things were in full swing on the desert.[27] The preceding three or four seasons had, for the most part, been long, mild and wet. Several valley communities had grown beyond the combined store-and-post-office stage into small trading and service centers for the surrounding population. In the Fort Rock Valley, there were three such centers—Fleetwood, Fremont, and Fort Rock. Fleetwood, located ten miles east of Fort Rock, had a population of about forty.[28] It had been named after the Fleets who "were the first ones that had the store and post office," according to Jo Godon. The village also comprised a blacksmith shop and a dance hall as well as the Cougar Valley school. It even supported a weekly newspaper—the *Fleetwood Tribune*—established by Luther Charles. "My sister used to help him set type," said Jo. At the western end of the Fort Rock Valley was Fremont, settled by people from Portland. Established as a post office in 1908,

INTERIOR OF A STORE IN SILVER LAKE, 1920s. *Courtesy of Anna Linebaugh.*

Fremont had a population of about thirty by 1915. It contained a store, a hotel, and a creamery, as well as a Union Church, a Commercial Club (a kind of chamber of commerce), and a cheese factory.[29]

Somewhat larger than either Fleetwood or Fremont was Fort Rock, with a population of nearly sixty in 1915. Beginning with a post office in 1908, Fort Rock had grown by 1911 into a prosperous village with at least two general stores, pool hall, barber shop, blacksmith shop, saloon, livery stable, garage, hotel, restaurant, and weekly newspaper, the *Fort Rock Times*, "with 500 subscribers." Eventually, the town also boasted a physician, three livery barns, a creamery and cheese factory, and a Methodist Episcopal Church.[30]

Both the Fleetwood and the Fort Rock newspapers, along with the *Silver Lake Leader*, focused their attention on local news and community events. At the Fort Rock school, the children staged "a Tom Thumb Wedding which was a big hit in the community, a front page write up in the *Fort Rock Times*," recalled Josine Jensen.[31] The papers also published smatterings of state, national, and international news; serial fiction; and articles on agriculture, health, and business. Each carried advertising for local businesses and services, but their chief source of revenue was from the publication of the legal notices required when a

MEN ON THE STORE PORCH IN FREMONT. *Courtesy of Shorty Gustafson.*

homesteader filed an initial claim and again when final proof was submitted. During the heyday of the homesteading era, as many as two dozen such notices might appear in a single issue.

The homesteading activity on the desert spilled over into and benefitted Silver Lake as well. By 1915, the population there was about one hundred sixty. It had three hotels, a boardinghouse, several general stores, livery barns, a meat market, a pharmacy, and a saloon. Dr. Thom and Dr. Keeney provided medical services; an itinerant dentist, Dr. Short, spent one week there each month. The town had a lively social life. Every week the newspaper announced baseball games and debates, ice cream socials and dances. "When we'd come up to Silver Lake for a dance," Anna Linebaugh recalled, "there was a supper, a dance supper at the Lewis Hotel. Then we'd dance the rest of the night and have breakfast before we'd go home." Special occasions, such as the Fourth of July, also brought people into Silver Lake. In 1909, for instance, the newspaper reported that five hundred attended the Fourth of July celebration there.[32] When the Odd Fellows Hall was dedicated in 1910, "people came from all over the desert for that dedication," said Anna. "There were three to four hundred people there. We lived at Christmas Lake then; I was about ten years old. We

ST. ROSE'S CHAPEL, FORT ROCK VALLEY. B. *Allen.*

came in a wagon with four horses and stayed a day or two, perhaps at the Chrisman Hotel."

"In those days," explained a woman from Silver Lake, "when they had a gathering, everybody came, *everybody* came. People had to come with horse and buggy, so if they lived very far away and especially in the cold weather, they'd stay over. So they'd stay with neighbors or stay in the hotel. Most of the ranch houses were fairly good-sized; they could always accommodate somebody else." She laughed as she remembered that her grandmother "used to tell about five and six little girls sleeping sideways in a bed. She'd say, 'We'd go to turn over and we'd holler, "Spoon!"' That's the way they'd do it in those days."[33]

Both Silver Lake and the desert villages provided focal points for an active community life. Fremont had a Commercial Club and Viewpoint a Homesteaders' Association. There was a nondenominational Union Church in Fremont and Sunday schools at Fleetwood and Lake.[34] "During that time, a minister would come to Christmas Lake once a month to preach," said Anna Linebaugh. "The church [service] was held in the schoolhouse. . . . We'd go to Sunday school on horseback [or] my folks would drive a team with a buckboard." Fort

Rock also had monthly church services led by a circuit-riding preacher. In Fleetwood, a Catholic priest visited the community at the same interval to say mass for about two dozen Catholics there. The Catholic services were held in the schoolhouse until Protestants in the community objected. Denied access to the schoolhouse and spurning an offer of the dance hall as a substitute location, the Catholics built their own chapel, St. Rose's, east of the village.[35]

A SOCIAL WHIRL

Together, the churches and the schools functioned as pivots around which much of the social activity in the valley revolved. For instance, near Christmas Lake, Anna Linebaugh recalled, "every Sunday, especially in the summertime, we'd go to each other's homes for dinner after Sunday school. . . . Everyone would just take their turn."

Going to church itself was an all-day affair, and often as much a social as a spiritual experience. A typical Sunday entry in Anna Steinhoff's diary reads:

> We got up before six o'clock, dressed and had breakfast and then at 7:45 we started for Sunday School. Got to Gooches at 9:50. When Mrs. G. was ready, Longs came by and we rode with them. There was a large crowd at S. School and after the lesson they had a nice programme. We went home with Longs. Mr. Post and Gooches also. She had a lovely dinner and we had a very nice time. Mr. Graves walked to the lake with us. We got home just before dark.

Sometimes Sunday socializing extended into Monday and Tuesday. One Sunday in June 1911, the Steinhoff sisters visited a friend, Jennie Anderson, in the afternoon following Sunday school; from there in the evening, "all went up to Mr. Morganstern's place. There Jennie played the organ and we sang and then Mr. M. showed us his souvenirs from the Phillipine Islands." The following morning at the Andersons, "we put on some of Jennie's clothes and helped Mrs. Anderson make garden, bake pies, and stitch a quilt." They had supper Monday with another neighbor, "then we all went with them to a surprise party at Remingtons. There was quite a crowd there. Mr. Pond and Mr. Watkins played the piano and several sang. They had a nice supper of pie, cake, and milk. We got back to Andersons about two o'clock." The Steinhoffs finally returned home Tuesday at noon.

School programs, attended by the entire community, were scheduled throughout the year, to celebrate such occasions as Thanksgiving and Christmas, Arbor Day and Washington's birthday.[36] The end of the school term was regularly observed with a program staged by the school children, followed by a supper.

On Decoration Day (Memorial Day) and the Fourth of July, the homesteaders staged pageants and organized community picnics. Anna and Millie Steinhoff attended Viewpoint's Memorial Day picnic in 1911. People gathered at noon

> at a cave on the side of the mountain. There the ladies spread a nice lunch and everyone seemed to enjoy the cool shade. Dinner over, the young folks set out to climb the mountain. It was a hard trip up over the steep rocks but very interesting.
>
> We got back to Bertha Hach's place before sunset and Mrs. Hach took the picture of the crowd. There were thirty-six. Three old soldiers. After the folks left Miss Hach got supper and then Mr. Porter entertained us with music on the phonograph. . . . It was midnight when we got to bed.

While a day in the outdoors was clearly pleasurable, it had its hazards. "Our clothes were full of sage-ticks," Anna Steinhoff noted, "so we had to look through them before we could go to bed."

In the Fort Rock Valley, the homesteaders congregated at the ice caves for ice cream socials on the Fourth of July. "You had to go into the cave fairly deep—I don't know how many hundred yards or more—to get to where the ice was," explained DeForest Stratton. "The men would carry out several hundred pounds of it, and there'd probably be a dozen freezers of cream." The Finnish families who had settled in the Fort Rock Valley, particularly around Connley and Arrow, celebrated special occasions in their own way. On New Year's, for instance, Ed Eskelin remembered, "They took some solder, maybe half-pound bar of solder, a wooden pail full of cold water and they'd fuse that solder 'til it was all liquid and they'd dump it in that cold water and it would immediately congeal." The resulting shape was then interpreted as representing what the year would bring for some member of the party. Another practice was to "put cups upside down on the table. One person would go into another room so they couldn't see. Then they'd place a little rag doll under a cup. . . . If a woman picked up the cup with the doll under it, it meant she was going to have a baby. If it was a single man, it meant he would find a bride."

FOURTH OF JULY CELEBRATION (WITH MAYPOLE) AT LAKE, 1914.
Courtesy of Anna Linebaugh.

Many of the neighborhoods, including Fleetwood, Fort Rock, Fremont, Horning Bend (at the foot of the Connley Hills in the Fort Rock Valley), and Viewpoint, had community halls in which a variety of social events were staged. "I was about ten years old [1910], when they built the hall at Viewpoint," Anna Linebaugh told me. "They dedicated it with a big basket social and dance. The women would make pretty baskets and fill them with pie, cake, salad, and sandwiches. Then they'd auction them off." For a basket social at the Lake school in January 1911, Anna Steinhoff decorated a basket to look like "a little cabin patterned after my own."

> There was a large crowd at the social. About ten o'clock they sold the baskets. Mine was the first sold so only brought forty cents. . . . After supper we played all kinds of games. Stayed until about 2:30.
> We rode home with Remingtons. There were ten of us and all sat flat in the wagon bed. We sang nearly all the way home in spite of the cold weather. It was about ten degrees below zero.

People often walked miles to go to dances; those who had buckboards or wagons brought the entire family—children and all. The babies were put to bed in an anteroom while their parents enjoyed the

A HOMESTEADERS' PICNIC. *Courtesy of Anna Linebaugh.*

festivities. At one dance, the musicians "got to fooling around one time and decided that with the kids, we'd mix up their shirts and coats and see what would happen," Lawrence Deadmond told me. "These affairs would go on all night. When it was time to leave, they just grabbed their kids and run. The people would get home just at daylight in time to milk the cows. The women would fix breakfast and go wake up the kids and they might have a kid from a couple up north of Christmas Lake! There were no means of communications but a few old phones on the barbed wire fence. Everyone had somebody else's kid! It was an uproar and went on for a long time, almost a year.

"Everyone was curious and accused us, but we said, 'I played the guitar and he played the violin and part of the time I played the piano. We couldn't have done it because we were playing.' About a year after that, it began to get funny to them. Then we told them."[37]

In addition to organized community events, homesteaders also made impromptu outings to the ice caves for picnics or to Fossil Lake to hunt fowl or search for arrowheads, or gathered in private homes in the evenings to play cards or checkers, sing or dance. The Godon home near Fleetwood, with five daughters in it, was a lively social center on Saturday nights.[38] In the Christmas Lake Valley, "we had parties every week," Anna Linebaugh told me. "In the wintertime they came to our place for skating and taffy pulls." The parties often comprised a large and motley assembly of people. One Friday evening in January 1912, Anna Steinhoff observed, the Longs entertained "four vacqueros, four borax miners, Prof. Tibbets, and ourselves."

A favorite pastime in the Christmas Lake Valley was the "surprise party." A number of people in the neighborhood would gather at a targeted house late in the evening and "surprise" its occupants, who were then expected to invite the visitors in and offer refreshments. On May 23, 1911, the Steinhoffs had supper with the Longs "and then went with them to the surprise party at Andersons. . . . Mrs. and Mr. Anderson had gone to bed so they were quite surprised. We had a jolly time." Anna and Millie themselves were once treated to a surprise party. They had already prepared for bed "at about 8:30 but before I was asleep a party of fifteen people from Viewpoint came and surprised us. We had a jolly good time playing games etc. and had a fine supper of coffee, sandwiches and cake besides two boxes of candy. Then we sang all sorts of songs and told jokes until 3:15 o'clock. Day was breaking when they started home."

In addition to filling the homesteaders' need for fellowship, socializing often served practical purposes. Pie suppers and basket socials helped raise money for church or school needs. Anna Steinhoff's frequent visits to her neighbors were usually spent sewing, embroidering, and quilting. Sometimes women visited each other simply to alleviate loneliness, boredom, or fear, especially when the men were away from the claims. "The womenfolks, they'd go visit one of the other families," said Mary Emery. "They'd load their kids in their buggy and stay all night with them." "Maybe stay two, three days," Russell added. "One time, Mrs. Owsley called up my mother and said, "Will's gone. I wish you'd come over and stay all night with me. I'm afraid to stay alone." So my mother, she loaded Jim and I on a horse, and she got on another horse, and we rode across the hill over there and stayed all night.

"Just about bedtime, this Mrs. Owsley, she took one of the kids outside. And she come back in, said, 'You know, I thought I heard somebody say "Get away!" to the dog.' So we went to bed and didn't think any more about it. Anyway, it wasn't long afterwards in bed 'til I heard a noise at the screen door. Mrs. Owsley, she was all excited,

GATHERING OF WOMEN IN THE CHRISTMAS LAKE VALLEY, 1910. IN
FRONT: JENNIE ANDERSON, MILDRED STEINHOFF, AND ANNA LONG.
BEHIND: BERTHA HACH, ETHEL JOHNSON, ANNA STEINHOFF, AND
MARY LONG. *Courtesy of Anna Linebaugh.*

she was going to go out. My mother said, 'Don't open the door, for
goodness sakes!' It kept rattling and knocking around there and finally,
he tore the screen off the door there. My mother said, [in a loud voice]
'Have you got a gun?' And Mrs. Owsley said, 'Yes, I've got a gun.'
"So my mother said, 'Well, get it.' And then this fellow left."[39]

THE DARKER SIDE

At first glance, the amount of energy the homesteaders
expended socializing seems out of proportion to the accomplishment
of their goals on the desert, making them seem a frivolous lot. In the
year and a half that Anna Steinhoff lived on her homestead, for
instance, she spent nearly a quarter of her time in social company.
But the intense level of activity in the Fort Rock–Christmas Lake Valley afforded not only a welcome but a psychologically necessary diver-
sion from the physical, emotional, and economic hardships that desert
life imposed on the homesteaders. Many had come from urban set-
tings where amenities such as electric lights and indoor plumbing were
taken for granted and had engaged in occupations far less physically

demanding or economically precarious than farming. Even the people who had agricultural experience had to adapt themselves to the peculiar conditions of the high desert. Everyone had to cope with the extremes of heat and cold and inadequate protection from either, with cramped living quarters and a monotonous diet, with hard work and limited rewards for its accomplishment, with separation from former homes and friends and isolation from the world at large. These conditions must have bred considerable tension. In at least one instance, domestic friction erupted in violence, when a man shot and killed his wife at Christmas Lake in 1918.[40] The desert witnessed other episodes of violence as well, including a lynching that stemmed from a robbery and murder.

"There was some guy that was more or less of a stranger in the country who tried to cast suspicion on some old German fellow that everybody thought well of," DeForest Stratton told me. "Nobody'd bought it and they got to thinking it over, 'Well, I just wonder if this guy himself might have been the one.'

"And whoever the fellow was, he got a little bit worried that they had him under suspicion, so he got on a horse and took out across the desert. People got more and more suspicious, so they took out after him. Finally the posse that went out after him, they came back to Silver Lake and people asked, 'Well, what happened?' All they'd say was, 'Well, the trail ended at such and such a place out there on the desert.' Somebody, out of curiosity, went out there to find out why the trail ended and they found out. They found the guy hanging from a tree out there."

Fred Eskelin's former trapping partner, DeMoss, also came to a violent end. "Mr. DeMoss's theft of Father's share of the [fur-trapping] money did him little good," wrote Ed Eskelin. "Later during the spring, he, along with two other men, were apprehended stealing horses. The other two men immediately surrendered to the three cowboys, but Mr. DeMoss grabbed his revolver and started to dodge behind his horse when one of the cowboys shot him. Mr. DeMoss was buried where he fell."[41]

In the winter of 1913–14, a Fort Rock Valley homesteader named C. E. Schafer was killed by a sheriff's posse in his own cabin. Jo and Alice Godon provided a vivid account of the event: "They killed Schafer down here," volunteered Alice. "The deputy killed him."

"I forget what Schafer done," said Jo.

"Oh, he was an outlaw. He'd give to the poor," replied Alice. "He'd steal from the rich and give to the poor. Drop of a hat, he'd shoot you."

"They thought he had a gun, see, and they went to arrest him," Jo told me. "He didn't have one, but they thought he had, so they didn't take a chance on him and they shot him."

"Shot him through the window."

"And it went through the horn on the phonograph."

"We used to have that horn," Alice remarked absently. "I don't know where it is now."

Nonviolent death was even more common on the desert. The only cemetery in the valley was established at Fort Rock in 1909, just south and east of the Rock itself. It was located on land donated by Charles Rice whose father, Nathan, was the first interment.[42] Thirty people were buried there during the homestead era, but numerous others were simply buried on various homesteads throughout the desert. Disease, primarily tuberculosis and influenza, was the leading cause of death during the homestead period. The flu epidemic toward the end of the decade, in particular, wreaked havoc among the population, killing at least a half dozen people in the Fort Rock–Christmas Lake Valley.[43] Accidents also took their toll. Raymond Duchaplay, as already noted, was killed by well gas in the winter of 1914. A sawmill accident claimed the life of a twenty-four-year-old man later that year. Another man died of exposure in 1917, lost in the woods north of Fort Rock. A nineteen-year-old was the victim of a self-inflicted gunshot wound that the newspaper reported as accidental but that oral tradition asserts was suicidal.

Within the homesteading population, the highest mortality rate was among children, especially infants. They made up nearly one-third of the homestead-era burials in the Fort Rock cemetery, and likely many others were interred on private property.[44] Marie Jetter's mother bore twin daughters prematurely and lost one almost immediately after birth.[45] Anna Steinhoff witnessed a poignant scene of childbirth and death in December 1910, less than two months after she arrived on the desert. Called to assist a neighbor woman in labor, she wrote,

> I quickly changed my clothes and went. I reached Bs' at 1:30 p.m. Mrs. B. was quite sick. An hour later a baby boy was born. Mrs. Remington and Mrs. Gooch washed and dressed him and I helped wherever I could. She had no shirts for the baby so we had to wrap him up

until evening when we made him a shirt out of some of his mother's old ones. All went well. The doctor came at about 10:30 p.m.

Anna remained at the Buchanans to care for the mother and baby, but two days later,

> the baby was crying so I took him to quiet and found that he had rup-
> tured the navel and was bleeding. Then I helped Mrs. B. dress him and
> feed him and put him to sleep. Then they insisted that I should go to
> bed. That was at 12:30 a.m. About an hour later Mr. B. called me again.
> The baby was bleeding terribly. I helped them put on a dressing of flour
> and alum and then took him to the stove to get warm. The sight of the
> blood and his pitiful crying was too much for me and I got sick. Handed
> the baby to Mr. B. and I went outdoors. When I came back the baby was
> sleeping and also Mrs. B. I sat down near the stove and watched the
> baby. The blood was flowing from him faster than ever and at about 2:30
> his breath began to come very slowly. Mr. B. handed him back to me
> and anxiously watched until life had left. Then I put the little corpse on
> a chair and waited until day light before washing him.

The family procured a casket in Silver Lake and buried the baby on the homestead, with only a few neighbors in attendance.[46]

Economic hardships compounded physical and emotional ones. Making a living from 160 or 320 acres of arid land was a difficult prop-osition at best. Even when the weather cooperated in producing a crop, transporting it to market was arduous and expensive, and the local market for grain and hay, as well as eggs, butter, and milk, was limited. One way that the homesteaders kept their cash outflow to a minimum was by trading work with neighbors—helping in house or barn construction, clearing and fencing, or plowing and harvesting. They bought costly equipment, such as threshing machines, in part-nership with each other, and used them cooperatively.[47] On the Eskelin farmstead, for instance, "Walter Peterson, a homesteader living 9 miles East of the folks' homestead, cut the hay [in the summer of 1914] with a mower and raked it with a dump rake. The surrounding neighbors exchanged work to get the hay stacked. Father sold hay at $12.00 per ton in the field, the first time any field crop was sold from the farm."[48]

Even with such efforts, however, nearly all those who took up homestead claims had to rely on a source of income other than the land itself. People who operated businesses in the valley had more or less steady incomes independent of their homesteads, but others had to find employment where they could. When Fred Eskelin first arrived in the Fort Rock Valley, he "went to work for a homesteader by the name of Bowman who had just taken a homestead 8 miles East of Father's homestead. The wages were $2.00 per acre and the land had to be 'clean,' i.e., every twig [and] root had to be removed and burned."[49] Some homesteaders used particular skills, such as carpentry or blacksmithing, to earn money within the valley. Lewis Haines, for instance, was a carpenter and worked on several buildings in the Fort Rock Valley, including houses, barns, and schools. For most of the homesteaders, making enough money to live on meant spending at least a few months of each year at work away from their claims. Some people found seasonal work in the immediate vicinity, including the Silver Lake Valley, especially during the haying season. One young couple worked side by side there one summer.[50] Johann Schimelpfenig spent three consecutive summers "at work harvesting for Dan Graf in Summer Lake." A few people found year-round employment in the area and commuted between their workplaces and their homesteads. Dick Schaub, for instance, who had a claim west of Connley, "used to go to work at Embody's mill. He walked back and forth all the time," Maurice Ward told me. "Sunday afternoon he'd start out right after noon and it'd take him 'til dark to get over there to the mill. And he wouldn't leave 'til maybe Friday afternoon—Friday evening if it was in the summertime—to go home to his homestead, or he'd wait 'til Saturday morning. He'd start early and it would take him half a day to walk straight across there [a distance of some twenty miles]."

Opportunities for finding work locally were limited, however, and many homesteaders were forced to go far beyond the bounds of the Fort Rock–Christmas Lake–Silver Lake area in search of a job. Peter Godon worked as a chef in hotels as far away as Reno and San Francisco while his family held down the homestead claim.[51] "The men would go away and work, earn some money and come home once in a while," said Maurice. "I've heard Ed Eskelin tell about his dad walking all the way to Klamath Falls to go to work in the mill there."

"Every spring, the Finns in the immediate area would go to Klamath Falls to work for Pellican Bay Lumber Co.," Ed Eskelin wrote, "then in July, they would return to put up the hay. The hay crops were excellent in 1916, but when Father was half through haying, Oscar Thiel, operator of the Connley store–post office, came with his 1914

Ford bringing a telegram from Pellican Bay Co., asking Father to come to work immediately and they will pay $4.00 [per day]. That very afternoon, Father started to walk the 120 miles to Klamath Falls. He hired August Jaskari to finish the haying. Father worked at Pellican Bay till mid Nov."[52] While the men were away working for wages, "that left the women and the kids to take care of the homestead," Hazel Ward commented. The marginality of the homesteaders' existence was stated most bluntly by the county agricultural extension agent: "During the summer the people are away earning money to live during the winter."[53]

The homestead law made the seasonal movement between work and land a relatively easy matter, as entrymen were allowed to spend five months out of twelve away from their claims, provided they notified the General Land Office promptly of their departures and returns. Ross Noel, following the letter rather than the spirit of the law, blithely proposed to the General Land Office that he take a five-month absence at the end of 1913 and another at the beginning of 1914. A no-nonsense reply from the General Land Office disallowed his scheme.[54]

Throughout the homesteading period, there was constant movement in and out of the area—homeseekers coming in to look the country over and leaving again, perhaps to return later as homesteaders; families arriving to take up residence on their claims; new arrivals finding the area and homestead life not to their liking and pulling out after six months or less; people coming in and buying relinquishments or patented lands; men shuttling between their homesteads and their jobs; families moving between town and the desert; entrymen giving up their claims before acquiring title and relinquishing them to neighbors or newcomers; people proving up on their land and moving on; others, after years of struggle, finally simply giving up and abandoning their land, patented or unpatented, to be taken over by those remaining or to revert to the government.[55] In the midst of this flux, however, more people stayed than left, with just under 7 percent of the land in the valley still in the public domain by 1916.[56]

In fact, settlement was thick. "Every piece of this ground here [in the Christmas Lake Valley] was homesteaded," said Shorty Gustafson. With homesteads established on every 160 or 320 acres, "Mr. Webster tells that in 1912, when they had nothing but kerosene lamps," said DeForest Stratton, "he could go out in his yard and count eighty lighted windows or something like that. Now, with the bright fluorescent lights that a lot of the farmers have, why, there's only eight or ten in sight."

"During the homestead days, you know," recalled May O'Keeffe of Silver Lake, "there was more people up in this end of the county than there were in the south. There was somebody on every 320 acres or so, homesteading. In fact," she added, "there wasn't as many people on this side of the hill [Silver Lake] as on the other side [the Fort Rock Valley]."[57]

By 1916, the tide had turned, however, and the great wave of enthusiasm that had carried people onto the desert began to recede as weather conditions worsened and economic lures beckoned the homesteaders elsewhere. Although railroad talk in northern Lake County grew heated in 1916, it was destined to remain only talk. A more concrete subject of discussion among residents during that year was the opening of sawmills in Bend, sparked by the war-induced boom in the timber industry. The mills offered employment for settlers on the desert who were tired of their hardscrabble existence, and many left their claims in the Fort Rock–Christmas Lake Valley for wages in Bend. The ensuing exodus marked the beginning of the end of the homesteading era.

Desert
Primose.

"Now there's nothing to show it was ever there."[1]

4

Aftermath

The greatest number of homestead entries in the valley in a single year was recorded in 1912, when 269 claims were filed. After that, the number of people entering the valley began to taper off. At the same time, the residence requirement on enlarged homesteads was reduced from five to three years, speeding up the process of perfecting land titles. And since the government did not require an entryman to live on his claim after he had proved up on it, there was little incentive to stay, given the valley's harsh environmental and economic conditions. The population drained away slowly from 1912 on; in 1915, there was a sharp drop in both initial and additional entries on homesteads to less than one-third of what they had been in the previous year. By 1916, a devastating "bust" that paralleled the explosive settlement "boom" in the area ten years earlier was under way. Actually, the decline occurred in two stages. First came the rapid exodus of most of the homesteaders from the valley between 1916 and 1920, followed by a more gradual decline of population, along with a shift in land use, through the 1920s and 1930s. By 1940, the population had shrunk to a tenth of what it had been in 1912, and 65 percent of the land had reverted to the federal government.[2]

NATURAL FORCES

A series of factors, both internal and external, contributed to the demise of homesteading in the Fort Rock–Christmas Lake Valley. The most influential was the weather. The first years of the homestead rush on the desert coincided with a cycle of relatively wet years extending from 1907 to 1916.[3] During these years, average annual rainfall was about nine and a half inches, which, while not abundant by any standard, compares favorably with the 8.6 inches at Fort Rock and 7.8 inches at Lake recorded between 1918 and 1945.[4] When the Eskelins first arrived in 1909, Ed told me, "we had quite a bit of stuff growing. In dry years that killed it all off. We had honeysuckle and soursap, wild flax and different kinds of flowers, wild flowers, that we don't have any more."[5] In neighboring Silver Lake Valley, the weather was also wetter than usual during the first part of the decade. In the years before Thompson Valley Reservoir, Marge Iverson remembered, "this Paulina Marsh down here was full of water. . . . When the water'd get high in the spring, we'd have to move out. I can remember coming out of there I don't know how many times in a boat."[6]

Not only was the average precipitation relatively high during the homesteading period, it was also fairly evenly distributed from one year to the next, varying less than two inches from the average between 1907 and 1916.[7] In more humid regions, such deviation would be irrelevant. But in an area of sparse rainfall, in which a minimum of nine inches is needed to make a crop, a variation of two inches in either direction is not a matter of a larger versus a smaller crop yield. When precipitation falls below the minimum amount needed, it means having no crop at all. Because rainfall levels were at or slightly above the critical amount almost every year between 1907 and 1916, the homesteaders had a reasonable chance to make their crops during the period when they most needed to—while they were trying to prove up on their claims.

Although somewhat more erratic than the rainfall patterns, the length of the growing seasons was still generally favorable during these same years. The shortest growing season occurred in 1909, with just thirty-nine frost-free days. Hazel Ward's father had homesteaded near Fremont that year. "When it froze his crop down on the Fourth of July," she said, "he went back to California and relinquished his homestead to his stepfather." In contrast, in both 1911 and 1912 the seasons were over one hundred days long, and in 1914 it was just slightly under that figure.[8]

Long-time residents, especially in the Silver Lake Valley, recognized that these relatively wet and mild conditions were aberrant from the norm. They explained the change as a response to the introduction of agriculture on the desert. "It is the general opinion that more extensive cultivation is lessening the tendency to early frosts," wrote geologist Gerald Waring in 1908, "and it is claimed that vegetables, such as tomatoes, can now be grown in several places in the county where formerly they could not."[9]

Similar beliefs about the weather changing in conjunction with farming activity in newly opened sections of the country were reported throughout the arid and semiarid West both before the turn of the century and after. Perhaps the best-known formulation of this belief was "Rain follows the plow," the rallying cry that sustained successive waves of settlers on the Great Plains for nearly thirty years.[10] The homesteaders in the Fort Rock–Christmas Lake Valley apparently subscribed to the cognate notion that "Frost flees the plow." The underlying principle in both cases is the same: sheer human will, bent to a purpose, can alter natural forces obstructing the fulfillment of that purpose. If the purpose is agriculture, then human activity on the land, in the form of cultivation, can change climatic conditions. In the Fort Rock–Christmas Lake Valley, this belief was hard to refute because weather records had not been kept there before the homesteaders began moving in. Thus there was no objective means of comparing perceptions of changed weather patterns with accumulated statistics. Nor had there been any agricultural activity in the area before the homesteaders' arrival, so that the impact of their activities on frost patterns could not be accurately judged.

Also working to the homesteaders' benefit, in addition to favorable weather conditions, was the fact that they were planting and harvesting crops in virgin soil, which may have accounted for the reported productivity of the land during that period.[11] Modern-day dry farming techniques show that land which lies fallow over a season rebuilds not only in moisture content but also in fertility; therefore, previously untilled land "would have been misleadingly productive at first."[12] Only after several crop years did the alkalinity of the soil—the "principal agricultural problem of the county," according to the county agricultural extension agent—fully manifest itself.[13] Extensive cultivation and,

in particular, irrigation only aggravated the problem by drawing salts to the surface through capillary action.

By 1916, the weather had begun cycling out of a wet, mild period into a harsher, drier one. In 1917, annual rainfall fell from an average of nine and a half inches for the preceding five years to just four and a half inches. In the following year it was little better—a total of approximately six inches.[14] After two years of drought, the lakes in the area began to dry up and the water in the wells to recede. "Silver Lake dried up completely that year," wrote Ed Eskelin, "and the ranchers from many parts of Fort Rock Valley farmed small acreages in the lake bottom."[15] Drought-induced crop failures pushed the homesteaders already living on the margins of economic viability over the edge. "Well, they didn't have any water. . . . Your dry land farming in this country is nothing. They tried to raise enough rye to feed their cows, but they just starved out," remarked May O'Keeffe. "They had more or less of a drought in those years," explained a woman from the Christmas Lake Valley, "and the only crop that they could raise was rye because there was no irrigation. And the rye didn't even make it, so the people didn't make it either."[16]

The deteriorating weather was not the only natural adversity impinging on the homesteaders' economic security after 1916. There were also the jackrabbits. These pests had plagued the homesteaders in their fields and gardens from the beginning, but the infestation reached an intolerable state in the Fort Rock–Christmas Lake Valley by the fall of 1915. In vegetable gardens, "the rabbits moved in," Jo and Alice Godon remembered. "Every night they took a row. The rabbits then moved into the rye and went down row by row."[17] Anna

RESULTS OF A JACKRABBIT DRIVE IN THE SILVER LAKE VALLEY, 1912.
Courtesy of Anna Linebaugh.

Linebaugh recalled their depredations as well. "This sounds fantastic, but I remember . . . the rabbits actually burrowed under the haystacks. They'd eat up just as far as they could eat." The most effective way of controlling the pests was to conduct periodic roundups or jackrabbit "drives." A rabbit drive involved setting up a long net or wire mesh trap in a semicircle at a designated point. Then the people taking part in the drive fanned out in a large arc, anywhere from a quarter to a half mile across and an equal or greater distance from the net, and began moving toward it, driving the rabbits ahead of them through the sagebrush in an ever-narrowing area until the animals were trapped in the waiting nets, where they were clubbed to death. The carcasses were then piled onto wagons, hauled away, and burned or buried in a vacant area of the desert.[18]

During the fall and winter of 1915–16, the *Silver Lake Leader* was full of jackrabbit news, carrying announcements such as "There will be a jackrabbit drive next Saturday one mile north and one and a half miles east of Fort Rock. Bring tin cans tied together" and "Rabbit drive next Sunday at Horning Bend School." Follow-up stories in the paper give some idea of the dimensions of the problem. In the Horning Bend drive, for instance, six thousand rabbits were killed. Just a week later, two hundred people took part in a second drive at the same location and rounded up another thirty-one hundred.[19] The county, through the agricultural extension agent's program, loaned neighborhood organizations the necessary netting for the drives and supplied poison to them as well.[20] It also briefly experimented with offering a bounty on rabbits. On February 23, 1917, the *Silver Lake Leader* reported that, during the preceding week, "five hundred rabbit ears have been sent from this post office" for bounties. The bounty program was popular among the homesteaders as it not only reduced the jackrabbit population but also enhanced their meager incomes. But the ranchers in the area, who paid the taxes that supported the bounty but did not benefit from it, eventually forced its cancellation.[21]

Obstacles posed by the desert environment were indeed formidable—drought, unseasonable frost, jackrabbits. The succinct histories of their farming activities the homesteaders provided to the General Land Office on their final proof applications reveal the extent to which they were at the mercy of these forces. One after another, these histories read like a litany of disasters:

> Arthur Donahue:
> 1909 - 1/2 acre planted in garden; no harvest due to July frost
> 1910 - 3 1/2 acres in garden and oats; no harvest due to July frost
> 1911 - 5 acres in rye; no harvest
> 1912 - 7 acres in rye; harvested 3 tons of hay
>
> Josiah J. Fox:
> 1912 - 6 acres planted in rye; destroyed by rabbits
> 1913 - 10 acres in rye, 23 acres in oats; destroyed by rabbits and frost
>
> John Schaub:
> 1912 - 4 acres planted in rutabagas; crop destroyed by rabbits
> 1913 - 6 acres in rye; harvested 2 1/2 tons of hay
> 1914 - 10 acres in rye; harvested 3 tons of hay
> 1915 - 40 acres in rye; harvested 6 tons of hay, rabbits destroyed balance
>
> John Sweem:
> 1913 - 40 acres planted in rye; failed due to drought and jackrabbits
> 1914 - didn't get crop planted on time due to lack of money to buy seed and prepare land
> 1915 - 40 acres in rye; completely destroyed by rabbits
>
> George King:
> 1913 - 1/2 acres in garden truck
> 1914 - 2 1/2 acres planted in turnips, 1/2 acre in potatoes; harvested 1 sack of turnips and 1/2 sack of potatoes
> 1915 - 24 acres in rye; crop destroyed by frost and rabbits[22]

Even to an outsider, the homesteaders' situation seemed hopeless. "I have seen many sorts of desperation," wrote a traveler along the Bend-Burns Highway, north of the Fort Rock–Christmas Lake Valley, in 1912, "but none like that of the men who attempt to make a home out of three hundred and twenty acres of High Desert sage."[23] Anna Linebaugh summed up the difficulties the homesteaders faced: "There was no electricity. There was no water, no way to get the water they had, no deep wells. And the drought came, and the rabbits came and ate up everything they did have. And there was nothing they could do but to move out. They just couldn't make it; they *had* to leave."

ECONOMIC FORCES

Economic forces, as much beyond the homesteaders' control as natural ones, also affected their destiny. One critical factor was the failure of promised rail lines through the area to materialize. In 1916, the nearest railroad was the Oregon Trunk in Bend, eighty miles away. The completion of that line from The Dalles to Bend in 1911 had cut the distance from the valley to a railhead in half and improved the prospect of making wheat farming in the area economically feasible. It had also raised hopes for the construction of the Oregon Eastern Railroad, the east-west line that had been surveyed through the Fort Rock–Christmas Lake Valley in 1907 and 1908. The promise of the railroad had been the lodestone attracting people to the Fort Rock–Christmas Lake Valley from the beginning and remained a staple item in the literature promoting the area throughout the homestead era and in local publications. The *Fort Rock Times*, for instance, crowed, "The Oregon Eastern Railroad will run through this territory!"[24]

In 1910, the holdings of the Oregon Eastern were transferred to the Oregon-Washington Railroad and Navigation Company, a subsidiary of the Union Pacific, which resurveyed the old Oregon Eastern route in 1913 and 1914.[25] Apparently anticipating imminent construction of the line, in 1913 some enterprising residents of the Fort Rock Valley platted a townsite called Ficksburg along the proposed railroad route north of Lake.[26] By 1916, however, the Oregon-Washington line had been completed only as far west as Vale in Malheur County with apparently no immediate plans to extend it into Lake County.

Railroad fever hit the Fort Rock–Christmas Lake–Silver Lake area in earnest, however, in 1915 when engineer/entrepreneur Robert Strahorn proposed his "Strahorn System," a network of rail lines based

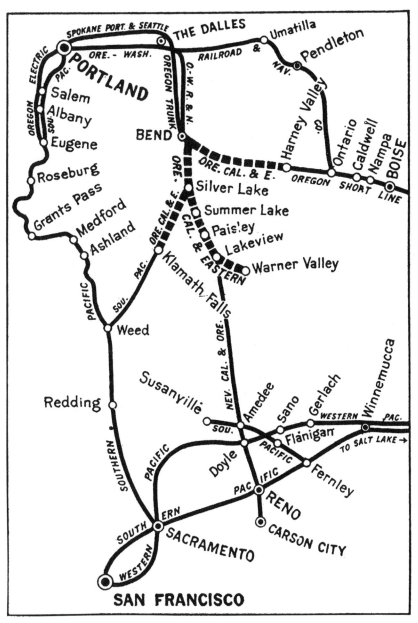

Proposed route of the Oregon, California & Eastern
Ry., and connections. Dotted line
shows proposed road.

FORT ROCK TIMES, NOVEMBER 11, 1915.

in Klamath Falls and extending into central Oregon, including the Silver Lake Valley.[27] In order to best develop central Oregon, Strahorn argued, "Lines particularly needed are, first, from Bend to the Klamath region by way of the productive Fort Rock and Silver Lake sections . . . ; second, a continuation of this line from the vicinity of Silver Lake through the Summer Lake and Paisley territory, to Lakeview and Warner Lake Valley."[28] For months, the *Silver Lake Leader* breathlessly kept its readers posted on the progress of Strahorn's Oregon, California and Eastern Railroad. On March 24, 1916, the paper excitedly announced, "Strahorn Engineers Making Survey Through Silver Lake." Nearly every issue of the newspaper for the rest of that year was devoted alternately to reporting railroad news and making glorious predictions for the future of the Silver Lake Valley. On April 28, 1916, for instance, under the headline "Silver Lake the coming Railroad Center," the editor prophesied that with the railroad (and the proposed Silver Lake Irrigation Project), "there is no good reason to doubt but what Silver Lake will be a city of 5,000 within four or five years." Although rights-of-way were secured through the valley in 1916, excitement began to die down as Strahorn, unable to secure financial backing for the entire network, concentrated his attention on the Klamath Falls component of the line. Only about sixty-five miles of track for the Oregon, California and Eastern were ever completed (all in the southern part of the state), and the rights-of-way in the Silver Lake Valley were eventually relinquished in 1928.[29]

The failure of both the Oregon Eastern and the Oregon, California and Eastern to come to fruition was due largely to the federal government's antimonopoly suit to separate the Union Pacific and the Southern Pacific, which owned interests in both the Oregon-Washington line and the Strahorn system.[30] But it was symptomatic as well of the American railroad industry in general at mid-decade. Having become overextended in the first years of the twentieth century, the railroads seem to have pulled in their horns by 1915. They were especially reluctant to extend lines into new territory by that time because of developing competition from commercial trucking and public buses. Railroad growth slowed significantly after 1915, particularly in the western United States; World War I brought it temporarily to a standstill. The proposed lines through northern Lake County were just two among dozens of lines throughout the West that were projected and never completed, leaving hundreds of farmers—like those

RAILROAD SURVEY CREW IN THE SYCAN MARSH SOUTH OF THE
SILVER LAKE VALLEY. *Courtesy M. K. Buick.*

in the Fort Rock–Christmas Lake Valley—stranded on marginal lands
without access to rail transportation for their produce. "You couldn't
make a living off 160 acres anyway," Maurice Ward pointed out. "Still
can't, so far as that goes. . . . But then transportation was a problem
in those days. . . . Everything had to go out in wagons and teams,"
and freight rates were high, as much as twenty-five to thirty cents per
mile per ton.[31]

Even when commercial motorized freight vehicles were introduced
into the valley, transportation remained problematic, for the roads,
until the early 1930s, were simply unimproved wagon roads. From the
Eskelin homestead, "it was thirteen miles to Silver Lake along a wagon
road across Hayes hills," wrote Ed Eskelin, "but that was too rocky
and steep for auto traffic." He graphically illustrated just how arduous
travel was during that period with a story about his father's experiences on a trip to Lakeview:

> In January 1918, three young men from the immediate neighborhood
> [Connley] had to register for the draft. . . . Father agreed to transport
> them to Lakeview (100 miles away). The last 18 miles was snow covered
> and it took several hours to traverse the distance. They left our place
> about 8:30 in the morning and arrived at Lakeview shortly after mid-
> night. . . . On the way home, the car broke through the ice [near] Thou-
> sand Springs area near Summer Lake and it took several hours to travel
> a quarter of a mile. Somehow they managed to get over Summer Lake
> hill but presently they ran out of gas. . . . [After obtaining gas from a
> rancher a mile away], the group arrived in time to eat breakfast at our
> place, 24 hours after leaving Lakeview.[32]

Climatic factors also limited travel beyond the immediate area. Winter storms and snow in the Cascades virtually cut off the eastern portion of the state from the western part. During the winter, in fact, "it was virtually impossible to get into [Lake] county by any other route than by way of Salt Lake City and Reno,"[33] a circuitous route indeed!

As the drought deepened and their hopes for promised railroads faded, the people in the Fort Rock–Christmas Lake–Silver Lake Basin turned for solace to the possibilities of developing the area through irrigation. Out of the national excitement over irrigation in the early part of the century had come the U.S. Reclamation Service, responsible for developing irrigation projects in the arid lands of the western United States. Several of these lay in eastern Oregon and were confidently predicted to "soon be supporting in comfort a large population of prosperous farmers with consequent towns, cities, schools and all the refinements of civilization."[34] One of the proposed federal projects lay in the Silver Lake Valley, but by 1906, the Reclamation Service had declared it unfeasible because ranchers there had established rights to all the available surface water, leaving none for a large-scale public project.[35] After the federal project was placed in abeyance, three private irrigation schemes were proposed. One was to divert water from Odell Lake, eighty miles west of the Fort Rock Valley, by means of cement-lined canals. The second was to dam the waters of Silver Creek in the Silver Lake Valley. The third scheme was to bring water from the Sycan Marsh, thirty miles south of Silver Lake, through the Silver Lake Valley and thence into the Fort Rock–Christmas Lake Valley.[36] None of the projects was practicable, and none went beyond the planning stages.

In 1915, however, the U.S. Reclamation Service, in cooperation with the State of Oregon, reopened the possibility of developing the Silver Lake Irrigation Project. The major component of the project lay in the Silver Lake Valley, just west of the lake and in Paulina Marsh, with subsidiary units in the Fort Rock area and in the Connley Hills southeast of Fort Rock to be supplied through a canal from the Paulina Marsh.[37] Irrigation engineers visited the area in 1915, but "before the irrigation plans could be implemented, water rights had been filed on all available waters in the Silver Lake water shed and a dry cycle approached which deprived the farmers in the Silver Lake area of sufficient water, so the plans to channel water into Fort Rock area had to be abandoned."[38] When the project was finally carried through, with the completion of the Thompson Valley Reservoir in 1922, the two Fort Rock Valley components were omitted.

In addition to forces at work virtually pushing the homesteaders off the land, others were pulling them from another direction. Vast timber resources on the eastern slope of the Cascades had prompted the completion of the Oregon Trunk Railroad into Bend in 1911. By 1916, at least two sawmills had opened there, and the town's population had increased tenfold from its 1910 level of 500. By 1918, six sawmills were in operation, one reportedly employing 1,000 people.[39] News of Bend's booming economy and of the jobs available there spread rapidly to the homesteaders in the desert lands to the east and southeast, including the Fort Rock–Christmas Lake Valley. Maurice Ward's family moved from Silver Lake to Bend in 1916 because "the mills were starting up. . . . They were using horses in those days and everybody who was ten, twelve, fifteen, sixteen years old, who could drive a team, they could get a job in the woods." Even though wartime demand sent the price of wheat soaring, the possibility of making a steady income earning wages was appealing to a number of homesteaders tired of trying to scratch a living from the land. The high industrial wages which resulted from the World War induced most of the professional people and many of the farm settlers [in the Fort Rock–Christmas Lake Valley] to move out," wrote Arnold Burrier in a U.S. Resettlement Administration report in 1936.[40] "The biggest exodus was probably in 1916 when they started construction on the two mills there in Bend, two big mills," said DeForest Stratton. "And, of course, World War I was on then in Europe and America was enjoying a lot of prosperity from it, so most of the homesteaders couldn't resist [the opportunity] to get wages that were available somewhere else." Perhaps the final straw was the influenza epidemic of 1917–18. The schools on the desert as well as in Silver Lake were closed, as the contagion spread and brought death throughout the area.[41]

THE EXODUS

The confluence of these adverse natural and economic conditions produced a general abandonment of the Fort Rock–Christmas Lake Valley between 1916 and 1920. Some people left their claims before acquiring title to them, others after their land had been patented. Of the approximately thirteen hundred homestead entries filed between 1900 and 1920, nearly 25 percent were relinquished.[42]

Relinquishment meant turning the land back over to the public domain before final patent. Entrymen who did so were allowed, "without prejudice," to file on other homestead claims, provided they were otherwise eligible.[43] Although early on in the homesteading period, people often relinquished claims on their original tracts in order to file other claims elsewhere in the valley, this practice seems to have diminished after 1912. After that year, people who filed relinquishments apparently left the area, as their names do not reappear on the General Land Office tract books. A homestead claim that was given up was supposed to revert directly to the Land Office, but people often tried to recoup the investments they had already made in their claims by selling relinquishments. Individuals who bought them paid the original entrymen an agreed-upon amount of money, were given credit for the time that had already been spent on the claims, and assumed responsibility for fulfilling the legal requirements for gaining title to the land under the appropriate land laws. Real-estate agents in the Silver Lake Valley actively solicited relinquishments as a means of building up their own landholdings.

More than half of the entrymen who had filed on homesteads between 1900 and 1920 gained title to their land, but a good many of them left their claims soon after patent. John Minderhaut, for instance, who had received the patent to his land in 1913, wrote to the General Land Office on June 20, 1915, as follows: "I left my Home Stead June 8 to work at Bend Ore."[44] People who were leaving patented homesteads often turned the land over to individuals who planned to stay in the area, sometimes as payment for a debt. "If they owed the store," explained one woman, "they deeded the property over to pay their grocery bill."[45] Storekeeper J. B. Fox of Fremont, for instance, was listed on the 1920 county tax rolls as responsible for tax bills on a half dozen properties.

While some homesteaders had spent a full five years on their claims before acquiring title to them, others had chosen to commute their entries by paying the government $1.25 per acre after three years in lieu of the remaining period of residence. About 10 percent of the initial homestead entries in the Fort Rock–Christmas Lake Valley were commuted. Once title had been gained in this manner, the homesteader—like his full-residence counterpart—was free to leave the land. Homesteader Arthur Donahue explained in a letter to the General

Land Office why he wished to gain patent to his land by commuting his claim:

> This water proposition coupled with the fact that the children must go three big miles to a very poor school decided me to bring the family to this place [LaPine]—60 mi. from the homestead, where there is a good school—and I might add, plenty of good water—and where I have had steady employment, which, in my case is a most important factor as I have seven children, and my wife and myself to support.[46]

In their exodus from the promised land that had become a land of bondage, people sold as many of their belongings as they could, packed what they needed most onto a wagon or pickup truck, and left the rest behind.

Ed Eskelin described his own family's departure from the desert in vivid detail.

> Mother became ill [in September 1918] and asked Father to return home from Bend where he was a timber feller. Mother regained her health before Father arrived home. Two days later, Father started to return to Bend, but he did not leave the Valley because it was Flu Winter and there was nobody for miles around. The closest telephone was in the store at Connley. About 11 o'clock he returned; he had found a buyer for the cows and chickens. Mother was not happy about leaving, but she could see Father's concern, so she started packing. Two days later, early in the morning, before daylight, we left with the Ford packed with essentials, John and I sitting on top of the load with our heads touching the roof of the auto. . . . I did not look back as we left. I was certain that we were going for a visit and before long would be returning home again. The sun was just rising when we were across the valley on the North side ready to make the first gradual ascent into the hills. A man was milking a cow next to the road and his breath could be seen in the frosty morning air.[47]

The *Silver Lake Leader* carried notice after notice of household furnishings for sale by those who had decided to leave. While the notices convey the pathos of the homesteaders' attempts to salvage something from their shattered dreams, the situation had its lighter side as well. Russell Emery, for instance, told a story about a local miser and a departing homesteader: "There was an old boy down here, he was a little bit stingy. He always wore whiskers and an old army overcoat, and he looked like a tramp, but he was pretty well-to-do.

"One time on the desert when people was moving out . . . , he rode into this place and he said [in a quavering voice], 'What would be the chance for an old fellow without any money to stay all night?'

" 'Oh, sure, sure. Get down, put your horse in the barn.' So he put his horse in the barn, and he stayed all night.

"This fellow [the host] was about ready to leave, and he had a nice team and a wagon and a harness. And he wanted to sell them. So he got to showing this fellow [the old man] the team, and he said, 'They're for sale.' And they was pretty cheap too. This old boy, he couldn't pass that up; he knew it was cheap. So he dug down in his pocket, got out an old dirty check, and he said, 'I got an old check here.' Said, 'I might have enough money to buy that.' He said, 'I'll give it to you if you want to.' So he wrote him out a check for this team and wagon and harness.

"This fellow rushed into Silver Lake and caught the stage and rode to Paisley and said, 'Is this check any good?' And he [the banker] said, 'Yes! When you can get that old boy to write a check, why, take it!' "[48]

Few homesteaders were lucky enough to find purchasers for their belongings, however. "A lot of them walked away and left their furniture and everything, didn't take it with them," said May O'Keeffe. "You'd find houses out there that looked like they just walked out." As a child in the 1920s, "a fun thing for us to do [was to] go around and look through these old shacks," said Hazel Ward. "And at that time many, many of those places had trunks full of things, cupboards full of dishes, clothes hanging in the closet or behind a curtain—many of them didn't have closets—where people had just gone away, maybe to go to work, and never came back. . . . The men went first and found jobs and then they no doubt decided to bring their families. Just left thinking they'd come back, but never did." Eleanor Long said, "When they left the most was in World War I. I've been told a lot of them just picked up and left . . . their little cabins with their things in them. And then when they came back, or if they did, there wasn't anything left." "The way I understood it, the way it's been told to me," said a woman who had arrived in the Christmas Lake Valley in the 1950s, "there was shacks where they even left the dishes sitting on the tables. . . . They just took their clothes and left."[49] Perhaps the most poignant account of the homesteaders leaving came from Ed Eskelin, who recalled the departure of his family's closest neighbors, the Nybecks

and the Alankos. "On the morning they left," he said, "when they were about ready to go, they drank a cup of coffee there. And then they left their coffee cups and plates on the table, just as if they were going to go out for a minute and come back. And those cups stayed there for years."

Shorty Gustafson, who came to the Fort Rock Valley in 1920, remembered seeing those cups "set there 'til the saucers were full of dust a-blowing in there on that table, 'til it was up within that much [an inch] of the top of the cup. 'Course, I know why they didn't wash the dishes," he added. "They didn't have any water!" Mac Buick described the fate of the vacated cabins. "The wind used to blow around those old cabins and beat the dirt out and the doors would blow open," he said. "Finally they just fell down. It was kind of sad in a way. A lot of people spent their life savings; a lot of them got good experience too, put in a lot of hard work and muscles."

That at least some of the homesteaders left a good many of their possessions behind indicates a hope or at least a desire to return. "A lot of them figured on coming back," said Maurice Ward, "but they got a hundred miles away or two hundred miles away and they got busy working and trying to make a living and there was no way to *get* back." But a woman in Silver Lake disagreed, "I think probably a lot just decided they'd had it and were glad of an excuse to get out and start over again."[50]

By the spring of 1920, the federal census enumerators found 765 persons living in the Fort Rock–Christmas Lake–Silver Lake area, 300 of them in the Fort Rock precinct, 41 in the Lake precinct, and 19 at Sink. (The Fort Rock Valley remained more heavily populated than the Christmas Lake Valley most likely because the quality of both the soils and the water supply was better there.) The 360 people left in the desert represent a sharp decline from the peak of 1,200 in 1912. The county tax rolls for the years 1915 and 1920 reveal the population drop in equally dramatic terms.[51] In 1915, 842 names appeared on the tax rolls as taxpayers with mailing addresses within the Fort Rock–Christmas Lake–Silver Lake area. The people in the Silver Lake Valley probably constituted about a quarter of the population in the area. But five years later, only 169 taxpayers with local addresses were listed. On page after page of the tax roll books for that year, the old addresses of people who had moved out of the Fort Rock–Christmas Lake Valley had been crossed off and new addresses pencilled in. Most of them were located elsewhere in Oregon, especially Bend and Portland; others were in Washington, California, Idaho, and various states in the Midwest.

The population drop was, of course, most visible on the landscape. In 1918, W. A. Rockie, conducting a land classification survey in the Fort Rock Valley for the U.S. Geological Survey, found that "the status of seventy-two 320-acre homesteads [in a typical township] was . . . practically 100 percent abandonment."[52] As a high-school youngster in Nebraska in 1907, Rockie had worked for a railroad company, placing promotional posters advertising central Oregon lands in Nebraska train depots. In an ironic quirk of fate, he noted that "while inspecting these abandoned farms, the writer found, nailed over a broken window in an empty house, a dirty and torn cardboard poster *identical with those placed by him in the Nebraska railroad stations* some twelve years earlier"—a bitter testament to the failure of a dream.[53]

As the homesteaders moved away, the institutions that had grown up around them also began to disappear. The post offices closed in rapid succession, the first in 1915, three more in 1918, four in 1920. By 1921, only three post offices were left—at Fort Rock, Wastina, and Lake.[54] The Wastina office closed in 1925, Lake's in 1943. Of the thirteen post offices established during the homestead era, Fort Rock is

SITE OF VIEWPOINT, LOOKING SOUTHEAST TOWARD TABLE ROCK.
L. Montell.

the only one still in existence. A woman who visited the Viewpoint post office vicinity in 1918, about the time it was discontinued, provided a vivid description of what remained: "All the people had left. The newspaper mail had not been distributed and was still scattered around. The office door had blown away, but the post office books were there."[55]

Schools suffered the same fate as post offices. Pupils were shuffled from school to school as student population declined and teachers left the valley. Where there had been twenty schools in operation at one time or another between 1907 and 1915, just five were left in 1919—at Fleetwood, Fort Rock, Fremont, Lake, and Sink—with a combined enrollment of eighty-four. The Fremont school closed the following year, and the school census in 1920 dropped to fifty-three. [56]

For those left behind, "it was an awful feeling. We had wonderful neighbors and they were all so good. It was an awful feeling when they began to move out," said Jo Godon. The people who remained on the desert after the exodus of homesteaders often salvaged the lumber from abandoned buildings or moved them intact to other locations.[57] Venita Branch said, "My dad's place had four buildings that he moved in." Hazel Ward, pointing out her kitchen window, identified the outbuildings surrounding the main house "as a lot of those old houses moved in." Ed Eskelin, who had returned to the valley with his parents in 1935, moved the Clover Leaf schoolhouse onto the family farmstead and converted it into a dwelling, where he lived until his death in 1981.[58] The Fort Rock Grange Hall was constructed in 1939 from the old Connley, Cougar Valley, and Loma Vista schoolhouses.[59]

THE GRANGE HALL IN FORT ROCK. *L. Montell.*

The astonishing durability of the homestead-era buildings, in spite of their apparent flimsiness and hasty construction, is attested to in their presence on virtually every older ranch or farmstead in the Fort Rock–Christmas Lake Valley today. "Whenever anybody wanted a house," said Roberta Miles, "they just went out and moved in a homestead house off the desert. That's the way we got our houses. . . . That was another big community project. When anybody wanted a house, everybody'd pitch in and go help them." The two homestead houses moved in to make her present dwelling "took an awful lot of wrenching, you know, twisting and jerking when they were moving them because they brought them through sagebrush that was higher than a man's head, as high as the tractors," she explained. "It was huge sage. And sand dunes. And they got stuck in the mud, and they got stuck in the sand, and everything else. And they'd jerk them to get the traction back up. They tore the end out of one house and jammed it up against the other one and put them together." When Roberta and her husband later had asbestos shingles put on the house, "the carpenters said . . . that every corner came out square on the chalk line. They said they were the best built houses to have been jerked, wrenched, and twisted and still come out square."

THE 1920s

Although the number of people living in the Fort Rock–Christmas Lake Valley dwindled through the 1920s, the rate of population erosion was less than during the preceding five years. In fact, the number of people on the tax rolls with local addresses rose from 169 to over 200 between 1920 and 1925, due largely to homestead lands being patented and therefore becoming taxable during that period. And there was still a good deal of activity on the desert. One of the first—and probably the most important—developments in the posthomestead period was the shift from dry farming to a search for a larger and more reliable water supply than had hitherto been available. Apparently, the threat of a sustained drought, coupled with the realization that weather conditions would never be more than marginally favorable for agriculture, finally drove the people in the Fort Rock–Christmas Lake Valley to experiment in 1921 with drilling deep wells that would provide sufficient water for large-scale irrigation. Dry farming had already revealed its limitations in this region of very low rainfall; by the late 1910s, its drawbacks, especially in promoting rapid soil erosion, had also become apparent.[60] Irrigation thus afforded the last hope of making permanent agricultural settlement of the area possible.

In 1921, the Oregon state legislature appropriated $40,000 to sink four test wells in the Fort Rock–Christmas Lake Valley in an attempt to tap into deep artesian water.[61] "The first well was drilled on the John Ernst place in 1922 . . . 5 miles east and 3 miles south of Fort Rock," wrote Ed Eskelin. "The 'testing' of that well was a memorable occasion, attended by a large crowd of people." Ernst built a mile-long flume system to irrigate his fields from the well. The flumes were constructed of lumber obtained, ironically, "from barns which had been abandoned by the homesteaders."[62]

The second well was tested at the Crampton brothers' place, attracting people "from Portland and a lot of people from Bend and Lakeview," said DeForest Stratton. "A lot of people that came to the Crampton well demonstration had homesteads here, and they had gone away. And they wanted to see what potential their property had. And it was a long time before anything came of it." The pump at the Crampton well was originally steam powered. "Old Frank [Crampton], he'd cut wood, 300 or 400 cords of wood a year to burn in that thing in the summer," remembered Bussie Iverson. Eventually, all the wells were outfitted with gasoline- or diesel-powered pumps. Although flood irrigation did not work well in all the vicinities in the desert, due to differing soils,[63] the prospect of a steady supply of water from deep irrigation wells went a long way toward reassuring the residents that their investments in land, stock, and equipment were reasonably secure.

Land transactions in the early 1920s reflect the confidence inspired by the development of water resources in the valley. Additional homestead entries, which had dwindled to virtually nothing during the second half of the 1910s, amounted to thirteen in 1919 and in 1920 rose to forty-four. Many of these entries were made under the 1916 Stock-Raising Homestead Act, which allowed an entryman to claim up to 640 acres of the public domain for use as livestock range. People who could afford to had acquired land by outright purchase from those who were leaving the valley or by buying tax-default land from the county, often for as little as twenty-five cents an acre.[64] By doing so they put themselves in a better position to turn their holdings into profitable agricultural operations, for additional land made both growing crops and raising livestock more economically feasible ventures than trying to do so on a 160- or 320-acre homestead allotment—provided, of course, that sufficient water was available. "Now there was one fellow up north here," said Shorty Gustafson, "he got a little headstart up, and he stayed and he just survived. He had a little money, and he bought some of those homesteads, bought them out. It just give him more land and he was just one of the lucky ones. Most of them had jobs so that's how they happened to survive. They just made enough and saved enough that they could buy out some of those others."[65]

Nevertheless, the 1920s were hard years. While deep-well irrigation had renewed the hope of putting the valley's economy on a solid foundation, the bottom fell out of the wheat market in the agricultural depression of the early 1920s. Jackrabbits continued to plague farmers. The loss of human population made rabbit drives harder to organize, so, with funds from the county extension agent, farmers turned to poisoning as a means of eradication. In the winter of 1921, J. B. Fox of Fremont killed 2,500 rabbits with strychnine. The county agent reported that "in the Wastina section, Wm. L. Dehne killed 1500 . . . , and at Silver Lake George M. Mayfield killed 2000."[66]

To add to the residents' problems, the dry spell that had begun in 1917 continued virtually unabated until 1925, drying up Silver Lake and turning its basin into "a great meadow where cattle grazed."[67] The cycle of dry years brought "worry and discouragement to the rural people," wrote the county extension agent.[68] The winter of 1924–25 was a particularly hard one, and hay was very scarce. But the following spring was both early and wet, causing grass to appear in time to save livestock "that otherwise might have been lost in case of a late spring. Continued spring rains have made the range the best it has been for many years." Reservoirs filled up. Much of the land that had been irrigated for the past several years was dry farmed in that year.[69]

For those remaining in the valley during the 1920s, life went on much as it had before the exodus began. People still engaged in cooperative work projects and socialized whenever possible. They still traveled over dirt (or, depending on the season, mud) roads, for there were no improved roads in the area—indeed in the entire county—before 1930. (State Highway 31 from LaPine to Lakeview was not graveled until 1931.[70]) The children still attended grade schools on the desert and went to high school in Silver Lake. And, as elsewhere in the nation during the Prohibition years, some people in the area turned to making and selling illegal whiskey to supplement their incomes. Moonshiners set up stills in caves or abandoned homestead buildings,[71] and sold their product in the immediate area or in Bend. Locally, it would bring a dollar a quart, according to one Silver Lake resident. He recalled a personal encounter with a moonshiner: "There was some people up around Bear Flat, three brothers, and they moonshined a lot. So this fellow had a ten-gallon keg cached up there. He bootlegged it; he'd buy it from these moonshiners and he'd bootleg it out, bottle it up. So he wanted me and another fellow, kids, to go up there with him one time to help get this moonshine. So we got this ten-gallon keg and got it in the car and started home with it. We seen a light, car light, coming around the edge of the timber there. We stopped, to take [the keg] out to hide it. They saw our light too. So, anyway, we found out who it was—it was these Shanahan brothers. So we said, 'Do you want a drink of moonshine?' We had a straw there that they could suck it out of the keg. And they had a drink and said, 'Bejesus, come on now, I'll give you a drink.' We went over there; they had a fifty-gallon barrel and one of these old tin cups with the handle hanging over the side of the bucket, to drink it out of! These old country Irishmen.

"But a sheriff down at Lakeview, a fellow by the name of Woodcock, he was kinda tough on them old moonshiners. He'd go out and look for them and stay for days until he found them."[72]

THE 1930s

By 1930, there were only 179 people living in the Fort Rock–
Christmas Lake Valley, barely half of the 1920 total. When geographer Isaiah Bowman visited the area in 1931, he sketched a verbal
picture of its desolation: "Some of the buildings have been overturned
by the wind. The wire has been removed from the fence posts. Gates
are warped out of shape or hang on the verge of collapse. The land
has returned to its wild state."[73] Bowman counted twenty-five houses
on the road between Silver Lake and Fort Rock, all of them empty
and boarded up. There were only two or three houses still inhabited
at Fort Rock; Fremont was totally abandoned. Traveling east through
the Fort Rock Valley, he noted: "Between Fort Rock and the eastern
border of the Deschutes National Forest in a distance of ten miles
there are 15 uninhabited and 2 inhabited houses on or quite near the
road that runs through the driest and worst part of the valley."[74] The
scene in the Fort Rock–Christmas Lake Valley mirrored that in other
locales in the Great Basin where dryland homesteading had been
attempted after the turn of the century. In 1925, a writer for the *New
York Times* had driven from Winnemucca to Denio, through land in
northwestern Nevada that had also been homesteaded in the 1910s,
and commented on what he found there:

> On all the desert there is nothing more pathetic than the abandoned
> shacks of hardy men and women who have filed on the sand and sought
> to force a living out of it. It can't be done. For three hundred miles these
> shacks are to be seen at infrequent intervals. In not a single instance did
> the writer see one that was the home of a human being.[75]

At least part of the loss of local population between 1920 and
1930 can be attributed to another dry cycle that began in 1928 and
persisted through the mid-1930s. During this period, the annual precipitation in the Fort Rock–Christmas Lake Valley averaged just under
eight inches.[76] "In 1929 it was another real dry year," said Ed Eskelin.
"Where people had sandy ground, they had to put two wheels on the
mower and tie another wheel to it because it would sink so deep that
the dirt was rolling ahead of the wheels; instead of turning the mower,
they would roll backwards. It was really a bad year." Like other lakes
throughout the Great Basin that dried up during this period, Silver
Lake in 1931 "was hard and firm, where not consisting of sand, and
largely overgrown with ordinary desert shrubs."[77]

Compounding the problem posed by drought was severe soil ero-sion caused by wind.[78] Because the soils had little weight to begin with, they simply blew away when the sagebrush cover was removed, creating true desert conditions even where they had not previously existed. "It would dry out and the wind would blow it away," Maurice Ward explained. "That's happened all over this country in the sand hills down there. That's what happened when people plowed up the land and then they didn't do anything with it." The wind erosion in some vicinities removed two to three feet of soil from the surface. In 1923, one visitor reported, there were few roads that could be driven because of drifting sand.[79] By the mid-1930s, the Fort Rock–Christmas Lake Valley became Oregon's version of the Dust Bowl. "The dust was blowing so hard, you couldn't see in front of you," recalled Marge Iverson. "We couldn't even eat at the table. My grandmother would throw a sheet over [our heads at] the table so we could eat, the dust was blowing so bad. It was really Dust Bowl days."

Soil erosion resulted not only from the dry farming practices that had been used in the valley for the previous twenty years, but also from overgrazing by livestock. Under the open range system prevail-ing on the desert during the late twenties and early thirties, ranchers competed with farmers and with each other for scarce forage. The struggle was a fierce one, as recounted by Maurice Ward: "In those days they just turned the cattle out and let them go. The guy that had the most cows had the most grass. If you had 500, 600 head, why, you had all of it. [If] another guy tried to crowd in there, you'd send some cowboys out there and run them off. They wore guns in those days, and if somebody started crowding in on you, you just sent two of your worst crummy-looking old hands out there and told them guys to 'move on now, it's ours.' That's the way they did it. The guy with the most money and the biggest outfit got the most feed for his cattle. You'd have to own a little bit at home to raise your hay on, but a lot of guys didn't get it legally. They just moved in on somebody. Those days, the law was pretty far away." The solution to the problem of range rights came with the passage of the Taylor Grazing Act in 1934. Under its authority, seventeen square miles of the valley were placed under government control and a system of permits was established to allow grazing on those lands.[80]

The hard times being felt all over the nation during the 1930s hit the valley as well, forcing residents to accept financial help from the federal government in the form of loans for seed and feed, funds for rodent control, and purchase of livestock they could no longer care for.[81] Even during these years, however, some ten or fifteen families moved into the Fort Rock Valley. Some, like the Eskelins, were returning landowners who had kept the taxes paid up on their patented lands.[82] Others were newcomers, like Bill and Maxine Mattis, who moved in from southern California. They had spent a summer in the Fort Rock Valley with Maxine's aunt and uncle in the late 1920s. After they returned to California, "we couldn't forget this country," Maxine said. "We'd just think, 'Oh, that big moon, and those sunrises and sunsets.' And we couldn't get it out of our systems—me too, as bad as him. . . . My aunt and uncle's health had broke and they were leaving. So we come back and homesteaded and stayed here." She went on to recount their journey: "We quit a job in California, had two little kids. My dad give us a little two-wheeled trailer; we had it on the back of our car, a roadster. We loaded up everything we could. And everyone was giving us things because they knew we were going up to ranch or farm. Somebody gave us a little crate with a rooster; somebody gave us a pair of rabbits; someone a couple of little pigs. We had some pigeons, I had my canary, our dog. We brought all those besides

"MAIN STREET, FORT ROCK." FORT ROCK IN 1936. FEDERAL WRITERS'
PROJECT, VERNE BRIGHT, PHOTOGRAPHER. *Courtesy of the Oregon State
Library.*

these two little kids. Of course, going through Los Angeles, here we'd
stop at the stop lights and all these animals are squawking. Talk about
your *Grapes of Wrath*—that was us!"

By 1935 there were an estimated ninety families living in the Fort
Rock–Christmas Lake–Silver Lake area, twelve in the Lake community, thirty-nine near Fort Rock, and thirty-eight in the Silver Lake
Valley. Together, they represented just 9 percent of the total population living there in 1914.[83] Maxine Mattis, accustomed to city life,
recalled how the sparseness of population affected her: "I'd not seen a
woman for so long. I'd seen men; they'd come to borrow something or
see Bill or something. I'd see men. But for six weeks or more, I hadn't
even seen a woman or talked to a woman. They had a road crew up at
the Horse Ranch [east of Fremont]. And this woman, she came over
with her husband. And I didn't even hardly know her. When I saw
her, I just flew out [of the house] and *cried*, I was so happy. And she
said, 'I know just how you feel!' I was so happy to see her—a *woman* to
talk to."

At mid-decade, more than 70 percent of the landowners in the
Fort Rock–Christmas Lake Valley lived outside the county.[84] The
county itself had acquired more than 25 percent of all the lands that
had ever been on the tax rolls, through the default of owners on their

tax bills.[85] Just under a third of the valley was being cropped, with the remainder—badly depleted though it was—used for range. Virtually the only crop being produced was rye hay, although a few people were experimenting with raising alfalfa by irrigation.[86] In 1936, the U.S. Resettlement Administration proposed the establishment of the Fort Rock Conservation Area and the relocation of valley residents elsewhere. Although resettlement never took place, the federal government, under the authority of the Bankhead-Jones Act, bought back eighty-two square miles of land in the valley from property owners in the late 1930s and early 1940s, returning it to the public domain as grazing range.

This development accelerated the practice of recycling the old homestead buildings as the government allowed residents to remove them or tear them down for the lumber. The rest of the buildings were either burned or used as targets during U.S. Army desert warfare maneuvers conducted in the area in 1943.[87] Present-day residents speak resentfully of a "firebug" (presumably a government employee) who reportedly delighted in burning the old "shacks." "They tried to pressure us into selling," one woman said, by burning the old buildings down. "If you didn't sell, you'd be in trouble. They had a man [who] went around and burned them down. He bought the land, set them on fire, and burned them up. . . . Some of the little shacks that didn't amount to anything they left. The saying was that if you could see the smoke, it meant he was burning another house." Many owners, tired of struggling to make a living from marginal land, accepted the government's meager offer of fifty cents an acre and left.

By 1939, only seventeen farm units remained in use in the Fort Rock Valley; 157 others had been abandoned.[88] The 1940 census reported just one hundred people living in the Fort Rock–Christmas Lake Valley. Little remained on the landscape to memorialize the struggles of the homesteaders. Their houses had been torn down, burned, or hauled away. Their fences were gone, and sagebrush had reclaimed the fields they had so painstakingly cleared twenty-five years before. They had failed in their dream to transform the desert into a garden; their effort to do so, in retrospect, seems futile.

From our vantage point some seventy years later, we cannot know what a man experienced walking over his frost-ruined wheat field late in June, nor how a woman felt trying to feed her family from a rabbit-ravaged garden. We can only imagine how they both prayerfully watched the thunderheads build up over Hager Mountain, then, help-lessly, saw them sweep across the valley to the west, blessing their neigh-bors with rain but leaving their own fields parched. We do not know how they responded to the sight of neighbors on the next section strapping their belongings onto their truck and slowly pulling away on the road to Bend. We will never know with what anxious hopes they arrived on the desert, nor in what tired despair they left. But, particularly in its poignancy as a failed effort, we can recognize and appreciate the homesteading on the high desert as an expression of the human spirit, manifested in a particular time and place, but part of a broader canvas. A fuller understanding of the homesteading can come only from a consideration of the larger context within which it took place.

Sego Lily

5

The Larger Context

From the perspective of the late twentieth century, homesteading the Fort Rock–Christmas Lake Valley appears to have been a
pathetic effort doomed to failure. If pity is our first response, then
wonder must be our second. *Why* did the homesteaders undertake
such a futile venture? To some extent these present-day responses derive
not just from hindsight, but also from a conventional understanding
of American frontier history. If we believe that the frontier stage of
the nation's development ended before the turn of the century, then
we are inclined to see the homesteaders on the Oregon desert as hope-
lessly anachronistic in their efforts to transform the last remnant of
the public domain into a productive agricultural region. But people
did not take up homesteads on the desert expecting to fail. We can
begin to understand what motivated them only when we shift our
perspective from the present to the past and our focus from the out-
come of the homesteading to its inception, when we concentrate not
on what became of the homesteaders but on how they came to be
homesteaders. We have already retraced their steps; now we need to
examine the map they used.

In addressing the question of why people chose to homestead the high desert, we need to separate it into two components: personal motives and external forces. In other words, the decision to engage in homesteading was made on two levels. The first was the individual's or family's immediate situation and ultimate goals; the second was the larger milieu of conditions and circumstances on the regional or national scale that affected the homesteaders directly or indirectly.

THE HOMESTEADERS' MOTIVES

Because the homesteaders left behind no explicit statements, oral or written, about their intentions, we can only make informed guesses about their reasons for moving to the desert and assume that, like other settlers in other sections of the arid and semiarid West both before and after the turn of the century, they were prompted by a variety of motives. First, there were those who were sincerely interested in acquiring land to provide a living for themselves and their families. Some were inexperienced innocents, like the Eskelins and the Godons, who had never farmed before. Others, like the peripatetic families on the 1910 census, were no strangers to the agricultural frontier. Of those who had farming experience, some had been successful in other places and came to the desert seeking more land and a new challenge; others, having met with failure elsewhere, were making one final desperate attempt to find "God's country."[1]

A second group comprised people interested chiefly in gaining title to a homestead claim as quickly as possible and then returning home. Some may have been gambling that the value of their land would increase as agricultural development in the area proceeded and that they would be able to sell it at a handsome profit. Others, like Millie Steinhoff who moved away in 1911 but held onto her land until the 1960s, may have wanted the security they believed was inherent in land ownership. And still others may have simply wished to exercise their rights as citizens to acquire a piece of the public domain. Indirect evidence that some homesteaders wished to gain title to land without permanently settling on it lies in the fact that 10 percent of all initial homestead entries were commuted. Those who did not intend to remain on the desert may have used the commutation provision of the law to minimize the time they spent there, for after a patent was gained by this means, an entryman was no longer required by law to live on his land.

Finally, for a few people, homesteading was simply a lark. It seems likely that at least some of the young single men and women who filed on their own claims regarded homesteading as an adventure in independence rather than a long-term commitment.

We can only speculate from external evidence what the homesteaders' real motives might have been, for each homestead entry represents a unique set of circumstances under which an individual decision was made. Yet, however varied the homesteaders' reasons for moving to the desert might have been, their decisions to do so were all made during the same time period and therefore under the same set of historical circumstances. Herein lies our point of entry into the past in which the Fort Rock–Christmas Lake Valley homesteaders operated: the very fact that so many people were involved in the homesteading there within such a short period of time suggests the presence of large-scale forces at work prompting their migration to the Oregon desert. Those forces operated within two spheres of influence. One was that of the Pacific Northwest region; the second, more encompassing, was that of the nation. Investigating both those spheres may bring us closer to an understanding of the homesteading as both a historical phenomenon and a human endeavor.

THE REGIONAL SCENE

Central Oregon entered the national spotlight just after the turn of the century when railroad magnates E. R. Harriman of the Union Pacific and James J. Hill of the Northern Pacific and Great Northern both set their sights on this previously undeveloped portion of the state, billed as the largest territory in the United States without rail service.[2] Both men were interested in tapping the great timber wealth on the eastern slope of the Cascades and, concurrently, in developing central Oregon as an agricultural region that would generate freight traffic. The quickest way to accomplish these two ends was to build a rail line from The Dalles on the Columbia River up the Deschutes River canyon to the village of Bend in the heart of the pine timber country. Amid much national as well as regional fanfare, Hill and Harriman both announced plans in 1906 to construct such a line. Their plans brought them into direct conflict in 1909 when each began laying tracks along the proposed route. Harriman's line, the Des Chutes Railroad, lay on the east side of the river; Hill's Oregon Trunk Railroad occupied the west side. When the tracks reached the mouth of the Crooked River, some fifteen miles north of Redmond, the terrain forced the Hill line to cross the river. But "Hill had set about vigorously to develop the virgin territory through which his railroad had been built, and he brooked no interfering with his grand scheme."[3] After some negotiation, Harriman conceded the rest of his route to Hill in exchange for the use of the Hill tracks into Bend and Hill's promise not to extend his line south toward San Francisco, a territory that Harriman jealously guarded for his Union Pacific. From that point, near Metolius, a single track was laid into Bend, reaching there in the fall of 1911.

Hill chose the occasion of the completion of the line to extoll the region which his railroad had opened to settlement and upon which it would be dependent for profitability. In a speech to a large crowd at the ceremonial driving of the last spike, Hill stated confidently, "There is no reason why Central Oregon should not produce enormous wealth." He urged those present to advertise the region's advantages and "get people into this country. You could not build a prosperous community in the Garden of Eden and we could not run a railroad there if there was nobody but Adam and Eve to use it."[4]

In order to generate freight traffic and therefore make their enormous investments in the Deschutes line profitable, the railroads mounted an active marketing campaign aimed not only at selling their own substantial land grant acreage,[5] but also at attracting farmers onto the surrounding lands. This kind of promotion by the railroads was a standard concomitant to the settlement of public lands in the West. While "the homestead law gave the land away . . . , the railroad was expected to market this land, promote its settlement, and carry its resources to the East."[6] Land promotion took a variety of forms. There were "news" items in newspapers and magazines about the expansion of rail service into new territories and the resulting economic development in those areas. These pieces were often illustrated with photographs that demonstrated visually the value and productiveness of the lands the new lines traversed. For instance, in the *Minneapolis Journal* for June 11, 1911, the Great Northern Railroad published photographs of wheat fields taken in the newly opened Crooked River country northeast of Bend, captioned as "transformed sage brush country."[7] There were promotional brochures, also lavishly illustrated, describing locales served or soon-to-be served by the railroad. In 1914 alone, the Northern Pacific published twenty-five such

booklets, including one on central Oregon.[8] Special railroad "exhibi-
tion cars" toured the agricultural Midwest, displaying the farm products of the western states served by the railroads and depicting the
land there in glowing terms, as a means of luring people out west.[9]

In promoting central Oregon, the railroads advertised heavily in
the Pacific Northwest, especially in Portland and Seattle, on the Great
Plains, and in cities back east. They even resorted to "point-of-sale"
promotion, so to speak, placing posters advertising the region in rural
midwestern train depots.[10] The railroads courted homeseekers assidu-
ously, offering special excursion rates and even conducting rudimen-
tary marketing surveys among travelers to and from central Oregon
to find out their reactions to the region, presumably with an eye toward
refining publicity strategies.[11]

While railroad activities in central Oregon generated a good deal
of interest in the area, attention was drawn there as well through the
promotional efforts of the Oregon Land and Colonization Company,
which purchased 800,000 acres of land in Crook, Harney, and Malheur
counties in 1910.[12] Part of the Willamette Valley and Cascade Mountain Military Wagon Road grant, this land had never been opened to
settlement. The Oregon and Western Land Colonization Company,
based in St. Paul, was headed by local businessman W. P. Davidson
with Louis Hill (James Hill's son) as silent partner. The company
announced the opening of the land for settlement in newspapers around
the country and pursued a multifaceted marketing campaign, publishing and distributing maps and brochures by the thousands and arranging special excursion trains to central Oregon, often with Davidson
himself serving as tour guide. Davidson recruited real-estate agents,
particularly in the upper Midwest, to find prospective buyers for the
company's central Oregon lands. Within the first year of operation,
Davidson was besieged with offers to serve as local land agents for the
company from people who were dissatisfied with their present situa-
tions or who already resided in central Oregon. One such offer, dated
March 8, 1911, came from H. H. Hach of Viewpoint in the Christmas
Lake Valley, describing his success as a locator in northern Lake County
and offering his services to the land company in the same capacity.

The promotion of central Oregon by both the land company and
the railroads focused on its potential as a wheat-producing region. "It
was advertised, as I remember stories, as a potential wheat country
when this opened up for homesteading," said Hazel Ward. "There was

much more moisture in the area at that time. . . . Well, I think they probably got one or two crops of wheat, depending on the year. You can still get a crop of wheat here sometimes. . . . But they hit a [bad] year or two and then, of course, they starved out." Eleanor Long remarked, "The railroad advertised what wonderful grain country this was . . . , where you could grow all kinds of things and make your fortune." Peter Godon had seen central Oregon lands advertised in Philadelphia. His daughter Jo painted a vivid picture of the impact of the ad and of its bitter fruit: "They evidently had this land advertised highly. You thought you was getting a gold mine—320 acres for nothing, you know. And we really thought we could pick up gold off the ground and fruit off the trees. And we're still hunting! Really, that's the way they had it advertised, and they was a lot of people got fooled. But a lot of them didn't come as far as we did. Some of them came from Portland and some of them still had their homes and their jobs and they could go back, but we couldn't 'cause we had sold everything and there was nothing to go back to."

The promotional literature "devoted a great deal of attention to the matter of precipitation,"[13] for the amount of rain that fell in any given year was of critical concern to a potential wheat farmer. Because experience in other sections of the West had demonstrated that wheat could be successfully grown with less than twenty inches of rain per year, promoters confidently quoted U.S. Weather Bureau statistics indicating that the precipitation in central Oregon was between ten and twenty inches per year.[14] (In the Fort Rock–Christmas Lake Valley, of course, the actual average rainfall was much less). The demand for information about the weather in this and other parts of the arid West during this period was so high that Weather Bureau officials were often called upon to write articles for advertising circulars. The serious homeseeker, however, was advised to go directly to government reports, for the advertising aimed at homeseekers by transportation companies, land agencies, and colonizers did not always give accurate pictures of weather conditions.[15]

The central Oregon promotional campaign drew much of its effectiveness from its glowing comparison of the sage lands there to the wheat lands of the Columbia River Basin. Superficially, the comparison was a reasonable one to make, for the Palouse region of southeastern Washington and northeastern Oregon had also been sage-covered before its conversion to a wheat- and fruit-producing area in the 1870s.

As fruit orchards were established and wheat fields sown there, the popular image of the Columbia Basin shifted from that of a sagebrush desert to a rich farming district, aided by statements from government officials. A "misapprehension" of the nature of lands in eastern Oregon existed, wrote the Director of the General Land Office in 1876, because of "the natural inference that the bunch grass regions of this State are essentially similar to the sterile uplands and desert plateaus notably characteristic of Utah, Wyoming, Colorado, Montana, Nebraska, and other States and Territories of the great West. Nothing," he asserted, "could be further from the truth. The division of Oregon lying east of the Cascades does not . . . consist of arid and unavailable lands. . . . [Instead] there are watercourses and luxuriant grasses."[16] The report went on to claim that every locale in that part of the state had an ample supply of surface water; those that didn't, it added stoutly, if not consistently, could be irrigated. Although the rainfall was admitted to be less than that of the Willamette Valley, it was still characterized as "considerable," and certainly within the range of the fifteen inches of rainfall a year said to be adequate to grow wheat.[17]

Transforming the image of the Palouse from that of desert to garden was the more easily accomplished because it paralleled a similar metamorphosis occurring on the Great Plains at the same time, particularly after the introduction of large-scale wheat farming in the Dakotas during the 1880s. In the Dakota "boom" of that decade, the practicality of one operator sowing, cultivating, and harvesting thousands of acres of wheat was demonstrated over and over again. The development of the Palouse thus seemed to afford the opportunity to repeat the American success story of conquering the Great American Desert and transforming it into the Garden of the World. George Palmer Putnam, in his tour of the Pacific Northwest in 1909, made the parallel explicit. In the Palouse, he wrote, "farming is upon a bonanza basis, and the bigness of it all is reminiscent of the Dakotas, were it not for the majestic skylines, blessed visual reliefs lacking altogether in the continental mid-regions."[18] From a comparison between the Plains and the Palouse it was no great leap to discover a similar parallel between the Palouse and the central Oregon desert.

The comparison was made not only on the basis of observed similarities in vegetation and conditions, but on the grounds of like soils as well. Drawing inspiration from a report published by the

Smithsonian Institution comparing the soil of the Palouse to that of Sicily,[19] Thomas Shaw extended the analogy to central Oregon, writing, "There is no more fertile soil to be found anywhere, for volcanic ash is more enduring than any other soil, and the entire Central Oregon country is volcanic ash. . . . Central Oregon will some day become one of the most famous wheat producing sections of the world."[20]

The posters that W. A. Rockie plastered on the walls of Nebraska train stations also made an explicit comparison between the lands in central Oregon and those in the Palouse.[21] What was not known either by potential settlers or by the promoters luring them onto the land, however, was that two critical differences existed between the two regions: the land in central Oregon stood higher above sea level and had a lower annual rate of precipitation. The high altitude made the danger of crop-damaging frosts greater, while the lower rainfall average made consistently profitable farming a chancy proposition. But the enthusiasm that had boosted the Dakota boom and the development of the Palouse seemed to be infectious when the central Oregon desert was being promoted.

Out of all the areas in the arid West being promoted and developed during this period, central Oregon may have had particular appeal. The popular American image of Oregon, after all, had always been one of a land of opportunity. The Lewis and Clark Exposition in Portland in 1905, celebrating the centennial of their expedition, tried to breathe new life into the image.[22] But, by itself, the mystique surrounding Oregon as an agricultural paradise was not a strong enough magnet to attract people to the central part of the state from other sections of the nation (and it certainly cannot explain people moving there from within Oregon). There must have been other, more deeply felt, compelling forces at work in the lives and minds of the Fort Rock–Christmas Lake Valley homesteaders to cause them to uproot themselves and their families and to travel hundreds, even thousands, of miles to the Oregon desert—forces that transcended the regional context of the development of central Oregon, that existed instead on a national scale.

THE NATION AT THE TURN OF THE CENTURY

What was the national mood at the turn of the twentieth century? A key element in what Americans at large were thinking about themselves and the state of their nation—the context within which the high desert homesteaders acted—was a belief that a significant period of American history was ending and a new one beginning. What was coming to a close, of course, was the frontier era, characterized by the continuous sweep westward of an agrarian population into new land. The frontier experience, Americans believed, had not only enabled the transcontinental settlement of the country but had also nurtured their best qualities as a people. The classic articulation of this idea was Frederick Jackson Turner's statement on the significance of the frontier as a shaping force in American history.[23] Inspired by the findings of the 1890 census, Turner interpreted the disappearance of an identifiable line of frontier settlement to mean that the frontier itself had closed. Presumably, since the frontier as *place* had vanished, the frontier as *process* had also come to an end. Turner's argument was published just a little more than ten years before the first homesteaders began moving onto the desert—long enough for its implications to have sunk into the American consciousness but recently enough to be still fresh in people's minds.

Turner's "frontier thesis" struck a resonant chord in American thought, judging from the enthusiastic response it generated in the popular press and the revolution it created in American historiography.[24] Its initial eager acceptance indicates the extent to which it explained to Americans their contemporary situation—poised as it were on the fulcrum between an agrarian and an industrial economic and social order.[25] Americans were ready to consider the frontier era as closed in order to move on to the bigger and better things promised by the new economic and social forces of industrialization and urbanization that had begun to transform the nation in the last third of the nineteenth century. But, in the process of generating change in Americans' lives, those forces also created uncertainty and anxiety among Americans over their future. Turner's thesis that the frontier had been the source of Americans' identity and strength as a nation in the past provided a source of solace in the midst of turmoil because it

> argued the case for the frontier as against foreign influences, for environment as against inherited factors, for the Western-agrarian origins of American democracy, at a time when national pride, biological and social Darwinism, anxiety over imported ideas and racial strains, and the spectacle of the Populist revolt in the rural West and South prepared both the public and himself for his arguments.[26]

Turner thus provided Americans with a way of putting the frontier behind them while still allowing it to be invoked as a kind of Golden Age.

Indeed, the romanticization of the frontier as a bygone era began in the post-Turnerian 1890s, as Americans "were moving into another life . . . and paused for the pleasant pangs of nostalgia."[27] To be sure, the frontier had been subject to romantic interpretation long before then, in the novels of James Fenimore Cooper, in pictorial renditions of Western landscapes and natural history by George Catlin, Alfred Jacob Miller, and Karl Bodmer, even in Henry Thoreau's formulation that "to the east lay history, while westward was the apocalypse, the future and 'adventure.' "[28] But Turner's thesis served as the catalyst for a shift from regarding the frontier as an arena within which Americans could find their future destinies to seeing it as the wellspring from which Americans had drawn their strength in the past. It thus facilitated the transformation of the frontier from a living experience into historical fact.

The view of the frontier as irrevocably a part of the past permeated all forms of American cultural expression. Francis Parkman, in his 1892 preface to *The Oregon Trail*, mourned, "The Wild West is tamed, and its savage charms have withered."[29] At the Philosophical Congress of the World's Columbian Exposition in Chicago in 1893, James A. Skelton pronounced, "This westward march of empire and freedom during the ages comes to an abrupt end [here and now]."[30] Owen Wister, in his 1902 novel *The Virginian*, transformed the common cowboy of the cattle frontier into an enduring romantic hero, a figure who appears as well in the paintings and sculpture of Wister's contemporaries, Frederic Remington and Charles Russell. Russell's first one-man show, mounted in New York in 1911, was called "The West That Has Passed."[31] Buffalo Bill Cody's Wild West performances, which did a booming business at the Columbian Exposition,[32] represented in spectacle form the passing of the West through the symbolic reenactment of the demise of the buffalo, the subjugation of Native Americans, and the imposition of lawful social order on the natural chaos of the western wilderness.

The perception of the frontier as a bygone era meant that it was no longer regarded as part of contemporary Americans' reality. But, while Americans celebrated its pastness, its demise also made them unsure of themselves and their future and "subtly wove a thread of uneasiness" through the late nineteenth century.[33] Part of that uneasiness stemmed from the realization that the "closing" of the frontier was linked to the concurrent shift in the nation's economic base from agriculture to manufacturing during the second half of the nineteenth century and a corresponding social change from a predominantly rural population to an urban one. Given the long-standing American view "that farmers were naturally virtuous and freedom-loving pillars of democracy, unlike the decadent aristocrats, wretched aliens, and greedy businessmen of urban America,"[34] the growth of an urbanized citizenry raised the specter of a nation bereft of its traditional, conservative values. One response to this potential threat was the Back-to-the-Land movement, aimed at creating a best-of-both-worlds synthesis of the city and the country. The chief promoters of the Back-to-the-Land movement—politicians, lawyers, educators, speculators, bankers, and the like—"proceeded from the assumption that the cities were overpopulated while the rural districts were correspondingly underpopulated."[35] Some reformers advocated redressing the imbalance by moving urban dwellers from all walks of life onto small plots of land in the outlying fringes of the city. There they could become largely self-sufficient by raising their own fruits and vegetables and by keeping chickens, hogs, and dairy cows, while remaining close enough to the city to work there as well as to obtain goods and services available only in urban areas. Other advocates focused on attracting people, especially unemployed urban workers and recent foreign immigrants,[36] to the arid lands of the West. Movement enthusiasts published a regular series of articles in *Collier's Magazine*, starting in 1910; the chief organ of the movement itself was a slick publication called *Country Life*, first published in 1900.[37] Initially, this literature simply offered cautious advice to people who were considering moving "back to the land," but it soon evolved into the wholehearted, enthusiastic promotion of the healthfulness of life in the country in contrast to the disease, pollution, and overcrowding characteristic of city life.[38]

The Back-to-the-Land promoters were true Progressives in their desire "to save the city by redeeming the countryside" through the efficient use of resources. In theory, the people who established themselves on minifarms would do double duty to this cause: first, by leaving the city, they would begin to reduce urban problems, and, second, by engaging in either subsistence or truck farming, they could help ease the burden on American farmers, whose numbers were thought to be diminishing while non-food-producing urban dwellers were increasing.[39]

Judged by the Progressive ideal of efficiency, American agriculture was believed to be grossly deficient, threatening Americans with the possibility of serious food shortages.[40] Alarm over the future adequacy of the national food supply stemmed from the cyclical pattern of success and failure that had marked farming endeavors on the Great Plains from the 1870s through the 1890s. Americans believed that the difficulty farmers had encountered in successfully transforming the Plains into fruitful agricultural land on a sustained basis was due to the inefficiency of current agricultural technology and practice. That belief was fueled not only by high consumer prices for farm products, but also by a vague anxiety about the depletion of the supply of virgin agricultural land in the public domain.[41]

Americans' fears about the imminent disappearance of the public domain were first raised by Turner's pronouncement that the frontier was closed. They were exacerbated in the first years of the new century by the conservation movement that advocated government control over the nation's natural resources, including public lands, in order to prevent wasteful exploitation by private enterprise and to guarantee their "wise"—i.e., efficient—use. Under the two major pieces of conservation legislation, millions of acres were set aside for national parks and forest reserves during the first years of the century—sixty million acres by 1902, eighty-six million acres by 1905.[42] Many Americans, particularly in the West, protested against this diminution of the useful public domain at the very time that the need for more agricultural land was apparently growing, complaining that "the forests were being tied up and withdrawn from serving the needs of the West."[43]

It was within this general atmosphere of anxiety over the demise of the frontier, the growing population of the nation, and the dwindling supply of farmland, that prices for both land and agricultural products began to rise. Grim predictions of skyrocketing costs and future shortages of food produced a buying spree of farmlands, the price of which rose over 100 percent between 1900 and 1910. The price of wheat rose from $.58 a bushel in 1898 to $.93 in 1909.[44] All of this activity meant that farming was again seen as a potentially profitable and therefore attractive economic venture. At the same time, the introduction of mechanized equipment, chemical fertilizers, and improved methods of cultivation, along with the establishment of the

U.S.D.A. County Agricultural Extension Agent program in 1913, were all improving the productivity of American agriculture after the turn of the century. The other chief source of hope, especially in the arid and semiarid West where most of the remaining vacant lands were located, was the promise of turning lands previously regarded as worthless into productive agricultural regions by two radically different means: irrigation and dry farming.[45]

IRRIGATION

The turn to irrigation as a possible solution to agricultural difficulties was late in coming for Americans. The reason lies in the fact that irrigation seemed for a long time to have denied one of the basic tenets of the American agrarian ideal: that the land needed only the touch of the plow to be transformed into a garden. Admitting that an American agricultural frontier might turn out to be unproductive "was an aberration, a denial of faith."[46] The attitude that the farmer need only "tickle the land with the plow and it will laugh to the harvest" was in the ascendancy when the Great Plains first began to be settled in the late 1860s and early 1870s. As a result, little if any heed was given to the environmental differences between the lands east of the 100th meridian, where virtually all American agricultural experience had been gained, and those to the west, where the annual precipitation fell below the twenty-inch minimum necessary to grow crops without irrigation. Americans in the mid-nineteenth century wanted to believe "that the American republic could transform any type of country through sheer force of will." The Great Plains, like all previous frontiers, "must eventually succumb" to that will. "It was manifestly destined."[47] The noteworthy exception to this prevailing view was Major John Wesley Powell's 1878 report on the arid lands of the western United States; it was a forthright assessment of their suitability for grazing rather than farming purposes.[48] Powell's report called for a radical overhaul of the homesteading system, including the institution of 2,560-acre claims to be taken up along existing watercourses rather than following the standard township-and-range grid pattern, the common use of unwatered range lands, and cooperative irrigation projects. But his proposals were shouted down with familiar rhetoric: "The Creator never imposed a perpetual desert upon the earth, but on the contrary, has so endowed it that men by the plow can transform it, in any country, into farm areas."[49]

This attitude was reinforced during the first years of homestead-ing on the Great Plains after the passage of the 1862 Homestead Act. Initial settlement on the Plains coincided with the onset of a cycle of several relatively wet years which helped foster the belief that "rain follows the plow"—that is, that human activity on the land was caus-ing a favorable change in the climate. Because the cyclical nature of precipitation patterns on the Great Plains was not fully understood, this belief developed as a means of explaining the successful raising of wheat in an area previously thought unsuitable for that purpose.[50] While there was general agreement—at least early on—that the weather on the Plains was indeed changing, opinion was divided as to what the exact causes were. One school of thought argued that breaking up the sod mysteriously—almost magically—drew moisture from the air to the ground in the form of heavy dew, rain, or snow. Others argued that newly planted trees were altering the weather patterns, not only by creating windbreaks in the ordinary sense of providing shelter, but also by forcing the wind out of its usual pattern and causing it to give up moisture in the process. Still others claimed that laying railroad tracks and stringing telegraph wires somehow advantageously affected the local electrical forces that controlled rainfall patterns. Irrigation ditches and reservoirs were also believed to influence the weather, as were fires, fireworks, or artillery explosions.[51] (Some people who moved to the Great Plains may have been convinced that their doing so would actually help increase the rainfall.[52]) No matter what the means, how-ever, the changes thought to be generated were invariably favorable. Adverse effects of human activity, on the other hand, such as soil ero-sion that ultimately led to the Dust Bowl conditions of the 1930s, were ignored. While the idea of increased rainfall helped destroy the desert image of the Great Plains, it also retarded changes in public land pol-icy. After all, if the climate were improving, there was no need to change the laws.

Unfortunately, the explanations advanced to account for appar-ently improving conditions during each of a series of wet cycles failed to hold water when the weather turned dry. Yet there was persistent, almost pig-headed resistance to admitting that precipitation on the Plains was cyclical in nature and not induced or produced by human instrumentality, resistance that came from the will to believe that the desert could be made to blossom like the rose through the agency of the ideologically symbolic farmer. As long as that belief persisted, it

was heresy to suggest that artificial means of producing adequate moisture, like irrigation or rainmaking, ought to be employed. Indeed, they
were considered absurd, injurious, or utterly ineffective. Those who
proposed such solutions to drought in the 1880s were denounced as
public enemies for "casting discredit upon the region by advertising
its disadvantages to the world."[53] Local boosters were especially concerned that the development of a negative image of the region would
hurt the chances for its settlement (and, consequently, their opportunities to profit from it). Early irrigationists were regarded as the agrarian equivalent of atheists, who denied the basic premise of the American ideal that human beings could conquer nature. By the turn of
the century, however, irrigation began to be seriously discussed as an
alternative to the suffering of Great Plains farmers and their families
during droughts in the 1870s, '80s, and '90s. In other words, the real
environmental limitations that kept the Great American Desert from
becoming the Garden of the World began to be openly recognized.

The irrigation movement that began to emerge in the 1890s was
led by William E. Smythe. His *Conquest of Arid America*, published in
1900,[54] was an impassioned argument for government involvement in
large-scale irrigation projects to transform lands hitherto useless for
agricultural purposes into fruitful homesites. Smythe helped initiate a
series of irrigation congresses that met annually in various western cities during the first years of the century. Together with the energetic
and enthusiastic irrigationists' writings, these meetings served as a lobby
for legislation, which came with the passage of the Newlands Act in
1902, a law involving the federal government directly in the planning,
construction, and operation of irrigation projects.

Once accepted as a suitable solution to the western problem of
aridity, irrigation was touted in the same optimistic tones that had
characterized the earlier Garden-of-the-World promotional literature
of the Plains. "Somewhat slowly and unwillingly public attention has
at last settled itself upon irrigation, and in this seems to be the salva-
tion of the country," rejoiced Frederick Newell in the U.S.D.A. *Yearbook* for 1896. With regard to irrigation on the Great Plains, he continued, "it is incredible that, with these great natural advantages of
soil and sunshine, American ingenuity and persistence cannot find a
way to overcome in some degree the evil results of deficient or capri-
cious rainfall."[55] The promise of irrigation to revitalize the vision of

the arid West as a garden was reflected in the exclusion of irrigable lands from entry under the Enlarged Homestead Act of 1909.

DRY FARMING

What made homesteading on nonirrigable land seem feasible in 1909—what in fact was instrumental in the formulation of the Enlarged Homestead Act—was the other major development in western American agriculture: the advent of dry farming which promised to turn desert lands to productive use. Dry farming as a systematic set of agricultural practices emerged from farmers' experience on the Great Plains in the wake of the disastrous droughts in the last quarter of the nineteenth century.[56] To the chastened farmers in the arid and semi-arid regions of the West, the dry farming techniques devised by Nebraska farmer Hardy W. Campbell and promulgated in a variety of forms, especially after the turn of the century, seemed to afford a serious alternative to the wishful thought that rain would follow the plow.

The thrust of dry farming as an agricultural method was to conserve and make maximum use of the moisture available in areas of limited rainfall. The basic practices of the system consisted of plowing deeply initially, harrowing after each rainfall to create a fine dust mulch over the surface, alternately compressing and loosening the soil, increasing the organic matter in it, and fallowing fields every other year.[57] All of these techniques were designed to trap moisture in the ground where it would be available for plants.

The manner in which the dry farming gospel was preached managed to make a subtle but powerful emotional appeal over and above its apparently offering a solution to a stubborn agricultural problem. First of all, while irrigation was often perceived as calling for large capital investments, cooperative efforts, or protracted construction, dry farming involved a minimum outlay of money on new equipment and could be carried out single-handedly. Nor did the acceptance of dry farming involve conceding that "artificial" means were necessary to make the land productive as did the insistence on the need for irrigation. All dry farming called for was the application of a set of relatively simple, "natural" techniques, and success or failure hinged on faithful performance of its precepts rather than on uncertainties of climate. If dry farmers failed, it was their own fault and not that of the land. As an agricultural method, then, dry farming supported rather

than subverted (as irrigation projects could be seen to do) the traditional American ideal of agriculture as a simple, natural, individualistic calling.[58] And it seemed to promise western farmers a means for
regaining full mastery over the land.

A second appeal of dry farming was, paradoxically, that it was scientific, efficient, and up to date. Advocates of the dry farming method
characterized it as "scientific soil culture"[59]—time-consuming and pains-
taking work, altogether different from the sloppy and wasteful agricultural practices of the humid zone farmer. But dry farming was well
worth the effort, farmers were told; according to some claims, it could
increase harvest yields from three to five fold.[60] Describing dry farming in these terms, of course, flatteringly depicted the farmers who followed its precepts as modern, skillful practitioners, not unlike scientists; those who resisted it or regarded it with suspicion, on the other
hand, were viewed as backward. Thomas Shaw, agricultural consul-
tant for the Northern Pacific and Great Northern railways, warned
that settlers rushing into the arid lands of the United States and Canada "will fail using older agricultural techniques," and capped his argument by resorting to snob appeal. "Dry farming," he said, "is in a
sense high-class farming."[61]

At the same time that promoters hailed dry farming as the latest
in agricultural science, they also stressed its antiquity, citing the use of
certain dry farming techniques by ancient Egyptian and other Near
Eastern agricultural peoples. This tack not only vouched for the
method's reliability, but imbued it with almost biblical authority. Nor
did boosters neglect to mention its American antecedents. The feasibility of applying dry farming to the arid portions of the United States
was shown, as Shaw pointed out in 1911, by the fact that it had been
practiced in some areas of the Great Basin (that is, within the Mor-
mon culture area) for forty years.[62] The promoters of dry farming thus—
deliberately or unwittingly—represented it as comprising both tradition and innovation, practiced by both the yeoman farmer and the
scientific agriculturalist. On the one hand, it seemed to leave the vir-
tues of rural life untouched; on the other, it placed the dry farmer
among the most progressive of Americans.

Although few farmers had access to the literature published by
agricultural scientists, they could learn about dry farming from articles that appeared in both national magazines and local news-

papers.[63] Or they could read one of the several handbooks on dry farming that appeared in quick succession in the first decade of the century, including Hardy Campbell's own *Soil Culture Manual* in 1902, William MacDonald's *Dry Farming: Its Principles and Practices*, John Widtsoe's *Dry Farming: A System of Agriculture for Countries under a Low Rainfall*, and Thomas Shaw's *Dry Land Farming*.[64]

The promulgation of the dry farming method struck an optimistic note at a time when Americans were undergoing a fundamental shift in their economic and social orientations. In light of the declaration that the frontier was closed, anything that seemed to promise a continuation of the way things were—especially one so deeply rooted in the American psyche as the agrarian frontier—was bound to meet with a favorable response. The resulting enthusiasm for dry farming seemed to rise, phoenix like, from the ashes of the belief that settlement on and cultivation of the Great Plains would effect a permanent and favorable change in the weather there. In a way, it simply clothed the old belief in new language, with the plow still the instrument by which sufficient moisture was to be assured. In fact, the notion that "rain follows the plow," which had been on the decline in the 1890s, enjoyed a revival after the turn of the century, in the wake of the development and promulgation of the dry farming method.[65] Throughout the northern Plains, in fact, "publicity bulletins of every state repeated the old legend that rainfall was increasing consequent to turning the sod."[66]

Government agricultural experts did their best to debunk the belief in changing weather. E. C. Chilcott, head of the U.S.D.A. Office of Dryland Farming, said flatly, "Many people acquainted with present conditions [1907] believe that the climate of this region is rapidly becoming more humid. This belief is without foundation in fact."[67] Richard Sullivan, writing a year later in the U.S.D.A. *Yearbook*, was equally emphatic: "The cultivation and forestation of the semi-arid region, even though they had proceeded much farther than they have, could not change the climate."[68]

Dry farming was regarded not only as a panacea for the troubled Great Plains, but as a means of opening undeveloped arid regions of the Northern Plains, the Columbia Basin Upland, and even the Great Basin.[69] In an article in *Century Magazine* in 1906, J. L. Cowan claimed that even areas with an annual rainfall of twelve inches per year could produce good crops without irrigation. "There is little arable land in the great West," he prophesied, "that may not be divided into 40-acre farms, each one of which will be capable of supporting an average-sized family."[70] Hardy Campbell himself believed that "the semiarid West was destined to be the last and best grain garden of the world."[71] Promoters of dry farming waxed visionary in their descriptions of what dry farming could accomplish, aiming their rhetoric at the heart of Americans' fears:

> This vast area [the arid West] of fertile, and as yet almost unutilized, land is the foundation upon which the American people must build for a continuance of their prosperity for at least a century to come. . . . It will relieve the congestion of cities, provide an outlet for superabundant capital, and afford opportunities for the enterprising and discontented for decades.[72]

Dry farming, of course, had its detractors. Skeptics explained the successes with which it was credited by its advocates as simply the result of dry farmers being more systematic and methodical than their humid-region counterparts. After all, as one observer noted, dry farming was more successful in a wet cycle than in a dry one.[73] The method seems, in fact, to have provoked a good deal of dry humor, especially among the people involved in it themselves. "You have to plant three crops of dry-farmers before you get a stand,"[74] asserted a Plains parody of proverbial agricultural lore. Repeated throughout the arid and semiarid West was the story of the drylander asked by the visitor why he remained on his land under such adverse circumstances. Astonished, the drylander replied, "Leave? Why, I've only been here forty years and had two good years already!"[75]

The most serious challenge to dry farming came from the U.S. Department of Agriculture. The U.S.D.A. established an Office of Dryland Agriculture in 1905 as a service to farmers on the Great Plains, and published articles about dry farming in its *Yearbook* from 1907 through 1911. While the articles attest to farmers' interest in the subject, the governmental experts' advice offers a contrast to the enthusiastic tone of the dry farming handbooks, cautioning farmers against putting too much reliance on the technique as a foolproof system for farming in arid regions. E. C. Chilcott called the dry farming method "still experimental and one that requires a good deal of capital investment." Only when development proceeded gradually from established agricultural centers "instead of by unsupported beginnings in the midst of dry land can success be assured," he warned. He went on to predict with grim accuracy that "the boundaries of existing settlements may be gradually extended, but any wholesale attempts to colonize large areas of this semiarid land with people accustomed to farming only in humid regions or not accustomed to farming at all must surely result in disastrous failure."[76] The chief benefit that dry farming had to offer, as far as the government experts were concerned, was that it encouraged American farmers, who had been notoriously profligate with their land up to that point, to practice more conservative methods of land use.

Although government experts expressed caution, the proponents of dry farming continued to trumpet its advantages through most of the first two decades of the twentieth century. Among its most vocal boosters were the railroad companies. They stood to gain substantially as the successful implementation of dry farming made the extension of their lines into new territories feasible. The Northern Pacific Railroad, for instance, hired dry farming promoter Thomas Shaw as one of their publicity agents. In 1910 Shaw toured central Oregon— the region then being most aggressively marketed by the company— making widely publicized stops in Crook, Harney, and Malheur counties. His description of that trip, published in 1911, was, not surprisingly, an enthusiastic encomium for the region.

Dry farming was also promoted by an organization devoted exclusively to that purpose—the Dry Farming Congress. Formed in 1906, this organization met initially in Denver, then in Salt Lake City, Cheyenne, and Spokane in subsequent years.[77] Its membership, curiously enough, did not include many actual practitioners. Instead, it comprised railroad executives, representatives of agricultural equipment manufacturers and other business people, and government and civic functionaries, all of whom were interested in using the dry farming gospel to promote agricultural settlement wherever it would do them the most good.[78] As a result, the congresses concentrated on promotion rather than on practice. They paid scant attention to sober experimentation, preferring instead to glory in reports of what had already been accomplished or, better yet, to indulge in rosy visions of what future achievements might be. They operated, in effect, as lobby groups, particularly in urging reform of the public land laws to encourage the spread of settlement into agriculturally marginal areas.

REFORMING THE LAND LAWS

By 1900, there was a confusing array of land laws governing the kind of land that could be claimed, for what purposes, how much could be taken up by an individual, and the conditions for acquiring title (such as the amount of acreage to be under cultivation at any given time and the length of residence required). Amid this welter, all the public land laws had two interrelated purposes: (1) to establish individual families on agricultural land, and (2) to prevent the accumulation of large holdings in the hands of a few people. The fear that the public lands were being used for speculative or monopolistic purposes intensified after the turn of the century, as the corporation came to dominate the American economy and the supply of usable land still remaining in the public domain was perceived as rapidly dwindling. Out of this atmosphere erupted cries that the existing homestead laws were being badly abused and needed reform.[79]

President Theodore Roosevelt responded to clamor for reform of the land laws by creating the Public Lands Commission in 1903, charged with investigating the actual operations of the land laws and making recommendations for needed changes. In its final report, submitted in 1905, the commission proposed three major changes. One was the reduction of desert land claims to 160 acres, along with proof not only that an adequate water supply existed to irrigate the claim but also that a crop had actually been produced. Another recommendation was that the lands still remaining in the public domain at that point, whose agricultural potential was unknown, be classified according to their suitability for farming before being indiscriminately opened to homestead entry. The third recommended change was the repeal of the commutation provision of the homestead law. As it stood, the law allowed entrymen to prove up on their claims in fourteen months by paying $1.25 per acre in lieu of the full three years of residence on the land. The commission discovered that many entrymen who commuted their claims either sold the land immediately or borrowed money on it and disappeared. In either case, the land often ended up in the hands of large landholders or—what was worse, from the government's viewpoint—speculators. These abuses of commutation, the commission pointed out, meant that "the number of patents is increasing out of all proportion to the number of new homes." Because the paramount purpose of the public land laws was to provide individual families with agricultural land "so that homes would be created in the wilderness," the commission hinted ominously, if somewhat vaguely, that the continuation of the system as it stood would have a "disastrous effect . . . upon the well-being of the nation as a whole."[80] At the same time that the Public Lands Commission was working toward land law reform, an experiment was under way on the Plains, designed to test the feasibility of homesteads larger than 160 acres in an agriculturally marginal area of the public domain. Under the provisions of the Kinkaid Act of 1904, which applied only to the sandhills area of Nebraska, people could file on homestead claims of 640 acres. The Kinkaiders' success rate was closely monitored, as the outcome of the experiment would weigh heavily in any proposed legislation calling for increasing the size of homestead claims. But even before the results were in, Congress was swamped with requests from people all over the arid West to extend the Kinkaid legislation into their localities.[81] Among the proposals for an enlarged homestead act was one from the General Land Office in 1907, which suggested that a 640-acre allotment supplant the 160-acre homestead claim. In 1908, Congress took up a bill to that effect.[82]

Debate there raged over the size of the claims, the length and conditions of residence, and the requirements for cultivation and improvements. The key issue, finally, was the most feasible size for a homestead on marginal land, especially land that could not be irrigated. The chief stumbling block to establishing an appropriate number of acres was that the potential productivity of the remainder of the public domain, almost all of which lay in the semiarid or arid regions of the West, was virtually unknown. If the land were to prove as productive as that in more humid areas, especially under irrigation, 160 acres might be too much land for the entryman and his household; if it were less productive, or if it could not be irrigated, 320 acres might not be enough to support them.

Contradictory claims made for the effectiveness of dry farming compounded the uncertainty. On the one hand, its boosters presented dry farming as a set of scientifically based agricultural techniques, while on the other the U.S.D.A. experts expressed caution over its use and skepticism about the claims made for its efficacy. To lawmakers, however, the very fact that there existed an apparently codified set of techniques for turning worthless acreage into valuable farmland was the overriding consideration. Although dry farming as a method had not been adequately tested through experimentation when the debate over larger homestead claims was going on, the promise it seemed to offer for transforming the remainder of the Great American Desert into a garden was too strong an appeal to resist and the Enlarged Homestead Act was passed in 1909. Thus the promotional campaign for dry farming was translated into public policy.[83]

The bill that finally passed allowed an entryman to claim 320 acres of land that could not be appropriated under any of the existing land laws, except the Homestead Act itself. The 320-acre allotment, which simply doubled the amount allowed under the 1862 act, was absurdly illogical, compensating for the poor quality of the land by allowing twice as much of it to be claimed.[84]

HOMESTEADING IN THE TWENTIETH CENTURY

The passage of the Enlarged Homestead Act took place in the wake of the panic of 1907—the first serious economic crisis since the depression of 1893—and of residual unemployment in 1908 of over 7 percent. It thus came in the midst of economic hard times, as well as on the heels of the announcement that the frontier era—with its complement of free, virgin land—was ended. The timing of the new law triggered an enormous response somewhat akin to last-minute shopping on Christmas Eve: Anything would do. People who had never considered homesteading, along with those who had tried it more than once before, became land-seekers, even though the lands opened under the Enlarged Homestead Act were, in the words of one bitter commentator, "the parings and scraps and crumbs of the Old West."[85] As Shorty Gustafson said, "Boy, 160 or 320 acres of free land, it don't make any difference where it is. It's land and here they come."

A combination of factors thus spurred the early twentieth-century homesteaders: the apparently diminishing supply of public land, the high prices for agricultural land and farm products, the expansion and promotional activities of the railroads, the publicity surrounding irrigation and dry farming, and, eventually, the Panic of 1907 and the passage of the Enlarged Homestead Act. The result was that more land was homesteaded between 1898 and 1917 than in the preceding thirty years (100 million vs. 70 million acres). In fiscal year 1909–10 alone, more than eighteen million acres were taken up, the largest yearly aggregate of land covered by entries in the history of the homestead law.[86]

While people who took up homesteads in the early twentieth century were undoubtedly responding to economic influences, there was an emotional component to their response as well. The atmosphere of nostalgia beginning to surround the frontier, with which homesteading had always been closely identified, heightened the economic appeal of free government land. That appeal was further intensified by the sense that, if the frontier era were indeed passing from the American scene, the Enlarged Homestead Act afforded one last chance to participate in it. Among the people who scrambled to take up the "last free land" from the public domain were both farmers "who needed land acquisition opportunities," and nonfarmers swept along by the rhetoric of the promotional materials published by both the railroads and the land companies. That literature "threw all caution to the winds to play upon the fact that homestead land was almost gone." One brochure, published by the Great Northern, warned, "The time is rapidly approaching when there will be no free land left." Another exhorted readers, "Why not go out and get your birthright, 320 free fertile acres . . . ?" By staying at home, Americans were told, "they would miss a chance to take advantage of their rights as citizens to file on government land."[87]

Having been told since the mid-1890s that the frontier was closed, Americans responded to the Enlarged Homestead Act as though it were a reprieve. And in a way it was, for it reopened a door to opportunity that Americans were beginning to believe had closed forever—the opportunity to take up virgin land and make a living from it. Even the amenities offered by an urbanized America—wage employment, manufactured consumer goods, utility services—were not strong enough, for a good many people, to outshine the promise of the frontier.[88]

People responded as they did to the opening of the last of the public domain because that was where, historically, opportunity had lain for Americans.[89] The homesteaders were not simply hoping to escape the perceived complexity of the present by turning to a life-style associated with the "simpler" age just past. They were actively denying the reality that the frontier era was past at all; they were affirming, in fact, its continuation by participating in the same process of carving a living from the land that Americans had been engaged in for generations. Caught in the tension between the older agricultural basis for economic opportunity and the newer forms afforded by industrial and commercial development, twentieth-century homesteaders chose the more traditional mode of making a living—all the more comforting, perhaps, in the face of the economic changes that were effecting massive social upheaval and dislocation. At the same time, they may not have perceived their choice to be a traditional one; they likely saw themselves rather as in the vanguard of the new American agriculture as dry farmers. Nevertheless, in the early twentieth century, farming still represented a reassuringly familiar way of making a living, much as in the late twentieth century owning one's own business is still regarded as the classic American economic enterprise. Government publications painted a realistic, even sobering, picture of homesteading then, just as they now state the cold, hard facts of operating a small business. But, no matter how warned we are about the difficulties of going into business for ourselves, we cannot imagine not being able to make a success of it, especially if we equip ourselves with the latest in electronic gadgetry. Perhaps the homesteaders, too, could not imagine being unable to make a living from the land, especially with the latest in advanced agricultural techniques at their fingertips.

In making their choice, the homesteaders created a paradox. On the one hand, they were "carving homes out of the wilderness" in the best American frontier tradition. But they were doing so in an age when the definitions of pioneering were changing. When Americans turned away from the frontier in its classical geographical sense, they translated pioneering into a metaphor for innovation, making Thomas Edison and Henry Ford—not Hardy Campbell or John Widtsoe—American heroes. The twentieth-century homesteaders were taking the same risks as their Great Plains forerunners. But the road they had chosen was apparently so well traveled by then, so thoroughly familiar, and on its way to becoming, economically, a secondary route, that its dangers were no longer perceived as real by the portion of the population not traveling with them. As farming became a decreasingly common way of earning a living, it became increasingly identified with the frontier past. Urbanites in the 1910s may have been tempted to smile fondly at the homesteaders in an appreciation of the traditional if anachronistic nature of their endeavors, much as we smile now at the craftsperson in the local folk arts festival, nudge our companions, and say, "Isn't it wonderful that people are still doing things that way?"

Seeing the twentieth-century homesteaders as anachronisms, borne along on the receding tide of the frontier movement reflects, of course, a bias introduced by hindsight. We recognize, as they could not (or perhaps refused to), that the national movement toward an industrial economic base and an urban-based population was irreversible and inescapable. The danger in regarding twentieth-century homesteaders in this way is that it tempts us to explain them away as vestigial, even misfit, elements in the population. This view emerges in descriptions of them as "primarily people discontented with their lives . . . , some even hoping to get away from the world as they knew it and lead isolated lives . . . , never feeling rooted in any one spot."[90] George Palmer Putnam described a land-seeking couple he encountered on the Oregon desert in these patronizing and derogatory terms:

> The horses are ill mated, the wagon decrepit. Baling wire sustains the harness and the patched canvas of the wagon top hints of long service. "How far to Millican's?" says the driver.
> He is a young man; at least, his eyes are young. His "woman" is with him and their three kiddies, the tiniest asleep in her mother's lap, with the dust caked about her wet baby chin. The man wears overalls, the woman calico that was gaudy once before the sun bleached it colorless, and the children nameless garments of uncertain ancestry. The wife seems very tired—as weary as the weary horses. Behind them is piled their household: bedding, a tin stove, chairs, a cream separator, a baby's go-cart, kitchen utensils, a plow and barbed wire, some carpet; beneath the wagon body swings a pail and lantern, and water barrel and axe are lashed at one side.
> We direct them to Millican's.
> "Homesteading?" we inquire.
> "Not exactly. That is, we're just lookin'."
> There are hundreds like these all over the West, "just lookin'," with their tired wives, their babies, their poverty, and their vague hopefulness. They chase rainbows from Bisbee to Prince Rupert. Some of them settle, some of them succeed. But most of them are discontented wherever Fortune places them, and forever move forward toward some new-rumored El Dorado just over the hill.[91]

Carlton Culmsee, whose father homesteaded in Utah in 1909, was equally vitriolic when he called those who arrived after his own family as "dregs of the back-to-the-farm surge; braggarts, spineless and ineffectual."[92] These are the people H. L. Davis depicts in his novel *Honey in the Horn*, set in eastern Oregon in the early years of the century, as "the backwash of a pioneer movement turned back at the edge of a continent to despoil a promised land which, as they discovered too late, lay behind them, not ahead."[93] Even historians tend to portray

FORT ROCK. B. *Allen.*

the homesteaders as passive victims "recruited [to the frontier] by those who knew their business" and "pulled by the prospects of free or cheap land, encouraged by railroads, enticed by private and official promotional agencies, and driven by the perennial hope of better things over the horizon."[94]

This one-dimensional and demeaning caricature of all those who tried their hand on the public domain during this period hardly serves as a description of the homesteaders we have seen in the Fort Rock–Christmas Lake Valley. It is an easy caricature to draw because, from the point of view either of the urbanites who were their contemporaries or of present-day historians, the homesteaders were at best shortsighted and at worst benighted fools in choosing to hitch their wagons to the fading star of the frontier. Either judgment is, of course, grossly unfair to what the homesteaders did, why they did it, and what their acts ultimately meant.

The homesteaders were neither blind nor foolish. Rather, in an age when Americans as a people were growing beyond and away from their traditional agrarian roots, the twentieth-century homesteaders were pursuing a more conservative and familiar course, choosing the old over the new, the known over the unknown—the last generation of Americans able to make that choice in an honestly unselfconscious manner. Paradoxically, in doing so, the homesteaders saw themselves as the innovative pioneers of the new American agricultural frontier, while we find it expedient to see them as the victims rather than the vanguards of progress. The failure of the homesteaders, from our contemporary viewpoint, brought the frontier to an end; their sacrifice allowed the industrialized, urbanized future to come to pass.

Desert Lupine

Epilogue

The people who live in the Fort Rock–Christmas Lake Valley today are aware—some vividly, some vaguely—of the history of the land they own. They can look out over their own lush alfalfa crops and see the homesteaders' skimpy stands of rye. They can pump thousands of gallons of deep-well water and still be acutely aware of the aridity that early settlers had to contend with. They can count their present neighbors on the fingers of one hand, yet imagine the valley once full of people. Living as they do in an intimate, sometimes hostile, always uncertain relationship with the land, they have a deep appreciation for the homesteaders' struggles with it, and describe their predecessors' experiences with pity and fellow feeling. Perhaps that sense of a common experience is one reason that people in the area emphasized the homesteading in talking to me about the past.

That focus on homesteading, as I suggested in the opening pages, was a direct expression of the insiders' perspective on local history. The nondirective strategy I employed in conducting interviews meant that the people I talked with were free to express their own views of the local past (within the constraints of what they thought I wanted to know and what they wanted me to know). I deliberately chose this method, rather than asking direct question about specific topics, including homesteading, which would have elicited more concrete and detailed answers, because the ability of oral history to garner historical data of a factual nature had been amply demonstrated. I was more interested in showing that it could make other, less tangible but no less meaningful contributions to historical research, particularly in allowing the expression of narrators' own perspectives on and evaluations of the historical experiences they were asked about. Along the way, however, I discovered that orally communicated history had a third contribution to make: It permitted the transformation of historical experience into narrative form. By narrative here I do not mean the individual stories that different people told me. I mean instead the larger narrative structure that emerges from the entire body of material I recorded—the homesteaders' *story*—that reveals not only what happened, but what narrators consider to be the meaning of what happened.

People conveyed to me a rich sense of the significance of homesteading through a process of distillation in which the complexity and variety of actual historical experience were compressed into a single, simple story line. This distillation process becomes apparent when we compare the information available from written and documentary sources with the story that contemporary residents tell.

The written record indicates that a number of forces drew the homesteaders to the Fort Rock–Christmas Lake Valley, including the promise of being able to raise wheat and ship it to market via a convenient rail line; the enthusiastic publicity surrounding dry farming; changes in the public land laws, particularly the passage of the Enlarged Homestead Act; generally favorable economic conditions for agriculture; and a fear that the public domain was disappearing. According to documentary evidence, some of the homesteaders were married, some were single. Some were experienced farmers, some were rank strangers to the plow. As far as motivations can be determined, some took up claims hoping to profit quickly from the development of the valley; others were looking for a place to settle permanently; still others simply wanted title to a piece of the public domain and never intended to stay. Some of the homesteaders managed to do well enough (or hang on long enough) to gain the patents to their land; others gave up within a few months. Of the people who left the valley, not all did so at the same time nor for the same reasons. Some people left after they proved up on their claims, having achieved their goals; others were forced out before patent by economic circumstances. Some of the homesteaders were satisfied with what they had accomplished; others were frustrated and embittered.

In the oral testimony I recorded, however, all of the complications, confusions, and contradictions of the past were smoothed away. The resulting composite story told by present-day residents skinned the homesteaders' experiences down to a skeletal outline. Lured to the desert through false advertising by the railroads and misleading information promulgated by the government, and without prior farming experience, the homesteaders arrived with high hopes of raising wheat and making permanent homes for themselves and their families. They struggled hard for a few years, raising rye and combatting drought, frost, and jackrabbits; the men were forced to leave their families alone a good deal of the time while they worked for a living outside the valley. In spite of the hardships they endured, the homesteaders found time to build schools for their children and socialize with their neighbors. Eventually, however, the homesteaders failed, unable to make a living from the land—innocent victims of circumstances they couldn't control, deceived by greedy capitalists and/or venal government officials, and defeated by a hostile environment. Reluctantly, in sorrow and despair, they left the valley to find their fortunes elsewhere.

This version of the homesteading represents the careful selection and arrangement of information about the homesteading into a coherent pattern. Each element in the story contributes to the characterization of the homesteaders as like-minded, hardworking, nobly motivated individuals, pitting their strength and desire and will against the wilderness to create an ordered society in true American pioneer fashion. The story of the Fort Rock–Christmas Lake Valley homesteaders thus becomes a local redaction of the classic American frontier narrative, one repeated in countless places throughout the trans-Mississippi West both before and after the turn of the century. As such, it has an emotional power that transcends the local scene by evoking themes and images associated with the westward movement on a national scale.[1]

One feature of the high desert homesteaders' story, however, distinguishes it from the traditional narrative of the frontier experience: It was a failed effort. Instead of triumph the desert homesteaders suffered ignominious defeat. For contemporary residents, they are more

THE SILVER LAKE VALLEY, WITH IRRIGATION SYSTEM IN THE
FOREGROUND. B. Allen.

to be pitied than honored. In the orally communicated history I
recorded, the homesteaders were clearly not the giants of the earth
who stalk the writings of Cather, Rølvag, and Sandoz. People regularly spoke of them in diminutive terms—describing their "little cabins"
and their few possessions, their small farms and their brief tenure—as
though the immensity of the desert had literally dwarfed them. Exam-
ining the homesteading through the lens of oral testimony is almost
like looking through the wrong end of a telescope: everything seems
small and very far away. This perspective on the past seems to be a
function of the parallels that present-day residents draw between their
own experiences on the land and those of the homesteaders.

On the one hand, narrators focus on homesteading as a key element of community history because it helps them account for their
own presence in the valley today: No one would be living there now if
the homesteaders had not moved in and tried to settle it. On the other
hand, the emphasis on the homesteading as a failed effort helps explain
why the land today is sparsely populated and—until very recently—
remained nearly in its natural state: in spite of the homesteaders' efforts,
they were unable to subjugate the land to their purposes. The story of
the homesteaders, as recounted locally, thus validates the present in
terms of the past. Finally, by compressing the varied experiences of
the homesteaders into streamlined form, characterizing their efforts as
failures, and thus reversing the success theme of the frontier myth,
narrators are not just creating historical truth out of contemporary reality. They are also symbolically keeping the frontier alive in
the present. If the homesteaders had succeeded—or rather, if the

dominant perception of their efforts were one of success—in making the desert blossom as the rose, there would be little glory in the present struggle of the people living in the valley now, for they would simply be following in the homesteaders' footsteps. The homesteaders' failure, however, means that there is still an opportunity to bring strength and desire and will to bear on conquering the wilderness; there is still a chance in the present to participate in the pioneer process.

The people in the Fort Rock–Christmas Lake Valley today, then, regard the homesteading there as a pivotal point of their community's history because it both explains the present and validates their own efforts on the land in historico-mythic terms. As the transformation of the area begun by the introduction of electricity in 1955 and the subsequent large-scale development of irrigation systems powered by electric pumps continues, the face of the desert will change, along with people's relationship to it. That change may alter the contours of local history so that homesteading is no longer perceived as its crux. When that happens, it will be time to visit the valley again, to listen to people talking about the past from a new perspective.

Notes

NOTES TO PROLOGUE

1. John Unruh, *The Plains Across: The Overland Emigrants and the Trans-Mississippi West, 1840–1860* (Urbana: University of Illinois Press, 1979), esp. chapters 10 and 11.

2. Gilbert Fite, *The Farmers' Frontier, 1865–1900* (Albuquerque: University of New Mexico, 1974), p. 145; Samuel Newton Dicken and Emily F. Dicken, *The Making of Oregon: A Study in Historical Geography* (Portland: Oregon Historical Society, 1979), p. 135.

3. The fieldwork resulted in my doctoral dissertation, "Talking about the Past: A Folkloristic Study of Orally Communicated History" (UCLA, 1980). The transcripts of the interviews are on deposit at the University of Oregon.

4. The books included Phil F. Brogan, *East of the Cascades* (Portland: Binfords and Mort, 1964); Raymond R. Hatton, *High Desert of Oregon* (Portland: Binfords and Mort, 1977); E. R. Jackman and Reuben A. Long, *The Oregon Desert* (Caldwell, Idaho: Caxton Printers, 1964); and F. A. Shaver et al., comps., *An Illustrated History of Central Oregon* (Spokane: Western Historical Publishing Co., 1905).

NOTES TO CHAPTER 1

1. W. Eugene Hollon, *The Great American Desert, Then and Now* (New York: Oxford University Press, 1966), p. 206.

2. Dicken and Dicken, p. 29; John T. Whistler and John H. Lewis, *Silver Lake Project: Irrigation and Drainage* (Salem: Office of State Engineer, 1915), p. 15.

3. Phil Brogan, p. 267; Northern Pacific and Great Northern Railway Companies, Annual Reports. Maps, 1880 (Minneapolis: Minnesota Historical Society, microfilm edition, 1979); Maps, State of Oregon, Department of the Interior, General Land

Office, 1910; Israel C. Russell, *Preliminary Report on the Ecology and Water Resources of Central Oregon* (Washington, D.C.: Government Printing Office, 1905), p. 17.

4. Dicken and Dicken, p. 93.

5. Brogan, p. 267; Stephen F. Bedwell, *Fort Rock Basin: Prehistory and Environment* (Eugene: University of Oregon Press, 1973), p. 4; Gerald A. Waring, *Geology and Water Resources of a Portion of South Central Oregon* (Washington, D.C.: Government Printing Office, 1908), p. 9; M. O. Leighton, E. C. LaRue, and F. F. Henshaw, *Surface Water Supply of the United States, 1909. Part X, The Great Basin* (Washington, D.C.: Government Printing Office, 1911), p. 156; Russell, p. 17.

6. Carrol B. Howe, *Ancient Tribes of the Klamath Country* (Portland: Binfords and Mort, 1968), p. 4; James Slama Buckles, "The Historical Geography of the Fort Rock Valley, 1900-1941" (M.A. thesis, University of Oregon, 1959), p. 8.

7. Bedwell, p. 4; Waring, p. 59.

8. Buckles discusses the various names applied to the Fort Rock–Christmas Lake–Silver Lake area, pp. 8–11.

9. Emery Castle and Carroll Dwyer, "Irrigation Possibilities in the Fort Rock Area," Circular of Information #558 (Corvallis: Agricultural Experiment Station, 1956), p. 5; Waring, pp. 71-76; Buckles, pp. 37-38; Ira S. Allison, "Work of Wind in Northern Lake County, Oregon," *Geographical Society of America Bulletin* 52 (1940): 1943; W. A. Rockie, "Backsight and Foresight on Land Use," *Northwest Science* 18 (May 1944): 40-41.

10. Arnold S. Burrier, "An Analysis of the Proposed Fort Rock Conservation Area" (unpublished ms., U.S. Resettlement Administration, July 1936), p. 3. The surveyors' field notes for many of the townships in the area make specific mention of the plentitude of bunchgrass; see, for instance, the general descriptions for Township 24 South, Range 15 East, Township 25 South, Range 16 East, Township 27 South, Range 15 East, and Township 28 South, Range 16 East, as well as Waring, pp. 17, 59 and Bedwell, pp. 7-8.

11. E. R. Jackman and Reuben A. Long, p. 194; Waring, p. 17.

12. Surveyors' field notes for Township 27 South, Range 18 East, June 1882. The locations of several smaller lakes are shown on present-day maps. Marie Jetter, who grew up in the desert during the homestead period, wrote of several shallow lakes in the Christmas Lake Valley on which children would ice skate in the winter but which dried up in the summer (*Contentment Yesterday— Why Not Today?* [Jericho, New York: Exposition Press, 1969], p. 42).

13. E. D. Cope, "The Silver Lake of Oregon and its Region," *American Naturalist* 23 (November 1889): 977.

14. Surveyors' field notes for Township 25 South, Range 17 East, July, 1882; Waring, p. 66.

15. Anna Linebaugh, tape-recorded interview, Silver Lake, August 1, 1978. Except as otherwise noted, all information attributed to her was recorded during this interview.

16. Luther S. Cressman, "Cultural Sequences at The Dalles, Oregon: A Contribution to Pacific Northwest Prehistory," *Transactions of the American Philosophical Society*, N.S. vol. 50, pt. 10 (Philadelphia, 1960), p. 12.

17. Waring, p. 67; Castle and Dwyer, p. 4; Buckles, p. 20.

18. Buckles, p. 22; Whistler and Lewis, p. 19; Russell, p. 21; Waring, p. 14. The weather-recording station at Fremont, in the northwestern part of the Fort Rock Valley, recorded an average annual rainfall of between eight and ten inches from 1910 to 1914, but measured only seven to eight inches per year from 1927 to 1940. Burrier's

Resettlement Administration report stated, "During the thirty-two years for which weather records have been collected in this section, the rainfall has been less than ten inches for two-thirds of the time" (Burrier, p. 5). See also F. D. Trauger, *Basic Ground-Water Data in Lake County, Oregon* (Portland: U.S. Department of the Interior, 1950), pl. 6.

19. Burrier, p. 5.

20. A study of the availability of water in the Fort Rock Valley in the 1950s demonstrated that the annual amount of rainfall might vary as much as 125 percent from the average in either direction.

21. Eleanor Long, in a tape-recorded interview in the Fort Rock Valley, August 24, 1978, remarked that one night in the 1950s her thermometer registered -57 degrees. All information attributed to Eleanor Long was recorded on this occasion.

22. DeForest and Esther Stratton, tape-recorded interview, Silver Lake, July 12, 1978. (Except as otherwise noted, all information recorded from them was recorded on this date.) See also Russell, p. 21.

23. Castle and Dwyer, p. 9.

24. Castle and Dwyer, p. 8. The danger of killing frosts is slightly mitigated by the dryness of the air. Because of its low moisture content, the air must reach a temperature several degrees below the freezing point (26–28 degrees) before it begins to inflict serious harm on crops, according to Whistler and Lewis, p. 33.

25. U.S. Weather Bureau, *Report of the Chief of the Weather Bureau, 1908–09* (Washington, D.C.: Government Printing Office, 1910), p. 199.

26. Whistler and Lewis, p. 79; Brogan, p. 166; F. A. Shaver et al., p. 868; Howe, p. 64.

27. Dicken and Dicken, p. 28; Waring, p. 10; Whistler and Lewis, p. 15.

28. "Topographically . . . , Silver Lake Valley is really a part of this wider area [i.e., Christmas Lake Valley], being connected with it by a broad, low passage extending eastward to Thorn Lake, into which, at periods of high water, Silver Lake overflows" (Waring, p. 58). See also Whistler and Lewis, p. 16; Bedwell, pp. 6–7.

29. Whistler and Lewis, pp. 19, 33.

30. Waring, p. 32; Whistler and Lewis, p. 16.

31. Whistler and Lewis, p. 17.

32. Waring, p. 12.

33. Ernest Antevs, *Rainfall and Tree Growth in the Great Basin* (New York: Carnegie Institution of Washington and the American Geographical Society of New York, 1938), pp. 17–18.

34. Roberta Miles, tape-recorded interview, Fort Rock, July 7, 1978. All information attributed to her was recorded during this interview.

35. Frank B. Harper, "Dust to Dust," *Oregon Journal*, January 28, 1940, p. 4.

36. Waring, p. 17.

37. Bedwell, p. 169; Cressman, p. 9.

38. Jackman and Long, pp. 163–64. See also Howe; Verne F. Ray et al., "Tribal Distribution in Eastern Oregon and Adjacent Regions," *American Anthropologist* 40 (1938): 384–415; Joel V. Berreman, *Tribal Distribution in Oregon* (Menasha, Wisconsin: American Anthropological Association, 1937), p. 52.

39. Howe, p. 51; Christmas Valley Women's Club, *Where the Pavement Ends* (Christmas Valley, Oregon, 1968), pp. 5–6.

40. Howe, p. 51; Cope, p. 979.

41. Cressman later published a popular account of the find, *The Sandal and the Cave: The Indians of Oregon* (Portland: Blaner Books, 1964).

42. Isa Corum Freeman, "History of the Silver Lake Valley" (unpublished ms., no date), p. 1.

43. Freeman, p. 2.

44. Gilbert C. Fite, *The Farmers' Frontier, 1865-1900* (Albuquerque: University of New Mexico Press, 1974), p. 140.

45. Russell and Mary Emery, tape-recorded interview, Silver Lake Valley, August 29, 1978. Except as otherwise noted, all information attributed to them was recorded on this date.

46. M. K. (Mac) Buick, tape-recorded interview, Fort Rock Valley, August 9, 1978. Except as otherwise noted, all information attributed to him was recorded on this date.

47. Peter Skene Ogden of the Hudson's Bay Company passed to the north of the Fort Rock Valley during a trapping and hunting expedition in 1826-27. Soon thereafter Ewing Young led a trapping party to the Columbia River from the upper end of the Sacramento Valley in 1833. One source claims that Young passed through the Silver Lake country in his travels, but it is likely that he never approached any closer to the valley than Klamath Marsh (Shaver et al., p. 805). In December 1843, ten years after Young's expedition, the energetic John C. Fremont of the Topographic Engineers of the U.S. Army traveled from The Dalles to Klamath Marsh and then turned eastward into central Lake County, where he discovered and named Summer Lake and Winter Rim *(Oregon Almanac, 1915* [Portland: Oregon State Immigration Commission, 1915], p. 186).

In the 1840s and 1850s, at least two overland emigrant trains traversed the central Oregon desert in search of a shortcut to the Willamette Valley, both of them skirting the Fort Rock–Christmas Lake–Silver Lake Basin to the north (Brogan, pp. 39ff.).

When gold was discovered in eastern Oregon near Canyon City in the 1860s, prospectors traveling from California found that the most direct route lay through the Fort Rock–Christmas Lake–Silver Lake Basin. The road they built was noted by surveyors in 1877:

> The Canyon City and Yreka Wagon Road passes through this township [Township 25 South, Range 18 East, between Sink and Cliff] from the southwest to the northeast. This road was made in the year 1862 by miners emigrating from Yreka, California to Canyon City, Oregon. It is but little traveled at the present

(Surveyors' field notes for Township 25 South, Range 18 East, September 1877).

48. Shaver et al., p. 916.

49. Brogan, p. 74; Freeman, p. 2.

50. Before the local land office at Lakeview was established in 1877, entrymen had to travel to Linkville (later renamed Klamath Falls) 130 miles away to file their land claims. Even after the Lakeview office was opened, they apparently considered the 200-mile round trip to the county seat too difficult an undertaking, for only one of the land claims in the valley was filed by 1877. It was not until the early 1880s that land claims in the Silver Lake Valley began to be filed in large numbers, indicating that, by then, there was a U.S. Land Commissioner in Silver Lake to whom applications for land claims could be submitted (Robert Harrison, "Statutory Opening Dates of District Land Offices in Various States," in Vernon Carstensen, ed., *The Public Lands: Studies in the History of the Public Domain* [Madison: University of Wisconsin, 1963], p. 501.

51. Surveyors' field notes for Township 28 South, Range 16 East, September 1874 and Township 28 South, Range 15 East, 1874.

52. Information about land claims is derived from the General Land Office tract books and the land status records at the Bureau of Land Management Office in Portland, Oregon. When the ranchers first arrived in the Silver Lake Valley, all the land there was in the public domain, although it was unsurveyed and therefore not yet open to legal entry. The first land surveys conducted by the General Land Office in the Silver Lake Valley were undertaken in 1874, beginning with four townships near Silver Lake (Township 27 South, Range 15 East, Township 27 South, Range 16 East, Township 28 South, Range 15 East, and Township 28 South, Range 16 East), and followed by the adjacent township Township 27 South, Range 14 East in 1875. The township in which the future site of Silver Lake town would lie (Township 28 South, Range 14 East) was surveyed in 1877, along with three townships in Christmas Lake Valley (Township 25 South, Range 18 East, Township 25 South, Range 19 East, and Township 25 South, Range 20 East). The piecemeal pattern of surveying resulted from the fact that settlers were moving onto lands all over the state so fast that the survey crews could not keep pace with them. The state surveyor-general's office in Portland was deluged with requests from entrymen all over Oregon who could neither file land claims nor establish legal title to their claims until the lands had been surveyed. This problem was endemic not just in Oregon, but throughout the West at that time. In 1877, the commissioner of the General Land Office established the policy of giving priority to surveys of land that had been already settled over land that was still vacant. "It is not intended," the commissioner stated in a letter to the surveyors-general of the western states, "to use the [monies] assigned to your district for the survey of public lands subserving pastoral interest merely [i.e., range lands]. . . . You will . . . always giv[e] preference to lands already settled upon."

In Oregon, the pressure for surveys was particularly acute in the eastern part of the state. The surveyor-general of Oregon reported in 1878 that his office was swamped with petitions from settlers who "in some instances claim[ed] residence of ten or more years, without having their lands surveyed." It is likely, then, that the surveys of the five townships in the Silver Lake Valley in 1874 and 1875 were the direct result of the settlement that took place there in 1873. There may have been a specific request for a survey of the townships in the Christmas Lake Valley in 1877 as well, although there is no oral or documentary evidence of settlement there at that time. The remainder of the area, except for a few townships in the Fort Rock–Christmas Lake Valley, was surveyed between 1880 and 1882 (General Land Office, *Annual Report of the Commissioner for 1878* [H. exdoc. 1, v. 9 (45-3) #1850], pp. 160, 365; General Land Office, *Annual Report of the Commissioner for 1877* [H. exdoc. 1 (45-2), #1800, pp. 7-8).

53. Marge and Lawrence (Bussie) Iverson, tape-recorded interview, Silver Lake, July 10, 1978. All information attributed to them was recorded on this occasion. Sid Morrison of Bear River Valley in northern California told me a similar story in July 1974 about the settlement of his community. It also occurs in John Steinbeck's *The Grapes of Wrath*.

54. Shaver et al., p. 854; Freeman, p. 2.

55. Freeman, p. 1.

56. Shaver et al., p. 851.

57. Freeman, p. 2.

58. The population of the Silver Lake Valley had at least two features in common with that of the Pacific Northwest as a whole. The first was the distribution of

the adult population with regard to origins, for "most of the pioneer farmers who migrated to Oregon and Washington in the period from 1870 to 1890 came from the midwestern states of Missouri, Iowa, Illinois, Indiana and Ohio," according to Fite (p. 149). The second feature was the varied birthplaces shown for the children. Within the Pacific Northwest at this time, there were many families whose settlement in that region represented their second, third, and even fourth moves from their original homes (Fite, p. 149). This seems to hold true for the population of the Silver Lake Valley as well, as the birthplaces listed for the children in a number of families reveal that the parents had moved from one state to another, generally in a westward direction.

59. Freeman, p. 5.

60. Shaver et al., p. 854.

61. Freeman, pp. 3-4; Shaver et al., p. 854.

62. Isa Corum Freeman, "Silver Lake Schools" (unpublished ms., no date), p. 1; Shaver et al., p. 854.

63. Richard W. Helbock, Oregon Post Offices, 1847-1982 (Las Cruces, New Mexico: La Posta, 1982), p. 92.

64. Lawrence Deadmond, tape-recorded interview, Silver Lake Valley, July 19, 1978. All information attributed to him was recorded on that date.

65. Fite, p. 148; Donald Meinig, The Great Columbia Plain (Seattle: University of Washington Press, 1970), p. 344.

66. George Palmer Putnam, In the Oregon Country (New York: G. P. Putnam's Sons, 1915), p. 41; Meinig, p. 377.

67. Russell and Mary Emery, tape-recorded interview, Silver Lake Valley, July 6, 1978.

68. U.S. Census Bureau, Tenth Census of the United States, 1880, Report on the Productions of Agriculture (Washington, D.C., 1883), Vol. 3, Table XI, p. 202, and Table XV, pp. 304-5.

69. Published accounts of the Christmas Eve fire appear in Shaver et al., pp. 854-57; WPA Writers' Project comp., Oregon, End of the Trail (Portland: Binfords and Mort, 1940), p. 437; Brogan, pp. 162-65; Jackman and Long, pp. 126-27; Hatton, pp. 111-12; and in the Lake County Examiner for March 12, 1970, pp. 15-18. In every general historical account of the area, the Christmas Eve fire is inevitably referred to. And in general discussions of eastern Oregon and in statewide publications, a mention of Silver Lake is usually made only in connection with the fire. As far as outsiders are concerned, the Christmas Eve fire is the tail that wags the dog; i.e., the fire put Silver Lake on the map. Admittedly, it remains the worst fire disaster in the history of the state.

70. Perry Williams, "Silver Lake, Oregon, fire of 1894, a Reminiscence" (University of Oregon Mss. Collection #1128, no date), pp. 1-2.

71. Hazel and Maurice Ward, tape-recorded interview, Fort Rock Valley, July 21, 1978. All information attributed to them was recorded then.

72. Ed O'Farrell's heroic ride has numerous parallels in other communities throughout the West. The strength of the tradition as a Western historical motif helps explain why in oral tradition O'Farrell passed through Paisley where Dr. Thompson was visiting a patient to find Dr. Daly. In fact, Dr. Thompson had been turned back by snow at Summer Lake and presumably met O'Farrell on the road. Both Dr. Thompson and Dr. Daly treated the victims of the fire.

73. "At Silver Lake—A Tragic Christmas Eve Story," Lake County Examiner, March 12, 1970.

74. "Owsley-Buick Families," Bicentennial Family History File, Lake County Public Library (no date), p. 2.

75. George L. Gilfry letter, Oregon Historical Society Ms. #1500.

76. Stratton interview.

77. It is locally believed that the Christmas Eve fire prompted the state legislature to pass a law requiring the doors in public buildings to open outward, a belief repeated in *Oregon, End of the Trail*, p. 437. The law was actually enacted in 1909, as reported in the *Silver Lake Leader* on November 19, 1909. William Ivey has told me that the people in Calumet, Michigan, have the same belief in connection with a similar event. See his " 'The 1913 Disaster': A Michigan Local legend," *Folklore Forum* 3 (1970): 100–114.

78. U.S. Census Bureau, *The Tenth Census of the United States*, 1880, Report on the Productions of Agriculture, Vol. 3, Table IX, p. 167; *Eleventh Census of the United States*, 1890, Report on the Statistics of Agriculture (Washington, D.C., 1895) Table 8, p. 263, and Table 10, p. 303; *Twelfth Census of the United States*, 1960, Agriculture (Washington, D.C., 1902), Vol. 5, pt. 1, Table 45, pp. 470–71.

79. While Basque shepherds oversaw most of the flocks in eastern Oregon, dozens of young men fresh from Ireland served in this capacity in Lake County. According to folk legend, "they had been shipped to Oregon with a tag around their necks that said simply, 'Lakeview, USA' " (Dicken and Dicken, p. 137). In the census of 1880, in fact, the Irish constituted the largest foreign nationality group in Lake County—69 of 229 foreign born.

80. Brogan, pp. 116–17.

81. Shaver et al., p. 827.

82. Ibid.

83. "Creed Conn Is Missing," *Lake County Examiner*, March 10, 1904, p. 1; "Body Is Found," *Lake County Examiner*, April 28, 1904, p. 1; Freeman, "Silver Lake Valley," p. 7.

84. Venita and Floyd Branch, tape-recorded interview, Fort Rock, August 24, 1978. All information credited to them was gathered in this interview.

85. Shaver et al., p. 827; Josephine and Alice Godon, tape-recorded interview, Fort Rock Valley, July 17, 1978. All the information attributed to them was obtained on this date.

86. Putnam, p. 51.

87. *Central Oregonian* (Silver Lake), November 26, 1903.

88. Cf. the pamphlet "Lake County, Oregon: description of its climate, soil, resources and its desirable opportunities for homeseekers and those seeking profitable investments" (Lakeview: Beach and Beach, 1889); Waring, p. 18; Shaver et al., p. 853. Isaiah Bowman called this claim inaccurate, but made the same claim for a small community in Montana, according to John A. Alwin, "Jordan Country—A Golden Anniversary Look," *Annals of the Association of American Geographers* 71(1981): 484.

89. Freeman, "Silver Lake Valley," p. 4; Emery interview, July 11, 1978.

90. Waring, p. 18.

91. Freeman, "Silver Lake Valley," p. 6; *Central Oregonian*, February 1, 1906; Shaver et al., p. 854; Waring, p. 18.

92. The *Central Oregonian* was published between 1903 and 1907, the *Silver Lake Bulletin* for thirty-eight weeks in 1903, and the *Silver Lake Leader* from 1907 until it was moved to Lakeview in 1928 (Shaver et al., p. 1067; Stratton interview).

93. Rev. C. H. Mattoon, *Baptist Annals of Oregon, 1886–1910*, vol. II (McMinnville: The Pacific Baptist Press, 1913), p. 396.

NOTES TO CHAPTER 2

1. Deadmond interview.

2. Isaiah Bowman, *The Pioneer Fringe* (New York: American Geographical Society, 1931), p. 94. Studies of homesteading in specific locales throughout the West during this period contain striking parallels to the homesteading in the Fort Rock–Christmas Lake Valley, especially in terms of the physical environments, the backgrounds and presumed motivations of the homesteaders, the attractions that drew them to the respective sites, the hardships they encountered, and the ultimate failure of their efforts.

3. Vincent P. DeSantis, *The Shaping of Modern America, 1877–1916* (St. Louis: Forum Press, 1977), p. 35; Fred A. Shannon, "The Homestead Act and Labor Surplus," *American Historical Review* 41 (1936): 637.

4. Naturalist E. D. Cope mentions a rancher living at Christmas Lake in 1879 ("The Silver Lake of Oregon and its Region," p. 977). Jackson's name did not appear on the 1880 federal census, indicating that he probably arrived after that date (or that the enumerator failed to find him). An Alexander Chase, however, does show up on the 1880 census as a stockman and the head of a household that included himself, his business partner Charles Marshall, and five hired men. From his location on the census, he seems to have had a residence in the Silver Lake Valley as well as the homestead claim in the Christmas Lake Valley.

5. Jackman and Long, p. 30.

6. Anna Linebaugh, "[Remarks]," unpublished ms., October 28, 1981, p. 1.

7. Jackman and Long, p. 32.

8. Anna Linebaugh, tape-recorded interview, Reno, Nevada, May 23, 1985; Oregon Tract Books, Section 32, Township 26 South, Range 18 East. Subsequent information about homestead entries in the Fort Rock–Christmas Lake Valley in this chapter is taken from the Oregon Tract Books of the General Land Office (on microfilm at the Bureau of Land Management regional office in Portland).

9. Linebaugh, "Remarks," p. 1; Jackman and Long, p. 34.

10. *The Central Oregonian*, November 26, 1903, makes mention of people in Silver Lake taking up homesteads on the desert.

11. Waring, pp. 59–60; cf. Oregon Tract Books, Township 25 South, Range 18 East, Township 26 South, Range 18 East, Township 27 South, Range 17 East, and Township 27 South, Range 18 East.

12. John Whistler and John Lewis, pp. 18, 80; *Deschutes Pioneer Gazette* (Bend, Oregon), January 21, 1956; Letter from H. B. Durrant of the Union Pacific Railroad to J. T. McCartney, August 17, 1984; right-of-way maps were filed with the Secretary of the Interior between 1906 and 1908.

13. Randall R. Howard, "The Awakening of Central Oregon," *Pacific Monthly* 24 (November 1910): 512. It may also be, as James Buckles argues, that the range war in 1904 had publicized the Fort Rock–Christmas Lake Valley and that "newspapers and reward circulars probably gave prospective homesteaders a mistaken idea of the value of the land" ("The Historical Geography of the Fort Rock Valley," p. 60).

14. Waring, p. 61.

15. Ibid., p. 60.

16. Ibid., p. 66.

17. Ibid., pp. 18, 60; Helbock, pp. 25, 40, 56; U.S. Weather Bureau, *Annual Report of the Chief for 1908–09* (H. doc. 120 [61–2], #5781, Washington, D.C.: Government Printing Office, 1910), p. 199.

18. Letter from W. L. Powers to Hon. W. H. Halley [Hawley], March 29, 1912, Department of the Interior Classified Files, General Land Office, Enlarged Homestead-Oregon. File 2–27, pt. 3, p. 2, National Archives.

19. These numbers represent all the entries that were recorded in the Oregon Tract Books for Townships 25–27 South, Ranges 14–18 East. For most purposes, these townships conform to the boundaries of and activities within the Fort Rock–Christmas Lake Valley.

20. E. Louise Peffer, *The Closing of the Public Domain: Disposal and Reservation Policies, 1900–1950* (Stanford: Stanford University Press, 1951), p. 18.

21. Waring, p. 63.

22. Because the Desert Land Act did not require residence, it was commonly abused in other areas of the West by individuals wishing to acquire large landholdings for personal use or for speculation. Enforcement of the law was notoriously lax. Witnesses called upon to testify that the provisions of the law had been met, for instance, would swear that the land was "under irrigation" after they had watched the entryman pour a cup or a bucket of water onto the claim. The law was often used by stockmen who wished to take in available water sources by arranging for their employees to file dummy claims on desert lands that could then be assigned to the employer before title to the land was acquired. A second fraudulent means of gaining control over large tracts was to subvert the law's provision that allowed individuals to pool their capital resources by banding together into private irrigation companies. Because each individual within the company could file a desert land claim and the organization itself was entitled to a claim, people formed companies in every conceivable configuration of membership and filed desert land claims under each corporate name. See *Report of the Public Lands Commission, with Appendix* (S. doc. 189 [58–3], #4766, Washington, D.C.: Government Printing Office, 1905), p. 10; Wallace Stegner, *Beyond the 100th Meridian: John Wesley Powell and the Second Opening of the West* (Boston: Houghton Mifflin, 1954); Mary W. M. Hargreaves, *Dry Farming in the Northern Great Plains, 1900–1925* (Cambridge: Harvard University Press, 1957), p. 339.

23. Powers letter, p. 3.

24. Waring, p. 77.

25. Powers letter, p. 2.

26. As reported by Katerina Maruska, in her application for relief under Act of March 4, 1915, in Homestead Serial Patent File 687732, National Archives.

27. Quoted by Laura Anderson, "Homestead on the Oregon Desert: The Diaries of Anna Steinhoff" (unpublished ms., 1984), p. 6.

28. Peffer, p. 147. The U.S. Geological Survey was responsible for surveying the lands to determine their suitability for designation under the Enlarged Homestead Act, a job it performed hastily and apparently not always accurately. "Between 3 March and 1 July 1909 the Geological Survey had designated 161,428,184 acres in nine states. . . . [This was] remarkably rapid but superficial work" (Paul W. Gates, "Homesteading on the High Plains," *Agricultural History* 51 [1977]: 123).

29. Map of "Lands designated by the Secretary of the Interior, April 27, 1909 under the Enlarged Homestead Act of Feb. 19, 1909"; subsequent maps published March 30, 1910, and April 1, 1911.

30. Whistler and Lewis, map opposite p. 16.

31. An example of this kind of letter, written by a homesteader in Montana, was published in the *Tompkinsville* (Kentucky) *News* on February 24, 1915. It reads in part,

Hesper, Mont.

. . . . I have 320 acres of good land in partnership with Uncle Sam, but it will all be my own in two years. : . . I like Montana fine. One would naturally think the winters were hard but they are not. We have a few cold days sometimes, but it don't last long.
    . . . There is lots of homesteads left, but is being taken up very rapidly. If any Monroe county boys wants a good farm here for a very small amount of money let him come to this state where he can get plenty of good land and have plenty of room. . . .

Ed Bryant

32. *Silver Lake Leader*, October 8, 1909.

33. By 1911, people in the western part of the Christmas Lake Valley, whose land was designated as irrigable by the General Land Office and therefore not eligible for entry under the Enlarged Homestead Act, began petitioning the Secretary of the Interior, through their congressmen, to have their land reclassified. Those who had taken up desert land claims and were unable to fulfill the conditions of the law by irrigating them were especially anxious to convert their claims to enlarged home-steads lest their time and investments be lost. One such petition read as follows:

Fort Rock, Ore, Jan. 10, 1911.

Mr. Jonathan Bourne
Washington D.C.

Dear Sir:
    We the undersigned petition your Honor to aid us in useing your influence with the Secretary of the Interior whom we have petitioned to investigate the land in Township 26 South Range 15 East Lake Co. Oregon and have the same placed in the Enlarged Home-stead Tract which borders said Township on the North, for the following reasons.
    First—The land in said Township is of the same nature as that in the Enlarged Home-stead Tract.
    Second—There is no known source of water supply to irrigate said land at a reasonable cost.
    Third—This land has produced profitable crops, without irrigation, under the so called Dry Farming Method.
    Fourth—The land and climatic condition being the same, we feel justly intitled to the same amount of land as our neighbors in the Enlarged Homestead Tract.
    Fifth—Said Township has been surveyed but is not yet open for filing, therefor we con-sider this the opportune time to have the said Township placed in the Enlarged Homestead Tract, which will give the undersigned squatters and coming homeseekers a fair chance at fileing time.
    The undersigned are all squatters seeking a home in said Township.

[17 signatures]

(Letter from F. C. Eickemeyer et al. to Hon. Jonathan Bourne, January 10, 1911. Dept. of the Interior Classified Files, General Land Office, Enlarged Homestead-Oregon File 2–27, pt. 3, Record Group 49, National Archives.)
    The argument most often used in these petitions was that there was not suffi-cient water to irrigate the land. On March 29, 1912, William Powers wrote to Sen.W. H. Hawley, describing in detail his fruitless attempts to secure an adequate supply of water to irrigate his desert land claim. He concluded his appeal by saying:

Now if we could get the benefit of the additional [i.e., enlarged] Homestead law we would be allright but we are informed that we are within an Irrigation Project consequently we are bard from the benefit of that act. We know that there is an irrigation company formed to bring water through the Silver Lake Valey and from there to Christmass Lake valey but they havent sufficient water this year to supply Silver Lake let alone comeing to Christmass Lake valey.

Now there ar scores of settlers in just the same condition that I am and unless we can get the benefit of the additional Homested law our desert claims will have to be canceled and go back to the Government.

Now Mr. Hawley we believe that if the Secretary of the Interior would send a fair minded man here to look the mater up that there would not be any hesitancy in giveing us the benefit of the additional Homested Bill. . . .

W. L. Powers

After lengthy correspondence with both the Geological Survey, which was responsible for classifying public lands, and the Reclamation Service, whose Silver Lake Irrigation Project was still on the drawing board, the Secretary of the Interior capitulated. In August 1911, he allowed parts of five townships in the eastern Fort Rock Valley and western Christmas Lake Valley to be designated under the Enlarged Homestead Act. In July 1912, most of the rest of the Fort Rock–Christmas Lake Valley was also opened. The remaining portions (in Township 26 South, Range 16 East and Township 27 South, Range 16 East) were designated in November 1913. ("Memorandum for Secretary Adams," January 4, 1912. Dept. of the Interior Classified Files, National Archives.)

34. This was common practice elsewhere in the semiarid West. Cf. Everett Dick, *The Lure of the Land: A Social History of the Public Lands from the Articles of Confederation to the New Deal* (Lincoln: University of Nebraska Press, 1970), p. 306; Gates, p. 122.

35. Bowman, p. 98.

36. Burrier, p. 7.

37. Edwin Eskelin, tape-recorded interview, Fort Rock Valley, July 23, 1978.

38. A study of homesteaders on the Canadian Plains revealed that 40 percent of the men were married. See John W. Bennett, *Northern Plainsmen: Adaptive Strategy and Agrarian Life* (Chicago: Aldine Publishing Co., 1969), p. 204; cf. Bowman, 127. But Bowman says that most of the entrymen in and around Bend during this period were unmarried (p. 98).

39. Anna Steinhoff, "Diary" (unpublished ms., 1910–1912), pp. 1–5. All information attributed to her derives from this source.

40. Anderson, p. 13.

41. Powers letter, p. 1.

42. "Homesteads in Oregon," *Oregon Voter* 3:9 (January 1, 1916), p. 285. John Bennett estimates that the Canadian Plains homesteaders laid out an average of $1,400 for a house and equipment to begin operations (p. 105).

43. Jackman and Long, pp. 41–42.

44. The applications for final proof on homestead claims are filed in the Serial Patent Files of the General Land Office, Record Group 49 (Civil Archives Division, National Archives Records Administration). Thirty-three such applications were selected at random, at least two from each township in the Fort Rock–Christmas Lake Valley. Each file included the entryman's statement, statements from two

witnesses, a copy of the original homestead application, affidavits from the local land commissioner, and any correspondence that had passed between the entryman and the Land Office.

The final proof application required an entryman to state the monetary value of all improvements that had been made on the claim. In order to demonstrate as well that they were actually living on their claims, people listed not just buildings and fences, but equipment, tools, and household furnishings, so that the proofs read like an inventory of property.

45. Whistler and Lewis, p. 79. Not all the homesteaders fit this description, of course. Some had substantial assets in their former homes, to which they returned after proving up on their claims.

46. Edwin Eskelin, "History of the Eskelin Farm, Located in Fort Rock Valley, North Lake County, Oregon" (unpublished ms., 1975), p. 4.

47. Brogan cites a fee of $100 in *East of the Cascades*. Cf. Hargreaves's discussion of the lack of experience of Northern Plains homesteaders during the same period (p. 539).

48. Putnam, pp. 43–44. Carlton Culmsee, in "Last Free Land Rush," *Utah Historical Quarterly* 49 (1981): 26–41, writes, "Homeseekers were driven over the land by men singing a parody of a popular song, 'Everybody's doin' it! Doin' what?—Dry-farmin' it!'" (p. 29).

49. *Silver Lake Leader*, June 25, 1909. Writing of locators in Utah during the same time period, Culmsee recalled, "Brisk salesman for the land-locators avoided using the word *Desert* . . . ; it was *Valley*" (p. 28).

50. Eskelin, "History of Farm," pp. 3–4.

51. Letter from Dwight L. Nash to Georgia Stephenson, June 20, 1971.

52. Jetter, p. 26.

53. Helmer (Shorty) Gustafson, tape-recorded interview, Fort Rock, May 21, 1985; Raymond R. Hatton, *Pioneer Homesteaders of the Fort Rock Valley* (Portland: Binfords and Mort, 1982), p. 20.

54. Linebaugh interview, May 23, 1985.

55. Jackman and Long, p. 19.

56. Both houses were still standing, although in very dilapidated condition in 1981, according to Stephen Dow Beckham, *Lake County Historic Sites and Buildings Inventory*, vol. 1 (Eugene: Heritage Research Associates, 1982).

57. Eskelin, "History of Farm," p. 4.

58. Anonymous narrator, tape-recorded interview, Christmas Valley, July 18, 1978.

59. Cf. Beckham. The descriptions of the houses that follow, where not otherwise noted, were extrapolated from the final proof applications referred to above.

60. Beckham, "Julian House"; Buckles, p. 83.

61. Buckles, p. 83.

62. Waring, p. 23; Buckles, p. 81; Beckham, "Julian House."

63. Buckles, p. 80.

64. Hatton, *Pioneer Homesteaders*, p. 21; Buckles, p. 80.

65. Beckham, "Julian House."

66. Branch interview, August 24, 1978. Cf. Beckham, "Gubser House."

67. Jackman and Long, p. 59.

68. Eskelin interview; Jetter (p. 26) and Hatton (*Pioneer Homesteaders*, p. 24) both mention homemade juniper furniture.

69. Manius Buchanan, final proof application, Serial Patent File 260653; Gilbert F. Smith, final proof application, Serial Patent File 181804; Lewis Haines, final proof application, Serial Patent File 215714; Ernest Fenn, final proof application, Serial Patent File 76942.

70. Eskelin, "History of Farm," p. 11.

71. Arthur Donahue, letter of March 5, 1912, in Serial Patent File 430390.

72. Bill and Maxine Mattis, tape-recorded interview, Fort Rock Valley, July 13, 1978. All subsequent information attributed to them was recorded then.

73. Waring, p. 78.

74. Waring, p. 64; Josiah J. Fox, final proof application, Serial Patent File 456470; Ross L. Noel, final proof application, Serial Patent File 555935.

75. Whistler and Lewis, p. 50.

76. Harry W. Baker, final proof application, Serial Patent File 453097; Frank Polte, affidavit of May 31, 1911, Serial Patent File 311772; Mary E. Ashworth, application for relief under Act of March 4, 1915, Serial Patent File 763033.

77. Jackman and Long, p. 62.

78. Edwin A. Eskelin, "A Brief History of Wells in the Fort Rock Valley, Both Domestic and Irrigation Wells" (unpublished ms., 1971), pp. 2–3.

79. Eskelin, "Wells," p. 2.

80. Fred W. Stratton, final proof application, Serial Patent File 497944; Josiah T. Rhoton, final proof application, Serial Patent File 667962; Lawrence Frizzell, final proof application, Serial Patent File 742163.

81. Eskelin, "Wells," p. 1.

82. Jackman and Long, p. 62; cf. H. L. Davis, "Back to the Land—Oregon, 1907," *American Mercury* 16 March (1929): 320.

83. Waring, p. 62.

84. Whistler and Lewis, p. 80. Isaiah Bowman stated flatly in 1931 that there was so little wind in the region that "irrigation through the recovery of ground water by windmills is therefore impossible. Pumping power must be supplied by internal combustion engines" (p. 103). The wind nevertheless must have been a considerable environmental factor in the area, judging from the wind erosion in the posthomesteading period (discussed in Chapter 4).

85. Powers letter.

86. Serial Patent File 76942.

87. Waring, p. 61.

88. Eskelin, "History of Farm," p. 6.

89. Ibid.

90. Whistler and Lewis, p. 80.

91. *Silver Lake Leader*, November 19, 1909; John A. Sweem, final proof application, Serial Patent File 557647.

92. Whistler and Lewis, p. 80.

93. Eskelin, "History of Farm," p. 9.

94. Serial Patent Files 456473 and 533641.

95. Buckles, pp. 58, 87.

96. Vincent F. Kasperonez, final proof application, Serial Patent File 411876.

97. Eskelin, "History of Farm," p. 9.

98. Eskelin interview.
99. Jetter, p. 36.
100. E. D. Cope, during his visit to the Silver Lake Valley in 1879, wrote that the "Jackass rabbit" was "most important as an article of food" compared to other animals in the area (p. 976).
101. Jetter, p. 35.
102. Eskelin, "History of Farm," p. 6.
103. Ibid., p. 10; Waring mentions "pools about 10 miles northwest of Christmas Lake" from which he obtained salt samples (p. 75). It is likely that these are the lakes to which Eskelin referred.
104. Waring, p. 75.
105. Jackman and Long, p. 54; Jetter also mentions the picnics at the ice caves (p. 35).
106. Jetter, p. 30.
107. Jetter, p. 31.
108. Anonymous narrator, tape-recorded interview, Silver Lake, August 3, 1978.
109. Jetter, p. 33.
110. Lake County Agricultural Extension Agent, *Annual Report for 1916*, Agricultural Extension Service files, Record Group 111, Reel 12 (Oregon State University Archives), p. 1.
111. This figure was calculated as follows: There were 746 people in the Fort Rock–Christmas Lake Valley in 1910, according to the federal census. With 434 initial entries made in the area up to April 1910, this means 1.7 persons per entry. Adding the entries for 1911 and 1912 and multiplying them by 1.7 yields a total population in 1912 of 1,221. This figure is roughly in accord with historical geographer James Buckles's estimate of 1,000 people living in the Fort Rock Valley in 1915. He did not include the Christmas Lake Valley in his study (p. 97).

NOTES TO CHAPTER 3

1. Jackman and Long, p. 34.
2. Helbock, *passim*. John A. Alwin has argued that the establishment of post offices can be studied to show how settlement patterns develop. See "Post Office Locations and the Historical Geographer: A Montana Example," *Professional Geographer* 26 (1974): 183–86.
3. Putnam, p. 49.
4. Nash letter.
5. Howard, "The Awakening of Central Oregon," p. 507.
6. Nash letter; cf. Buckles, p. 73.
7. Eskelin interview.
8. *Silver Lake Leader*, August 20, 1909.
9. Eskelin, "History of Farm," p. 5.
10. Buick interview, August 9, 1978.
11. Ward interview.
12. Edwin Eskelin, "History of Schools in Fort Rock Valley" (unpublished ms., no date), p. 11.
13. They included Fremont, Fort Rock, Glendale, Wastina (Pine Grove), Mayfield, Valley View, Connley, Pleasant Valley, Fleetwood (Cougar Valley), Sunset, Horning Bend, Woodrow, Arrow, Garden Butte, Ludi, and Loma Vista in the Fort Rock Valley, and Lake, Sink, and Cliff in the Christmas Lake Valley (Eskelin, "Schools," *pas-*

sim). The county school records date back only to 1919. Eskelin's account, which draws upon his considerable personal knowledge of the area, as well as the memories of other residents, is the only source of information about the schools in the northern part of the county. Eskelin was a passionately meticulous amateur historian and all of his manuscripts—mimeographed and full of misspellings though they be—are invaluable sources of information.

14. Eskelin, "Schools," p. 1.

15. Eskelin, "History of Farm," p. 11; Hatton, *Pioneer Homesteaders*, pp. 34–36.

16. Hatton, *Pioneer Homesteaders*, p. 34; Eskelin, "Schools," p. 2.

17. Eskelin, "Schools," p. 11.

18. Beckham, "Cloverleaf School" and "Sunset School" in volume 1. It is worth noting that the homesteaders apparently spent more time, effort, and care on the school buildings than they did on their own houses, for shiplap (or weatherboard) construction is a more permanent and weatherproof method of construction than the board-and-batten method used in the homestead houses. For a consideration of how such architectural differences reflect community values, see Charles E. Martin, *Hollybush: Folk Building and Social Change in an Appalachian Community* (Knoxville: University of Tennessee Press, 1984), chapter 5.

19. Eskelin, "Schools," p. 7.

20. Jetter, p. 29.

21. Eskelin, "Schools," p. 12.

22. Ibid., p. 8.

23. Letter from Roberta Miles to Barbara Allen, March 12, 1985.

24. Eskelin, "Schools," p. 4.

25. Eskelin interview.

26. Eskelin, "Schools," p. 7.

27. Bowman notes that 1914 was a peak settlement year in central Oregon (p. 97).

28. Buckles, p. 70.

29. Frank B. Harper, "Dust to Dust," *Oregon Journal*, January 28, 1940, p. 4; *Oregon Almanac, 1915*, p. 187; Buckles, pp. 71–72.

30. *Oregon Almanac, 1915*, p. 187; Jetter, p. 33; Buckles, p. 71; "Fort Rock on the High Desert," Historic Towns—Homesteaders of the High Desert (WPA files, Series 1, Box 74, Folder 3, Oregon State Library), pp. 3–4. Buckles doubts the circulation figure for the newspaper, although such periodicals were often sent to other locales within the state, especially to other newspaper editors, as a means of "boosting" their home communities (p. 71). Hatton mentions a second paper in Fort Rock, the *Fort Rock News (Pioneer Homesteaders*, p. 44).

31. Quoted in Eskelin, "Schools," p. 5.

32. Whistler and Lewis, p. 17; *Silver Lake Leader*, passim for years 1909–1916.

33. Anonymous narrator, Silver Lake, Oregon, August 3, 1978.

34. Hatton, *Pioneer Homesteaders*, p. 50; Linebaugh interview, August 1, 1978.

35. Hatton, *Pioneer Homesteaders*, pp. 52–53.

36. Eskelin, "History of Farm," p. 16.

37. Although told as a personal experience narrative, this story seems to be a migratory legend, told in communities throughout the West as a "true" local anecdote. Perhaps its best-known version is the one that appears in Owen Wister's *The Virginian*. See James Bratcher, "The Baby-Switching Story," in Wilson M. Hudson and Allen Maxwell, eds., *The Sunny Slopes of Long Ago* (Dallas: Southern Methodist University Press, 1966), pp. 110–17.

162 NOTES TO PAGES 78–87

38. Hatton, *Pioneer Homesteaders*, p. 49.
39. Emery interview, July 11, 1978.
40. *Silver Lake Leader*, October 18 and November 8, 1918.
41. Eskelin, "History of Farm," p. 6.
42. Information about the cemetery, deaths, and burials is taken from Edwin A. Eskelin, "Fort Rock Cemetery Association" (unpublished ms., 1974), pp. 8–9.
43. The exact numbers are hard to come by, as people were buried on private ground as well as in the cemetery, and their graves are unmarked and unrecorded.
44. Shorty Gustafson has marked several of these graves, as well as making metal markers for some of the graves in the Fort Rock cemetery.
45. Jetter, p. 32.
46. Shorty Gustafson has marked the Buchanan baby's grave in recent years. In May 1985, he explained to me how one of the Buchanan children returned in later years, looking for the grave: "We just happened to be driving by there and she said, 'Stop just a minute.' And I stopped and she said, 'My little brother's buried right there in that corner.' So we got out and there's nothing, not even a rock, but you can tell just a little bit. It's not very big because she said they just put him in a box, not a casket, just a box and took him out there and buried him."
47. Eskelin, "Wells," p. 4.
48. Eskelin, "History of Farm," p. 10.
49. Ibid., p. 4.
50. Claude Stewart, final proof application, Serial Patent File 327026; Johann Schimelpfenig, final proof application, Serial Patent File 190292.
51. Hatton, *Pioneer Homesteaders*, p. 103; Beckham, "Godon House."
52. Eskelin, "History of Farm," p. 13.
53. Lake County Agricultural Extension Service, *Annual Report of the County Agent for 1916*, p. 1.
54. Serial Patent File 555935. According to Hargreaves, many homesteaders throughout the West spent only the period between planting and harvesting actually living on their claims; the rest of the time they lived elsewhere working for wages (p. 341). Cf. also John C. Hudson, "Migration to an American Frontier," *Annals of the Association of American Geographers* 66 (1976): 260.
55. Cf. Marshall E. Bowen, "Dryland Homesteading on Tobar Flat," *Northeastern Nevada Historical Society Quarterly* 4 (1981): 127.
56. Buckles, p. 65.
57. May O'Keeffe, tape-recorded interview, Silver Lake, July 28, 1978. All information attributed to her was recorded then.

NOTES TO CHAPTER 4

1. Godon interview.
2. Buckles, p. 108.
3. Burrier, p. 5.
4. Calculated from U.S. Weather Bureau reports for 1907–1916, and "Climatic Summary of the United States [1930], Section 4—Eastern Oregon," pp. 4–7, 4–11, 4–17; F. D. Trauger, pl. 6; Ira S. Allison, *Fossil Lake, Oregon* (Corvallis: Oregon State University Press, 1966), p. 8.
5. Eskelin interview, July 23, 1978.
6. Cf. Antevs, p. 17.

7. Ibid. Geographer Isaiah Bowman, in his 1931 study of pioneer "fringes," remarked on the favorable precipitation levels in the Fort Rock–Christmas Lake Valley during the settlement period. "The settlers came in a time of good seasons: after the peak of settlement, 1912–1917, precipitation was above normal in four out of six years [1912–1914, 1916] and only slightly below normal in the other two years [1915, 1917]. If the land were productive under tillage it would have been demonstrated then." Bowman, p. 94.

8. Castle and Dwyer, p. 8. These figures are taken from the Silver Lake weather-recording station.

9. Waring, p. 19. In 1978, some of the people I talked to reported that the recent large-scale introduction of sprinkler-irrigation systems in the Fort Rock–Christmas Lake Valley had reduced the amount of frost ordinarily experienced there.

10. See Henry Nash Smith, "Rain Follows the Plow: The Notion of Increased Rainfall for the Great Plains, 1844–1880," *Huntington Library Quarterly* 10 (February 1947): 169–94; Charles Robert Kutzleb, "Rain Follows the Plow: The History of an Idea" (Ph.D. diss., University of Colorado, 1968); Arnold C. Plank, "Desert versus Garden: The Role of Western Images in the Settlement of Kansas" (M.A. thesis, Kansas State University, 1962), pp. 66–87; John W. Hafer, "The Sea of Grass: The Image of the Great Plains in the American Novel" (Ph.D. diss., Northern Illinois University, 1975), pp. 23–33.

11. Burrier, p. 5.

12. David B. Green, "Irrigation Potential and Agricultural Settlement in Submarginal Land: An Example from Weld County, Colorado" (Ph.D. diss., University of Northern Colorado, 1980), p. 40.

13. Lake County Agricultural Extension Service, *Annual Report of County Agent for 1914–15*, p. 2.

14. Trauger, pl. 6.

15. Eskelin, "History of Farm," p. 14.

16. Anonymous narrator, Christmas Valley, July 18, 1978. Ernest Antevs, investigating the weather history of the Great Basin in the 1930s, considered the shift in environmental conditions to be the leading cause of the homesteader's difficulties:

> The drought of 1918–20 had important consequences and taught a severe lesson. Encouraged by the heavy precipitation beginning in 1904, the Enlarged Homestead Act of 1909, intensive advertising, cheap land, and high prices of wheat and other products, settlers had come into the region in great numbers. . . . The hazard of drought was not given sufficient consideration, and the first dry spell proved the impossibility of the attempted colonization and started an exodus that continued till 1926 or later, leaving hundreds of abandoned homesteads.

Antevs, p. 18.

17. Hatton, *Pioneer Homesteaders*, p. 25.

18. Jetter, p. 37.

19. *Silver Lake Leader*, December 31, 1915.

20. Lake County Agricultural Extension Service, *Annual Report of County Agent for 1916*, pp. 1–2.

21. Anderson, p. 15; Hatton, *Pioneer Homesteaders*, p. 73.

22. Serial Patent File 430390; Serial Patent File 456470; Serial Patent File 583678; Serial Patent File 557647; Serial Patent File 533641.

23. Dallas Love Sharp, *Where Rolls the Oregon* (Boston: Houghton Mifflin, 1913), pp. 57–58.

24. Hatton, *Pioneer Homesteaders*, p. 14. No date is given for the issue of the paper in which this announcement appears, although a railroad promotional pamphlet, owned by a woman in Christmas Valley, had been published in 1913.

25. Hatton, *Pioneer Homesteaders*, p. 45.

26. Buckles, p. 75. The townsite was most likely in Section 31 of Township 26 South, Range 17 East, through which the railroad had been surveyed and where William Fick had taken up forty acres in September 1911.

27. David F. Myrick, "Oregon, California, and Eastern," *The Ferroequinologist* (Central Coast Railway Club, San Jose, California), September 1, 1957, pp. [3-6].

28. Quoted in W. D. Cheney, *Central Oregon* (Ivy Press, 1918), p. 139.

29. Myrick, p. 2; letter from H. B. Durrant to J. T. McCartney, August 17, 1984.

30. Randall V. Mills, "A History of Transportation in the Pacific Northwest," *Oregon Historical Quarterly* 47 (1946): 298.

31. Bowman, pp. 98-99; Waring, p. 18.

32. Eskelin, "History of Farm," p. 16.

33. State Agricultural Extension Service, "Report of County Agent Work for 1917," *Annual Report*, Agricultural Extension Service Files, Record Group 111, Reel 12 (Oregon State University Archives), p. 9.

34. Joseph Gaston, *The Centennial History of Oregon, 1811-1912* (Chicago: S. J. Clarke Publishing Co., 1912), p. 481.

35. "Memorandum for Secretary Adams," January 4, 1912. Dept. of the Interior, General Land Office Classified Files. Enlarged Homesteads-Oregon. File 2-47 (pt. 3). National Archives.

36. Buckles, p. 76.

37. Whistler and Lewis, p. 78, map opposite p. 17.

38. Eskelin, "Wells," p. 4.

39. Brogan, p. 252; Thomas D. Murphy, *Oregon, the Picturesque* (Boston: The Page Co., 1917), p. 115; Cheney, p. 8.

40. Burrier, p. 7; cf. Brogan, p. 97.

41. Eskelin, "Schools," p. 7.

42. These and other land record figures are taken from the General Land Office Oregon Tract Books for Townships 25-27 South, Ranges 13-19 East.

43. U.S. Senate, 62nd Congress, 2nd Session. "[Advice to Homesteaders]" (Sen. Rpt. #633, vol. 2, #6121, Washington, D. C.: Government Printing Office, 1912).

44. John Minderhaut, Serial Patent File 411873.

45. Anonymous narrator, Christmas Valley, July 18, 1978.

46. Arthur Donahue, Serial Patent File 430300.

47. Eskelin, "History of Farm," pp. 14-15.

48. Emery interview, July 11, 1978. Lynwood Montell has told me of similar anecdotes about local characters in his home community in south-central Kentucky, indicating the story's nature as a migratory narrative.

49. Anonymous narrator, Christmas Valley, July 18, 1978.

50. Anonymous narrator, Silver Lake, July 31, 1978.

51. The county tax rolls are extant, after 1900, for only every fifth year (e.g., 1900, 1905, 1910, etc.); the others have been destroyed because they were deemed by the state legislature to have "no historical significance," according to the personnel of the Oregon State Archives.

52. Rockie, p. 36.

53. Ibid., p. 35.

54. Helbock, passim.

55. Lewis A. McArthur, "Oregon Geographic Names: II, Additions since 1944," *Oregon Historical Quarterly* 47 (1946): 72.

56. Lake County Superintendent of Schools, "Clerk's Annual Census Reports" for 1919 and 1920 (on file in Lake County Superintendent of Schools Office, Lakeview, Oregon).

57. Beckham notes this recycling of homestead buildings in *Lake County Historic Sites*, vol. 1, passim.

58. Eskelin, "Schools," p. 8.

59. Ibid., p. 4.

60. Buckles, p. 91.

61. Jackman and Long, pp. 351–52.

62. Eskelin, "Wells," pp. 4–5; Stratton interview.

63. Cf. Castle and Dwyer, "Figure 1: Generalized Soil and Irrigability Map," p. 7.

64. Ward interview.

65. The tendency for those remaining in the valley after 1916 to acquire more land is reflected in the agricultural census for 1920 which shows a decrease in the number of farms countywide between 1910 and 1920, but an increase in the total amount of acreage being farmed during the same period. By 1936, landholdings in the Fort Rock Valley, according to one report, averaged 2,300 acres per farmer. Burrier, p. 9.

66. Lake County Agricultural Extension Service, *Annual Report of County Agent for 1921*, p. 22.

67. Antevs, p. 18.

68. *Annual Report for 1926*, p. 11.

69. *Annual Report for 1926*, pp. 4–5, p. 14.

70. Dicken and Dicken, p. 141; Stratton interview.

71. Brogan, p. 222.

72. Emery interview, July 11, 1978.

73. Bowman, p. 93.

74. Ibid., pp. 93, 106, 108.

75. L. C. Speers, "Nevada-Oregon Desert Still Defies Pioneers," *New York Times*, Sept. 27, 1925, Sec. 8, p. 6.

76. Burrier, p. 5; Trauger, pl. 6.

77. Antevs, p. 18.

78. Burrier, p. 3.

79. Allison, p. 11, pl. 8; cf. Hollon, p. 176.

80. Buckles, p. 108.

81. Burrier, p. 12.

82. Buckles, p. 103.

83. Burrier, pp. 9, 16.

84. Ibid., p. 16.

85. Most of the defaulted land lay in the parts of the valley with the most alkaline soils (Buckles, p. 96).

86. Burrier, p. 9.

87. Ward interview; Brogan, p. 272.

88. Buckles, p. 110.

NOTES TO CHAPTER 5

Cf. Martha L. Smith, *Going to God's Country* (Boston: Christopher Co., 1941).

2. Putnam, p. 54. The information on the Hill-Harriman activity in central Oregon comes from several sources, including Mills, "A History of Transportation in the Pacific Northwest," pp. 296–98; Jerry A. O'Callaghan, *The Disposition of the Public Domain in Oregon* (Washington, D.C.: Government Printing Office, 1960), pp. 13–14; Barbara Pierce, "Economic and Geographical Determinants of Railroad Routes in the Pacific Northwest" (M.A. thesis, Reed College, 1937), pp. 70–79; and Brogan, *East of the Cascades*, pp. 234–45.

3. Mills, p. 297.

4. Quoted in Carlos A. Schwantes, ed., "Problems of Empire Building: The Oregon Trunk Railway Survey of Disappointed Homeseekers, 1911," *Oregon Historical Quarterly* 83 (1982): 372–73.

5. The Northern Pacific alone had 450,000 acres of land in Oregon in 1907. (General Land Office, *Annual Report of the Commissioner for 1907* [H. Doc. 5 (60–1), #5295], p. 145).

6. David M. Emmons, *Garden in the Grasslands: Boomer Literature of the Great Plains* (Lincoln: University of Nebraska Press, 1971), p. 25.

7. Great Northern Railway Co., *Annual Reports* (Minnesota Historical Society, 1979), microfilm roll #6, vol. 1, frame 103.

8. Roy V. Scott, "Land Use and American Railroads in the Twentieth Century," *Agricultural History* 57 (1979): 691; Northern Pacific Railway Company, records, Minnesota Historical Society.

9. Northern Pacific Railway Company, advertising records, Minnesota Historical Society.

10. Rockie, p. 35. H. L. Davis sketches in satiric terms a homesteading "rush" in central Oregon precipitated by railroad advertising in "Back to the Land—Oregon, 1907," pp. 314–23.

11. Schwantes describes these informal surveys and their results.

12. Information on the Oregon and Western Land Colonization was taken from the company records and the W. P. Davidson papers at the Minnesota Historical Society.

13. Scott, p. 692.

14. Buckles, p. 58.

15. Edward L. Wells, "The Weather Bureau and the Homeseeker," *U.S.D.A. Yearbook for 1904* (Washington, D.C.: Government Printing Office, 1905), p. 354.

16. General Land Office, *Annual Report of the Commissioner for 1876* (H. exdoc. [44–2], #1749), p. 324.

17. Meinig, pp. 314–15.

18. Putnam, p. 5.

19. Meinig, pp. 316–17.

20. Thomas Shaw, *Report of Trip through Central Oregon during the Fall of 1910* (St. Paul: McGill-Warner Co., 1911), p. 7.

21. Rockie, p. 38.

22. Henry E. Reed, *The Lewis and Clark Centennial* (Portland: Irwin-Hodson Co., 1905).

23. Frederick J. Turner, "The Significance of the Frontier in American History," paper read at the meeting of the American Historical Association in Chicago, July 12, 1893, published in *Proceedings of the State Historical Society of Wisconsin*, December

NOTES TO PAGES 122–26

14, 1893, and reprinted in numerous places, including Turner's *The Frontier in American History*.

24. Theodore Roosevelt wrote to Turner after the publication of his paper on the frontier, praising him for "put[ting] into definite shape a good deal of thought that [had] been floating around rather loosely." Quoted in Ray Allen Billington, *The Genesis of the Frontier Thesis* (San Marino, California: Huntington Library, 1971), p. 82. Rodman W. Paul and Michael P. Malone, in "Tradition and Challenge in Western Historiography," *Western Historical Quarterly* 16 (1985): 27–54, discuss Turner's impact on the writing of American history.

25. Walter Nugent outlines this shift in *Structures of American Social History* (Bloomington: Indiana University Press, 1981).

26. Earl Pomeroy, "The Changing West," in John Higham, ed., *The Reconstruction of American History* (London: Hutchinson & Co., 1962), p. 67.

27. Pomeroy, p. 67.

28. Quoted by Leon Baritz in "The Idea of the West," *American Historical Review* 66 (1961): 639.

29. Quoted in Roderick Nash, *Wilderness and the American Mind*, 3rd ed. (New Haven: Yale University Press, 1982), p. 100.

30. R. Reid Badger, *The Great American Fair: The World's Columbian Exposition and American Culture* (Chicago: Nelson Hall, 1979), p. 100.

31. David C. Hunt, *Legacy of the West* (Lincoln: University of Nebraska Press, 1982), p. 231.

32. Badger, p. 88.

33. Robert H. Wiebe, *The Search for Order, 1877–1920* (New York: Hill and Wang, 1967), p. 65.

34. William L. O'Neill, *The Progressive Years: America Comes of Age* (New York: Harper and Row, 1975), p. 6.

35. Richard White, *Land Use, Environment and Social Change: The Shaping of Island County, Washington* (Seattle: University of Washington Press, 1980), p. 114.

36. White, p. 117.

37. Stanford J. Layton, "The Politics of Homesteading in the Early Twentieth-Century American West: The Origin and Supersession of the Enlarged Homestead Act and the Stock Raising Homestead Act" (Ph.D. diss., University of Utah, 1972), pp. 73, 80–81.

38. Layton, pp. 75–76, 87.

39. White, pp. 116, 117.

40. David B. Danbom, "Rural Education Reform and the Country Life Movement, 1900–1920," *Agricultural History* 53 (1979): 465.

41. Howard L. Dickman, "James Jerome Hill and the Agricultural Development of the Northwest" (Ph.D. diss., University of Michigan, 1977), p. 7.

42. E. Louise Peffer, p. 57.

43. Peffer, p. 56.

44. Hargreaves, p. 71; Ray Allen Billington, *Westward Expansion*, 2nd ed. (New York: Macmillan, 1960), p. 754; Jeffrey B. Roet, "Agricultural Settlement on the Dry Farming Frontier, 1900–1920" (Ph.D. diss., Northwestern University, 1982), p. 10, Table 1.2.

45. Paul W. Gates, pp. 120–21.

46. Emmons, p. 4. Merle Wells has pointed out, however, that "The plains farmers' reluctance to consider irrigation has no application to Utah, southern Idaho, and eastern Oregon, where farmers could take great pride in their achievements through

irrigation. After 1890, their missionary efforts to convert backwards plains farmers to a superior agricultural system finally began to produce results." Letter to Barbara Allen, January 15, 1986.

47. Emmons, pp. 6-7.

48. John Wesley Powell, *Report on the Lands of the Arid Regions of the United States* (Washington, D.C.: Government Printing Office, 1878).

49. Quoted in Hollon, *The Great American Desert*, p. 147.

50. Meinig, p. 307; the fullest flowering of this idea was Samuel Aughey and C. O. Wilber, *Agriculture Beyond the 100th Meridian, or a Revision of the U.S. Public Land Commission* (Lincoln, Nebraska: Journal Co., 1880).

51. Frank G. Roe, reminiscing about homesteading on the Canadian Plains, intimated the prevalence of the belief in changing weather there by speculating that the extensive breaking of the sod had somehow produced more rainfall. See "The Alberta Wet Cycle of 1899-1903: A Climatic Interlude," *Agricultural History* 28 (1954): 112-20. Soil scientist E. W. Hilgard argued that the increased moisture in the soil was the result of tillage rather than precipitation ("Origin, Value, and Reclamation of Alkali Lands," *U.S.D.A. Yearbook for 1895* [Washington, D.C.: Government Printing Office, 1896], pp. 103-22). See also Meinig, p. 313 and Kutzleb, p. 33. An extended discussion of the purported relationship between rainfall and trees is contained in Plank, "Desert versus Garden," pp. 63ff. The Timber Culture Act of 1873, which allowed an entryman to claim 160 acres, provided he planted one-quarter of it in trees, was predicated upon that belief. See Hollon, p. 144; Everett N. Dick, *Conquering the Great American Desert*, p. 123; Kutzleb, p. 58; Emmons, p. 129.

52. Kutzleb, pp. 389-90.

53. Frederick H. Newell, "Irrigation on the Great Plains," *U.S.D.A. Yearbook for 1896* (Washington D.C.: Government Printing Office, 1897), p. 173.

54. New York: Harper and Brothers, 1900.

55. Newell, pp. 171-72.

56. There were, of course, earlier antecedents for dry farming, most notably in the Cache Valley of northern Utah and elsewhere in the Great Basin. But the deliberate promotion of dry farming as an agricultural method appropriate all over the arid West stems from Hardy Campbell's efforts.

57. Thomas Shaw, *Dry Land Farming* (St. Paul: The Pioneer Co., 1911), pp. 75ff.

58. Merle Wells notes that while "farmers in areas of severe cultural lag might have regarded irrigation as inconsistent with traditional simple individualistic agriculture, eastern Oregon farmers—or at least any farmers bold enough to go dry farming at Fort Rock—hardly would have been that backward. Development without having to bother with expensive canals, however, was an important advantage for anyone who would accept a substantial, but known, risk of dry farming." Letter to Barbara Allen.

59. J. L. Cowan, "Dry Farming—The Hope of the West," *The Century* 72 (1906): 437.

60. Cowan, pp. 440, 446.

61. Shaw, preface, p. 22.

62. Ibid., p. 29.

63. An article on dry farming, in fact, appeared in the *Silver Lake Leader*, November 12, 1909.

64. Hardy W. Campbell, *Campbell's 1902 Soil Culture Manual* (Holdrege, Nebraska: H. W. Campbell, 1902), followed by subsequent editions in 1905, 1907, and 1909; William MacDonald, *Dry-Farming: Its Principles and Practice* (New York: Century, 1909);

John Widtsoe, *Dry Farming: A System of Agriculture for Countries under a Low Rainfall* (New York: Macmillan, 1913). Shaw's book was dedicated to Louis Hill, then president of the Great Northern Railroad, "in recognition of the great work he is doing for the development of the agricultural resources of the American Northwest."

65. Meinig, p. 420; Smith, "Rain Follows the Plow," p. 191.

66. Hargreaves, p. 271.

67. E. C. Chilcott, "Dry-Land Farming in the Great Plains Area," *U.S.D.A. Yearbook for 1907* (Washington D.C.: Government Printing Office, 1908), p. 451.

68. Richard H. Sullivan, "The So-Called Change of Climate in the Semi-Arid West," *U.S.D.A. Yearbook for 1908* (Washington, D.C.: Government Printing Office, 1909), p. 291.

69. MacDonald, p. 163.

70. Cowan, p. 437.

71. Quoted in Layton, p. 47.

72. Cowan, p. 437.

73. Dick, p. 373.

74. Ibid., p. 381.

75. Mattis interview.

76. Chilcott, pp. 452, 467.

77. MacDonald, p. 37.

78. Hargreaves, pp. 96ff.

79. Among those calling for change were the railroads whose best interests were served by laws favoring small rather than large landholdings. James J. Hill, in fact, reportedly wanted all public land laws but the original 160-acre Homestead Act repealed (Hargreaves, p. 338).

80. *Report of the Public Lands Commission*, with Appendix (S.doc. 189 [58:37] #4766, Washington, D.C., 1905).

81. *Public Lands Commission*, p. 2.

82. Peffer, p. 144.

83. Layton, p. 45; Hargreaves, p. 542.

84. Peffer, p. 322.

85. Emerson Hough, *The Passing of the Frontier: A Chronicle of the Old West* (New Haven: Yale University Press, 1918), p. 160.

86. Peffer, pp. 134, 147.

87. O'Callaghan, pp. 14–15; Everett Dick, *The Sod-House Frontier* (Lincoln: University of Nebraska Press, 1979), p. 186.

88. See David Potter's discussion of the relationship between late settlement on the frontier and shifting notions of access to resources in *People of Plenty* (Chicago: University of Chicago Press, 1954), pp. 142–65.

89. Cf. Dale E. Courtney, "The Oregon Desert, 1967: A Pioneer Fringe?," *Association of Pacific Coast Geographers Yearbook* 29 (1967): 8.

90. Nancy Burns, "The Collapse of Small Towns on the Great Plains: A Bibliography," *Emporia State Research Studies* 31 (Summer 1982): 13.

91. Putnam, pp. 64–65.

92. Culmsee, "Last Free Land Rush," p. 32.

93. Dayton Kohler, "H. L. Davis: Writer in the West," *College English* 14 (December 1952): 134.

94. Hudson, p. 252; Fite, p. 216; cf. Courtney, p. 8.

NOTES TO EPILOGUE

1. William Kittredge, in "New to the Country," *Montana, Magazine of History* 36 (Winter 1986): 2-11, uses "story" in this large sense of a narrative framework within which the past is perceived.

Bibliography

BOOKS AND ARTICLES

Allison, Ira S. "Work of Wind in Northern Lake County, Oregon." *Geographical Society of America Bulletin* 52 (1940): 1943.

_____. *Fossil Lake, Oregon.* Corvallis: Oregon State University Press, 1966.

Alwin, John A. "Jordan Country—A Golden Anniversary Look." *Annals of the Association of American Geographers* 71 (1981): 479–98.

_____. "Post Office Locations and the Historical Geographer: A Montana Example." *Professional Geographer* 26 (1974): 183–86.

Anderson, Clifford B. "The Metamorphosis of American Agrarian Idealism in the 1920's and 1930's." *Agricultural History* 35 (1961): 182–88.

Antevs, Ernest. *Rainfall and Tree Growth in the Great Basin.* New York: Carnegie Institution of Washington and the American Geographical Society of New York, 1938.

Aughey, Samuel, and C. O. Wilber. *Agriculture Beyond the 100th Meridian, or a Review of the U.S. Public Land Commission.* Lincoln, Nebraska: Journal Company, 1880.

Badger, R. Reid. *The Great American Fair: The World's Columbian Exposition and American Culture.* Chicago: Nelson Hall, 1979.

Baldwin, Ewart M. *Geology of Oregon.* Ann Arbor: Edwards Brothers, 1964.

Baritz, Leon. "The Idea of the West." *American Historical Review* 66 (1961): 618–40.

Beckham, Stephen Dow. *Lake County Historic Sites and Buildings Inventory.* 3 volumes. Heritage Research Associates Report #12. Eugene: Heritage Research Associates, 1982.

Bedwell, Stephen F. *Fort Rock Basin: Prehistory and Environment.* Eugene: University of Oregon Press, 1973.

Bennett, John W. *Northern Plainsmen: Adaptive Strategy and Agrarian Life.* Chicago: Aldine Publishing Company, 1969.

Berreman, Joel V. *Tribal Distribution in Oregon.* Memoirs of the American Anthropological Association No. 47. Menasha, Wisconsin: American Anthropological Association, 1937.

Biddle, H. J. "Notes on the Surface Geology of Southern Oregon." *American Journal of Science* 35 (1888): 475–82.

Billington, Ray Allen. *The Genesis of the Frontier Thesis.* San Marino, California: Huntington Library, 1971.

————. *Westward Expansion*, 2nd ed. New York: Macmillan, 1960.

Bowden, Martyn J. "The Great American Desert in the American Mind, 1890–1972: The Historiography of a Geographical Notion." In *Geographies of the Mind: Essays in Historical Geosophy*, edited by Martyn J. Bowden and David Lowenthal. New York: Oxford University Press and the American Geographical Society, 1975, pp. 119–47.

Bowen, Marshall E. "Dryland Homesteading on Tobar Flat." *Northeastern Nevada Historical Society Quarterly* 4 (1981): 118–40.

Bowers, William L. *The Country Life Movement in America, 1900–1920.* Port Washington, New York: Kennikat Press, 1974.

Bowman, Isaiah. *The Pioneer Fringe.* American Geographical Society Special Publication #13. New York: American Geographical Society, 1931.

Bratcher, James. "The Baby-Switching Story." In *The Sunny Slopes of Long Ago*, edited by Wilson M. Hudson and Allen Maxwell. Publications of the Texas Folklore Society #33. Dallas: Southern Methodist University Press, 1966, pp. 110–17.

Brogan, Phil F. *East of the Cascades.* Portland: Binfords and Mort, 1964.

Burns, Nancy. "The Collapse of Small Towns on the Great Plains: A Bibliography." *Emporia State Research Studies* #31. Emporia, Kansas: Emporia State University, 1982.

Campbell, Hardy W. *Campbell's 1902 Soil Culture Manual.* Holdrege, Nebraska: H. W. Campbell, 1902; subsequent editions in 1905, 1907, and 1909.

————. *The Campbell System of Soil Culture.* Lincoln, Nebraska: Campbell Soil Culture Publishing Co., 1912.

Carstensen, Vernon, ed. *The Public Lands: Studies in the History of the Public Domain.* Madison: University of Wisconsin Press, 1963.

Cashman, Sean D. *America in the Gilded Age: From the Death of Lincoln to the Rise of Theodore Roosevelt.* New York: New York University Press, 1984.

Castle, Emery, and Carroll Dwyer. "Irrigation Possibilities in the Fort Rock Area." Circular of Information #558. Corvallis: Agricultural Experiment Station, Oregon State College, and the Soil Conservation Service, July 1956.

Cheney, W. D. *Central Oregon.* Ivy Press, 1918.

Chilcott, E. C. "Dry-Land Farming in the Great Plains Area." *U.S.D.A. Yearbook for 1907.* Washington D.C.: Government Printing Office, 1908, pp. 451–68.

Christmas Valley Women's Club. *Where the Pavement Ends.* Christmas Valley, Oregon, 1968.

Cope, E. D. "The Silver Lake of Oregon and its Region." *American Naturalist* 23 (November 1889): 970–82.

Corning, Howard M., ed. *Dictionary of Oregon History.* Portland: Binfords and Mort, 1956.

Coulter, John Lee. "Agricultural Development in the United States, 1900–1910." *Quarterly Journal of Economics* 27 (1912): 1–26.

Courtney, Dale E. "The Oregon Desert, 1967: A Pioneer Fringe?" *Association of Pacific Coast Geographers Yearbook* 29 (1967): 7–19.

Cowan, J. L. "Dry Farming—The Hope of the West." *The Century* 72 (1906): 435–46.

Cressman, Luther S. *Archaeological Researches in the Northern Great Basin.* Carnegie Institution of Washington Publication #538. Washington, D.C.: Carnegie Institution of Washington, 1942.

_____ . "Cultural Sequences at The Dalles, Oregon: A Contribution to Pacific Northwest Prehistory." *Transactions of the American Philosophical Society,* N.S., vol. 50, pt. 10. Philadelphia: American Philosophical Society, 1960.

_____ . *The Sandal and the Cave: The Indians of Oregon.* Portland: Blaner Books, 1964.

Cressman, Luther S., Howel Williams, and Alex D. Krieger. *Early Man in Oregon: Archaeological Studies in the Northern Great Basin.* Eugene: University of Oregon, 1940.

Crook, General George. *His Autobiography.* Edited by Martin F. Schmitt. Norman: University of Oklahoma Press, 1946.

Culmsee, Carlton. "Last Free Land Rush." *Utah Historical Quarterly* 49 (1981): 26–41.

Danbom, David B. "Rural Education Reform and the Country Life Movement, 1900–1920." *Agricultural History* 53 (1979): 462–74.

Davis, H. L. "Back to the Land—Oregon, 1907." *American Mercury* 16 (March 1929): 314–23.

DeSantis, Vincent P. *The Shaping of Modern America, 1877–1916.* St. Louis: Forum Press, 1977.

Dick, Everett N. *Conquering the Great American Desert: Nebraska.* Lincoln: Nebraska State Historical Society, 1975.

_____ . *The Lure of the Land: A Social History of the Public Lands from the Articles of Confederation to the New Deal.* Lincoln: University of Nebraska Press, 1970.

_____ . *The Sod-House Frontier.* Lincoln: University of Nebraska Press, 1979.

Dicken, Samuel Newton, and Emily F. Dicken. *The Making of Oregon: A Study in Historical Geography.* Portland: Oregon Historical Society, 1979.

Emmons, David M. *Garden in the Grasslands: Boomer Literature of the Great Plains.* Lincoln: University of Nebraska Press, 1971.

Fite, Gilbert C. *The Farmers' Frontier, 1865–1900.* Albuquerque: University of New Mexico Press, 1974.

Gaston, Joseph. *The Centennial History of Oregon, 1811–1912.* Chicago: S. J. Clarke Publishing Company, 1912.

Gates, Paul W. "Homesteading on the High Plains." *Agricultural History* 51 (1977): 109–33.

Hargreaves, Mary W. M. "Dry Farming, Alias Scientific Farming." *Agricultural History* 22 (1948): 39–56.

_____ . *Dry Farming in the Northern Great Plains, 1900–1925.* Cambridge: Harvard University Press, 1957.

Harper, Frank B. "Dust to Dust." *Oregon Journal,* January 28, 1940, p. 4.

Harrison, Robert. "Statutory Opening Dates of District Land Offices in Various States." In *The Public Lands: Studies in the History of the Public Domain,* edited by Vernon Carstensen. Madison: University of Wisconsin Press, 1963, pp. 499–504.

Hatton, Raymond R. *High Desert of Central Oregon.* Portland: Binfords and Mort, 1977.

_____ . *Pioneer Homesteaders of the Fort Rock Valley.* Portland: Binfords and Mort, 1982.

Hedges, James B. "The Colonization Work of the Northern Pacific Railroad." *Mississippi Valley Historical Review* 13 (1926): 311–42.

———. "Promotion of Immigration to the Pacific Northwest by the Railroads." *Mississippi Valley Historical Review* 15 (1928–29): 183–203.

Helbock, Richard W. *Oregon Post Offices, 1847–1982*. Las Cruces, New Mexico: La Posta, 1982.

Hibbard, Benjamin. *A History of Public Land Policies*. New York: Peter Smith, 1939.

Hilgard, E. W. "Origin, Value, and Reclamation of Alkali Lands." *U.S.D.A. Yearbook for 1895*. Washington, D.C.: Government Printing Office, 1896.

Hofstadter, Richard. *The Age of Reform*. New York: Alfred A. Knopf, 1955.

Hollon, W. Eugene. *The Great American Desert, Then and Now*. New York: Oxford University Press, 1966.

Hough, Emerson. *The Passing of the Frontier: A Chronicle of the Old West*. New Haven: Yale University Press, 1918.

Howard, Randall R. "The Awakening of Central Oregon." *Pacific Monthly* 24 (November 1910): 497–514.

———. "The Present and Future of Eastern Oregon," *Pacific Monthly* 25 (1911): 77–89.

Howe, Carrol B. *Ancient Tribes of the Klamath Country*. Portland: Binfords and Mort, 1968.

Hudson, John C. "Migration to an American Frontier." *Annals of the Association of American Geographers* 66 (1976): 242–65.

Hunt, David C. *Legacy of the West*. Lincoln: University of Nebraska Press, 1982.

Ivey, William. " 'The 1913 Disaster': A Michigan Local Legend." *Folklore Forum* 3 (1970): 100–114.

Jackman, E. R., and Reuben A. Long. *The Oregon Desert*. Caldwell, Idaho: Caxton Printers, 1964.

Jetter, Marie E. *Contentment Yesterday—Why Not Today?* Jericho, New York: Exposition Press, 1969.

Kincer, Joseph B. "The Climate of the Great Plains as a Factor in Their Utilization." *Annals of the Association of American Geographers* 13 (1923): 67–80.

Kittredge, William. "New to the Country." *Montana, Magazine of History* 36 (Winter 1986): 2–11.

Kohler, Dayton. "H. L. Davis: Writer in the West." *College English* 14 (1952): 133–40.

Lamar, Howard. "Persistent Frontier: The West in the Twentieth Century." *Western Historical Quarterly* 4 (1974): 5–26.

Leighton, M. O., E. C. LaRue, and F. F. Henshaw. *Surface Water Supply of the United States, 1909, Part X, The Great Basin*. U.S. Geological Survey Water Supply Paper #270. Washington, D.C.: Government Printing Office, 1911.

Loy, William G., Stuart Allan, Clyde P. Patton, Robert D. Plank. *Atlas of Oregon*. Eugene: University of Oregon Books, 1976.

Luper, Rhea. *Water Resources of the State of Oregon, 1914–1924*. Salem: Office of State Engineer, 1925.

MacDonald, William. *Dry-Farming: Its Principles and Practice*. New York: Century, 1909.

Martin, Charles E. *Hollybush: Folk Building and Social Change in an Appalachian Community*. Knoxville: University of Tennessee Press, 1984.

Mattoon, Rev. C. H. *Baptist Annals of Oregon, 1886–1910*. 2 volumes. McMinnville, Oregon: The Pacific Baptist Press, 1913.

McArthur, Lewis A. *Oregon Geographic Names*. Portland: Oregon Historical Society, 1974.
_____. "Oregon Geographic Names: II, Additions since 1944." *Oregon Historical Quarterly* 47 (1946): 61–98.
Meinig, Donald. *The Great Columbia Plain*. Seattle: University of Washington Press, 1970.
Mills, Randall V. "A History of Transportation in the Pacific Northwest." *Oregon Historical Quarterly* 47 (1946): 281–312.
Murphy, Thomas D. *Oregon, the Picturesque*. Boston: The Page Company, 1917.
Myrick, David F. "Oregon, California, and Eastern." *The Ferroequinologist* (Central Coast Railway Club, San Jose, California), September 1, 1957, pp. 3–6.
Nash, Roderick. *Wilderness and the American Mind*. 3rd ed. New Haven: Yale University Press, 1982.
Nesbit, Robert C., and Charles M. Gates. "Agriculture in Eastern Washington, 1890–1910." *Pacific Northwest Quarterly* 37 (1946): 279–302.
Newell, Frederick H. "Irrigation on the Great Plains." *U.S.D.A. Yearbook for 1896*. Washington D.C.: Government Printing Office, 1897, pp. 167–96.
Newell, J. P. *Report on Railroad Extensions to Serve Western and Central Oregon*. Salem: State Printing Department, 1925.
Norris, Frank. "The Frontier Gone at Last." *World's Work*, 3 (1902): 1728–1731. Reprinted in *Call of the Wild*, edited by Roderick Nash. New York: George Braziller, 1970, pp. 69–78.
Nugent, Walter. *From Centennial to World War: American Society 1876–1917*. Indianapolis: Bobbs-Merrill, 1977.
_____. *Structures of American Social History*. Bloomington: Indiana University Press, 1981.
O'Neill, William L. *The Progressive Years: America Comes of Age*. New York: Harper and Row, 1975.
Oregon Almanac, 1915. Portland: Oregon State Immigration Commission, 1915.
Oregon State Board of Higher Education. *Physical and Economic Geography of Oregon: A Compendium*. Salem, 1940.
Paul, Rodman W., and Michael P. Malone. "Tradition and Challenge in Western Historiography." *Western Historical Quarterly* 16 (1985): 27–54.
Peffer, E. Louise. *The Closing of the Public Domain: Disposal and Reservation Policies, 1900–1950*. Stanford: Stanford University Press, 1951.
Pomeroy, Earl. "The Changing West." In *The Reconstruction of American History*, edited by John Higham. London: Hutchinson & Company, 1962, pp. 64–81.
Portland Chamber of Commerce. *Oregon, the Land of Opportunity*. Portland, 1911.
Potter, David. *People of Plenty*. Chicago: University of Chicago Press, 1954.
Powell, John Wesley. *Report on the Lands of the Arid Regions of the United States*. Washington, D.C.: Government Printing Office, 1878.
Putnam, George Palmer. *In the Oregon Country*. New York: G. P. Putnam's Sons, Knickerbocker Press, 1915.
Ray, Verne F., George P. Murdock, Beatrice Blyth, Omer C. Stewart, Jack Harris, E. Adamson, and D. B. Shimkin. "Tribal Distribution in Eastern Oregon and Adjacent Regions." *American Anthropologist* 40 (1938): 384–415.
Reed, Henry E. *The Lewis and Clark Centennial*. Portland: Irwin-Hodson Company, 1905.
Rockie, W. A. "Backsight and Foresight on Land Use." *Northwest Science* 18 (May 1944): 35–42.

Roe, Frank G. "The Alberta Wet Cycle of 1899–1903: A Climatic Interlude." *Agricultural History* 28 (1954): 112–20.

Russell, Israel C. "A Geological Reconnaissance in Southern Oregon." *U.S. Geological Survey Annual Report* 4 (1884): 431–64.

————. *Preliminary Report on the Ecology and Water Resources of Central Oregon.* U.S. Geological Survey Bulletin #252. Washington, D.C.: Government Printing Office, 1905.

[Sayre, James V., and Lair H. Gregory]. *Pictorial Oregon, the Wonderland: An Invitation to Visit Oregon Extended by the Portland Press Club.* Portland: Portland Press Club, 1915.

Schmitt, Peter J. *Back to Nature: The Arcadian Myth in Urban America, 1900–1930.* New York: Oxford University Press, 1969.

Schwantes, Carlos A., ed. "Problems of Empire Building: The Oregon Trunk Railway Survey of Disappointed Homeseekers, 1911." *Oregon Historical Quarterly* 83 (1982): 371–90.

Scott, Roy V. "American Railroads and Agricultural Extension, 1900–1914: A Study in Railway Development Techniques." *Business History Review* 39 (1965): 74–98.

————. "Land Use and American Railroads in the Twentieth Century." *Agricultural History* 57 (1979): 683–703.

Seaman, N. G. "An Amateur Archaeologist's 50 years in Oregon." *Oregon Historical Quarterly* 41 (1940): 147–59.

Shannon, Fred A. "The Homestead Act and Labor Surplus." *American Historical Review* 41 (1936): 637–51.

Sharp, Dallas Love. *Where Rolls the Oregon.* Boston: Houghton Mifflin, 1913.

Shaver, F. A., Arthur P. Rose, R. F. Steele, and A. E. Adams, compilers. *An Illustrated History of Central Oregon.* Spokane: Western Historical Publishing Company, 1905.

Shaw, Thomas. *Dry Land Farming.* St. Paul: The Pioneer Company, 1911.

————. *Report of a Trip through Central Oregon during the Fall of 1910.* St. Paul: McGill-Warner Company, 1911.

Smith, Henry Nash. "Rain Follows the Plow: The Notion of Increased Rainfall for the Great Plains, 1844–1880." *Huntington Library Quarterly* 10 (February 1947): 169–94.

Smith, Martha L. *Going to God's Country.* Boston: Christopher Company, 1941.

Smith, Warren D., and Carl Swartzlow. "Mt. Mazama: Explosion versus Collapse." *Bulletin of the Geological Society of America* 47 (1936): 1809–1830.

Smith, Warren D., and F. G. Young. "Physical and Economic Geography of Oregon. XI: The Southeastern Lake Province." *The Commonwealth Review* (University of Oregon), 4 (1926): 199–253.

Smythe, William A. *The Conquest of Arid America.* New York: Harper and Brothers, 1900.

Speers, L. C. "Nevada-Oregon Desert Still Defies Pioneers," *New York Times,* Sept. 27, 1925, Sec. 8, p. 6.

Stegner, Wallace. *Beyond the 100th Meridian: John Wesley Powell and the Second Opening of the West.* Boston: Houghton Mifflin, 1954.

Sullivan, Richard H. "The So-Called Change of Climate in the Semi-Arid West." *U.S.D.A. Yearbook for 1908.* Washington, D.C.: Government Printing Office 1909, pp. 289–300.

Taylor, Paul S. "Reclamation: The Rise and Fall of an American Idea," *American West* 7 (1970): 27–33.

Trauger, F. D. *Basic Ground-Water Data in Lake County, Oregon.* Portland: U.S. Geological Survey, 1950.

Turner, Frederick J. "The Significance of the Frontier in American History," *Proceedings of the State Historical Society of Wisconsin,* December 14, 1893.

Unruh, John D., Jr. *The Plains Across: The Overland Emigrants and the Trans-Mississippi West, 1840–1860.* Urbana: University of Illinois Press, 1979.

Valde, Gary, compiler. *Lake County, Oregon, Resource Atlas: Natural, Human, Economic, Public.* Corvallis: Oregon State University Cooperative Extension Service, 1973.

Walker, Robert H. "The Poets Interpret the Western Frontier." *Mississippi Valley Historical Review* 47 (1960–61): 619–35.

Waring, Gerald A. *Geology and Water Resources of a Portion of South Central Oregon.* U.S. Geological Survey Water-Supply Paper #220. Washington, D.C.: Government Printing Office, 1908.

Wells, Edward L. "The Weather Bureau and the Homeseeker." *U.S.D.A. Yearbook for 1904.* Washington, D.C.: Government Printing Office, 1905, pp. 353–58.

Whistler, John T., and John H. Lewis. *Silver Lake Project: Irrigation and Drainage.* Salem: Office of State Engineer, 1915.

White, Richard. *Land Use, Environment, and Social Change: The Shaping of Island County, Washington.* Seattle: University of Washington Press, 1980.

———. "Poor Men on Poor Lands: The Back-to-the-Land Movement of the Early Twentieth Century—A Case Study." *Pacific Historical Review* 49 (1980): 105–31.

Widtsoe, John. *Dry Farming: A System of Agriculture for Countries under a Low Rainfall.* New York: Macmillan, 1913.

Wiebe, Robert H. *The Search for Order, 1877–1920.* New York: Hill and Wang, 1967.

WPA Writers' Project. *Oregon, End of the Trail.* Portland: Binfords and Mort, 1940.

UNPUBLISHED MANUSCRIPTS

Anderson, Laura. "Homestead on the Oregon Desert: The Diaries of Anna Steinhoff." 26 pp. Eugene, 1984.

Eskelin, Edwin A. "A Brief History of Wells in the Fort Rock Valley, Both Domestic and Irrigation Wells." 10 pp. Fort Rock Valley, 1971.

———. "Fort Rock Cemetery Association." 9 pp. Fort Rock Valley, 1974.

———. "History of the Eskelin Farm, Located in Fort Rock Valley, North Lake County, Oregon." 17 pp. Fort Rock Valley, 1975.

———. "History of Schools in Fort Rock Valley." 14 pp. Fort Rock Valley, no date.

Freeman, Isa Corum. "History of the Silver Lake Valley." 7 pp. Silver Lake, no date.

———. "Silver Lake Schools." 2 pp. Silver Lake, no date.

Garrett, Elma Linebaugh. "Pioneer Sketches of the Linebaugh Family in Central Oregon." 3 pp. 1982. Bicentennial Family History File, Lake County Public Library, Lakeview, Oregon.

Gilfrey, George L. "Letter to aunt," February 3, 1895. 2 pp. Ms. #1500, Oregon Historical Society, Portland.

Linebaugh, Anna. "[Remarks on the Occasion of Issuing a Christmas Commemorative Stamp at Christmas Valley, Oregon]." 2 pp. October 28, 1981.

"Owsley-Buick Families." 2 pp. No date. Bicentennial Family History File, Lake County Public Library, Lakeview, Oregon.

Riisberg, Mabel O. "Pioneer Women on the High Desert." 275 pp. Muskegon Heights, Michigan, no date. Ms. #2650, Oregon Historical Society, Portland.

Shaw, Les. "Bernard Daly, Rancher, Banker, Farmer, Etc.," 8 pp. No date. Bicentennial Family History File. Lake County Public Library, Lakeview, Oregon.

Steinhoff, Anna. "Diary." 164 pp. November 1910–March 1912.

Williams, Perry. "The Silver Lake, Ore. fire of 1894, a reminiscence." 8 pp. No date. Ms. #1128, University of Oregon, Eugene.

PAMPHLETS

"Lake County, Oregon: description of its climate, soil, resources and its desirable opportunities for homeseekers and those seeking profitable investments." Lakeview: Beach and Beach, 1889. University of Oregon Library.

THESES AND DISSERTATIONS

Allen, Barbara. "Talking about the Past: A Folkloristic Study of Orally Communicated History." Ph.D. dissertation. UCLA, 1980.

Buckles, James Slama. "The Historical Geography of the Fort Rock Valley, 1900–1941." M.A. thesis. University of Oregon, 1959.

Dickman, Howard L. "James Jerome Hill and the Agricultural Development of the Northwest." Ph.D. dissertation. University of Michigan, 1977.

Green, David B. "Irrigation Potential and Agricultural Settlement in Submarginal Land: An Example from Weld County, Colorado." Ph.D. dissertation. University of Northern Colorado, 1980.

Hafer, John William. "The Sea of Grass: The Image of the Great Plains in the American Novel." Ph.D. dissertation. Northern Illinois University, 1975.

Kutzleb, Charles Robert. "Rain Follows the Plow: The History of an Idea." Ph.D. dissertation. University of Colorado, 1968.

Layton, Stanford J. "The Politics of Homesteading in the Early Twentieth-Century American West: The Origin and Supersession of the Enlarged Homestead Act and the Stock Raising Homestead Act." Ph.D. dissertation. University of Utah, 1972.

O'Callaghan, Jerry A. "The Disposition of the Public Domain in Oregon." Ph.D. dissertation. Stanford University, 1951. Published as *Memorandum of the Chairman to the Committee on Interior and Insular Affairs*, United States Senate. Washington, D.C.: Government Printing Office, 1960.

Picht, Douglas R. "The American Farmer: an Interdisciplinary Examination of an Image." Ph.D. dissertation. University of Minnesota, 1968.

Pierce, Barbara. "Economic and Geographical Determinants of Railroad Routes in the Pacific Northwest." M.A. thesis. Reed College, 1937.

Plank, Arnold C. "Desert versus Garden: The Role of Western Images in the Settlement of Kansas." M.A. thesis. Kansas State University, 1962.

Roet, Jeffrey B. "Agricultural Settlement on the Dry Farming Frontier, 1900–1920." Ph.D. dissertation. Northwestern University, 1982.

Simpson, Peter K. "A Social History of the Cattle Industry of Southeastern Oregon." Ph.D. dissertation. University of Oregon, 1973.

GOVERNMENT REPORTS

Burrier, Arnold S. "An Analysis of the Proposed Fort Rock Conservation Area." Unpublished ms., U.S. Resettlement Administration, Region XI. July 1936. Oregon State Library.

General Land Office. *Annual Reports of the Commissioner*, 1870–1910.

Lake County Agricultural Extension Service. *Annual Reports of the County Agent*, 1913–1928. Oregon State University Archives; Lake County Extension Service Office, Lakeview, Oregon.

Public Lands Commission. *Report with Appendix*. 58th Congress, 3rd session, Senate doc. 189. Washington D.C.: Government Printing Office, 1905 (#4766).

U.S. Census Bureau. Tenth Census of the United States, 1880; Eleventh Census of the United States, 1890; Twelfth Census of the United States, 1900; Thirteenth Census of the United States, 1910; Fourteenth Census of the United States, 1920; Fifteenth Census of the United States, 1930.

U.S. Weather Bureau. *Annual Reports of the Chief, 1900–1920*.

ARCHIVAL RECORDS

Private

Northern Pacific and Great Northern Railway Companies. *Records*. Minnesota Historical Society.

Oregon and Western Land Colonization Company. *Records*. Minnesota Historical Society.

W. P. Davidson papers. Minnesota Historical Society.

Public

Department of the Interior. Oregon Eastern Railroad Rights-of-Way Maps. Cartographic and Architectural Services Branch, National Archives. Alexandria, Virginia.

General Land Office. Classified Files. Record Group 49, Scientific, Economic, and Natural Resources Branch, National Archives. Washington, D.C.

General Land Office. *Oregon Tract Books*. Microfilm rolls 46–49. Bureau of Land Management. Portland, Oregon.

General Land Office. Serial Patent Files. Record Group 49, Civil Records Division, General Branch, National Archives. Suitland, Maryland.

General Land Office. Surveyors' Field Notes for Townships 24–28 South, Ranges 13–19 East. Microfiche. Bureau of Land Management. Portland, Oregon.

Lake County, Oregon, Superintendent of Schools. *Clerk's School Census Reports*, 1919–1940. Lakeview, Oregon.

Lake County, Oregon, tax rolls, 1875–1930. Oregon State Archives.

WPA Writers' Project Files, Lake County, Oregon. Oregon State Library; University of Oregon Library.

LETTERS

Durrant, H. B. Letter to J. T. McCartney, August 17, 1984. 2 pp. Union Pacific Railroad, Omaha, Nebraska.

Miles, Roberta. Letter to Barbara Allen, March 12, 1985. 1 p.

Nash, Dwight L. Letter to Georgia Stephenson, June 20, 1971. 4 pp.

Stratton, DeForest. Letter to Barbara Allen, March 2, 1985. 2 pp.

Wells, Merle. Letter to Barbara Allen, January 15, 1986. 10 pp.

NEWSPAPERS

Bend Bulletin (Bend, Oregon), 1909–1915. Deschutes County Public Library.

Central Oregonian (Silver Lake, Oregon), 1903–1907. Microfilm. University of Oregon Library.

Deschutes Pioneer Gazette (Bend, Oregon), 1956, 1968–1973. Central Oregon Community College.

Lake County Examiner (Lakeview, Oregon), 1900–1920. Microfilm. University of Oregon Library.

Silver Lake Leader (Silver Lake, Oregon), 1909–1920. Microfilm. University of Oregon Library.

ORAL SOURCES

Branch, Venita and Floyd. Tape-recorded interview, Fort Rock, Oregon. August 24, 1978.

Buick, M. K. (Mac). Tape-recorded interviews, Fort Rock Valley. July 6, August 9, August 23, 1978; May 21, 1985.

Deadmond, Lawrence. Tape-recorded interview, Silver Lake Valley, Oregon. July 19, 1978.

Emery, Russell and Mary. Tape-recorded interviews, Silver Lake Valley, Oregon. July 6, July 11, August 29, 1978.

Eskelin, Edwin. Tape-recorded interviews, Fort Rock Valley. July 23, August 27, 1978.

Godon, Josephine and Alice. Tape-recorded interview, Fort Rock Valley. July 17, 1978.

Gustafson, Helmer (Shorty). Tape-recorded interviews, Christmas Valley and Fort Rock, Oregon. July 24, August 28, 1978; May 21, 1985.

Iverson, Marge and Lawrence (Bussie). Tape-recorded interview, Silver Lake, Oregon. July 10, 1978.

Linebaugh, Anna. Tape-recorded interviews, Silver Lake, Oregon, and Reno, Nevada. August 1, 1978; May 23, 1985.

Long, Eleanor. Tape-recorded interview, Fort Rock Valley. August 24, 1978.

Mattis, Bill and Maxine. Tape-recorded interview, Fort Rock Valley. July 13, 1978.

Miles, Roberta. Tape-recorded interview, Fort Rock Valley. July 7, 1978.

O'Keeffe, May. Tape-recorded interview, Silver Lake, Oregon. July 28, 1978.

Pendleton, Jack. Tape-recorded interview, Lakeview, Oregon. May 20, 1985.

Stratton, DeForest and Esther. Tape-recorded interviews, Silver Lake. July 12, August 25, 1978.

Ward, Hazel and Maurice. Tape-recorded interview, Fort Rock Valley. July 21, 1978.

Index

e item below is now available for pickup at designated location.

SGCL Cluster
Springfield Greene Library Center

StCharles Second Floor
CALL NO: F 882 .L15 A44 1987
AUTHOR: Bogart, Barbara Allen,
Homesteading the high desert
BARCODE: 39835000218457
REC NO: i10289112
PICKUP AT: SGCL Lib Center

MICHELLE R SWIFT
Library Center

201:1